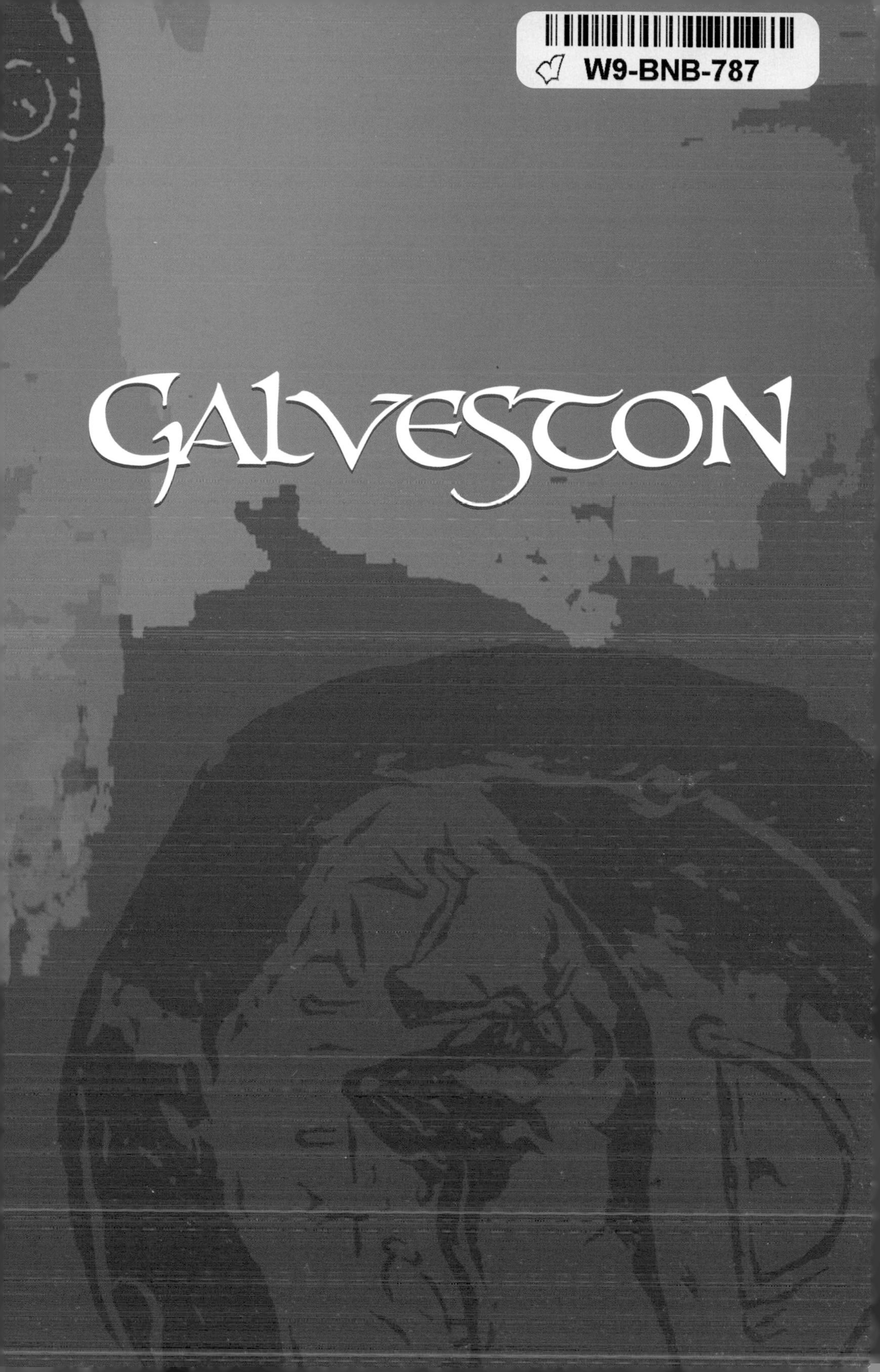
GALVESTON

BOOM!
STUDIOS

ANDREW COSBY
ROSS RICHIE
founders

MARK WAID
editor-in-chief

ADAM FORTIER
vice president,
new business

CHIP MOSHER
marketing &
sales director

MATT GAGNON
managing editor

ED DUKESHIRE
designer

GALVESTON — April 2009 published by BOOM! Studios. Galveston is copyright © 2009 Boom Entertainment Inc. and Johanna Stokes. BOOM! Studios™ and the BOOM! logo are trademarks of Boom Entertainment, Inc., registered in various countries and categories. All rights reserved. The characters and events depicted herein are fictional. Any similarity to actual persons, demons, anti-Christs, aliens, vampires, face-suckers or political figures, whether living, dead or undead, or to any actual or supernatural events is coincidental and unintentional. So don't come whining to us. Office of publication: 6310 San Vicente Blvd, Ste 404, Los Angeles, CA 90048-5457.

First Edition: April 2009

10 9 8 7 6 5 4 3 2 1
PRINTED IN KOREA

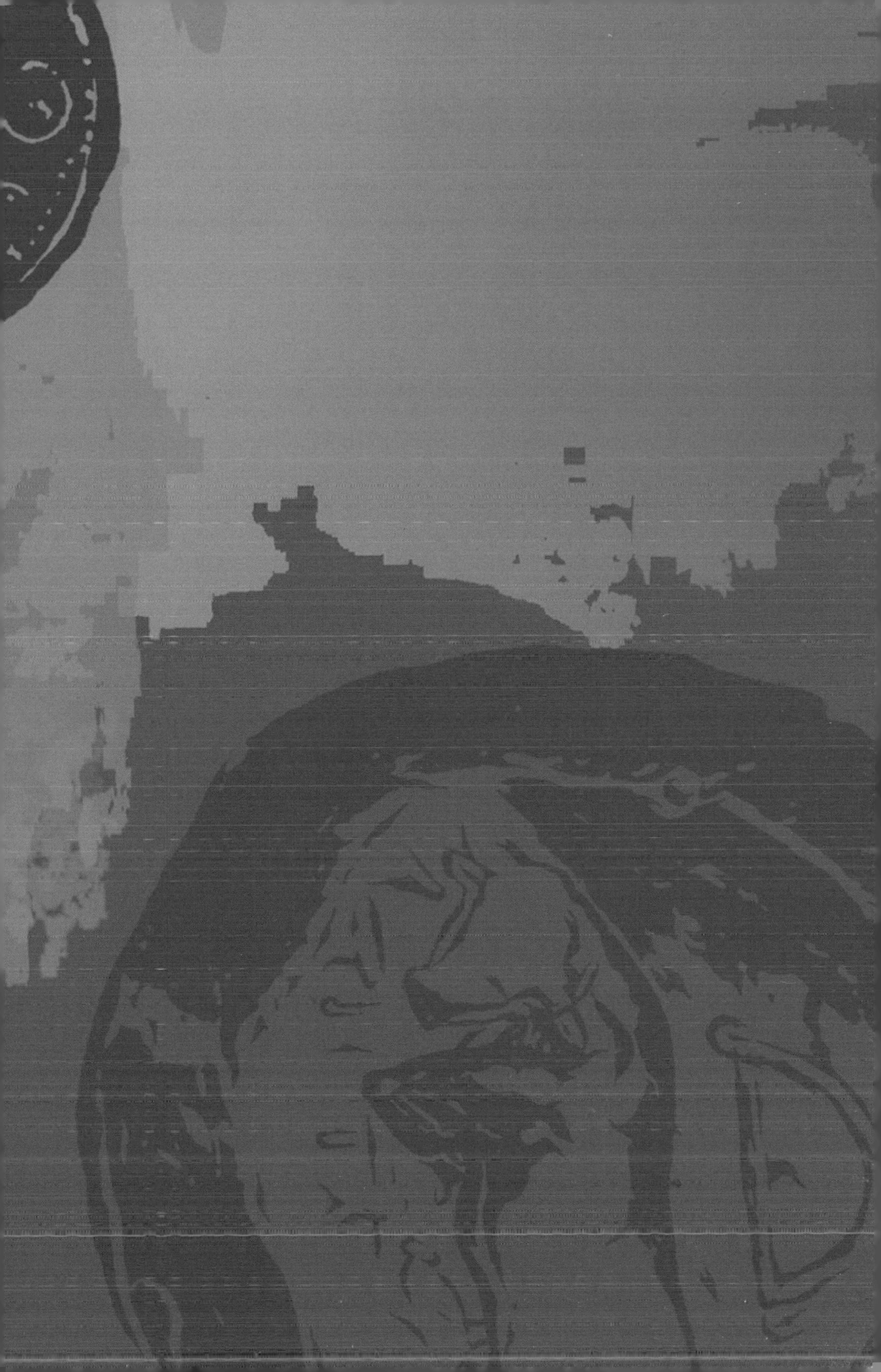

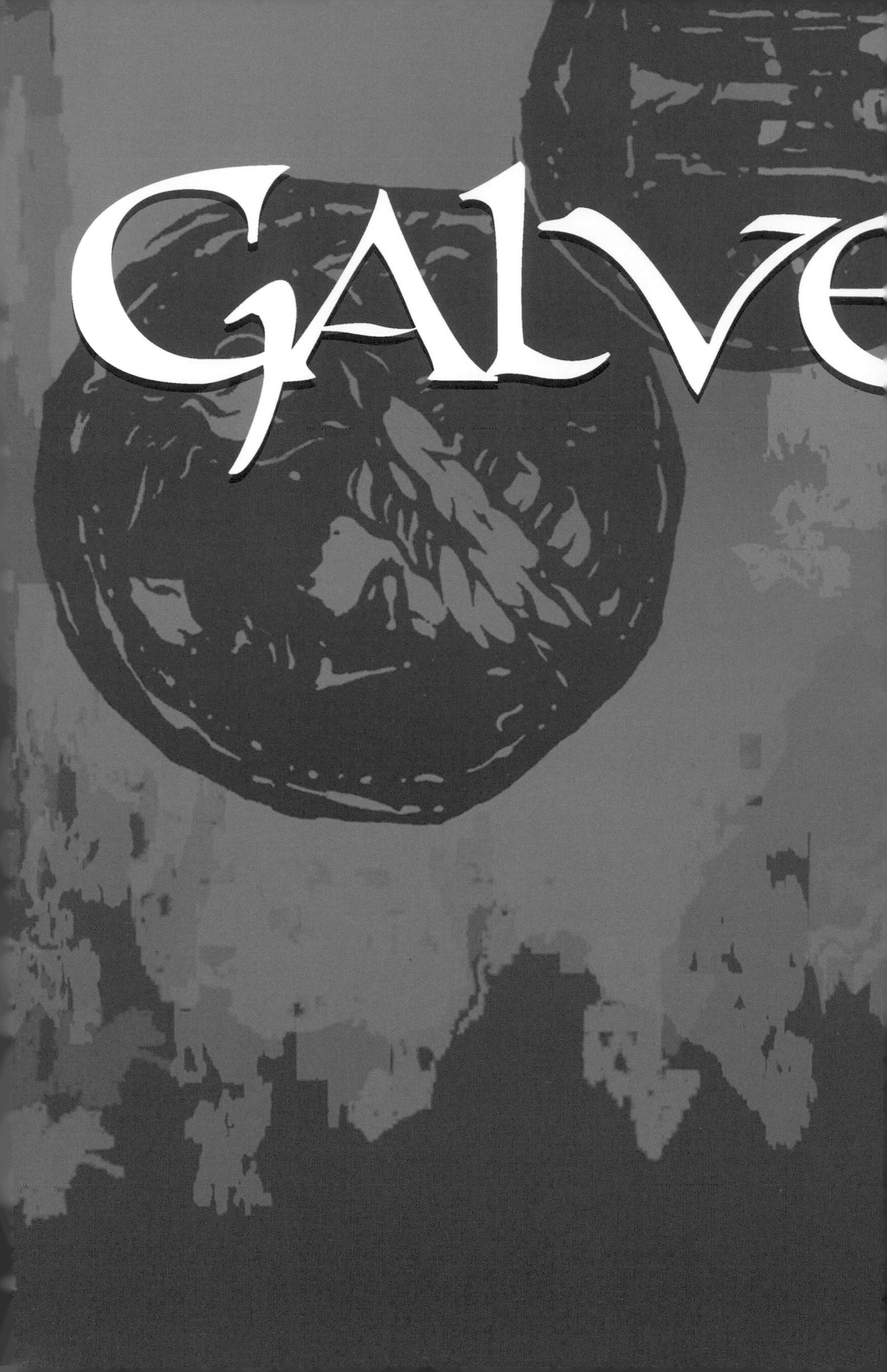
GALVE

STON

CREATED BY **JOHANNA STOKES**
and **ROSS RICHIE**

WRITTEN BY **JOHANNA STOKES**
ART BY **TODD HERMAN**

COLORS BY **DIGIKORE STUDIOS**
CHAPTER 2 ASSISTS BY **ANDRES LOZANO**

LETTERED BY **MARSHALL DILLON**
EDITOR: **MATT GAGNON**

FIRST ISSUE PLOT BY **Tom Peyer**
and **Mark Rahner**

CHAPTER I

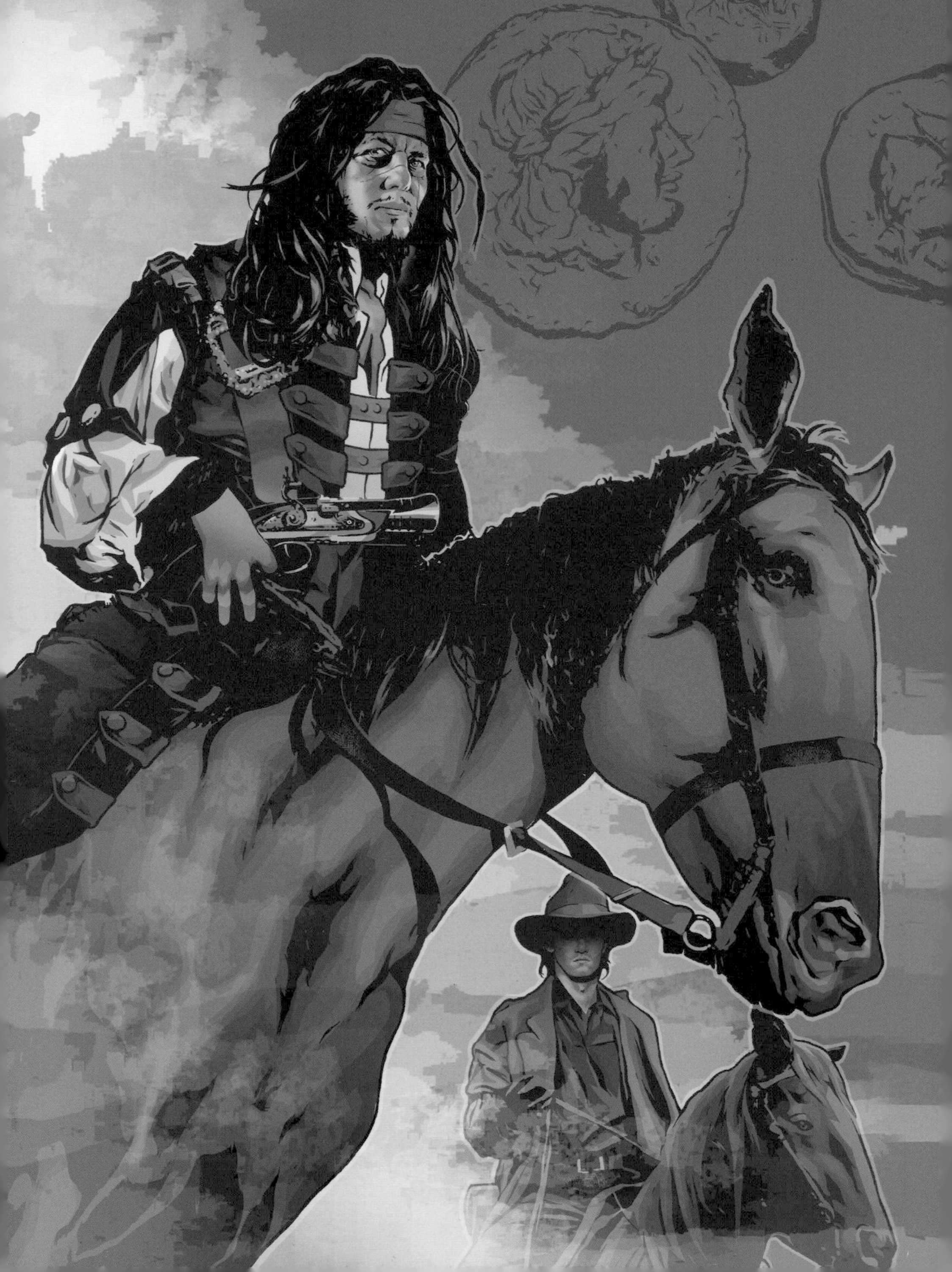

THE GULF OF MEXICO, 1817.

FAMOUS KNIFE-FIGHTER JIM BOWIE IS STILL YEARS AWAY FROM ATTAINING NOTORIETY IN THE SANDBAR FIGHT IN WHICH, AFTER BEING SHOT AND STABBED SEVERAL TIMES AND, WITH A SWORD CANE STILL PROTRUDING FROM HIS CHEST, STILL MANAGED TO DISEMBOWEL ONE OF HIS OPPONENTS WITH HIS NINE INCH BLADE.

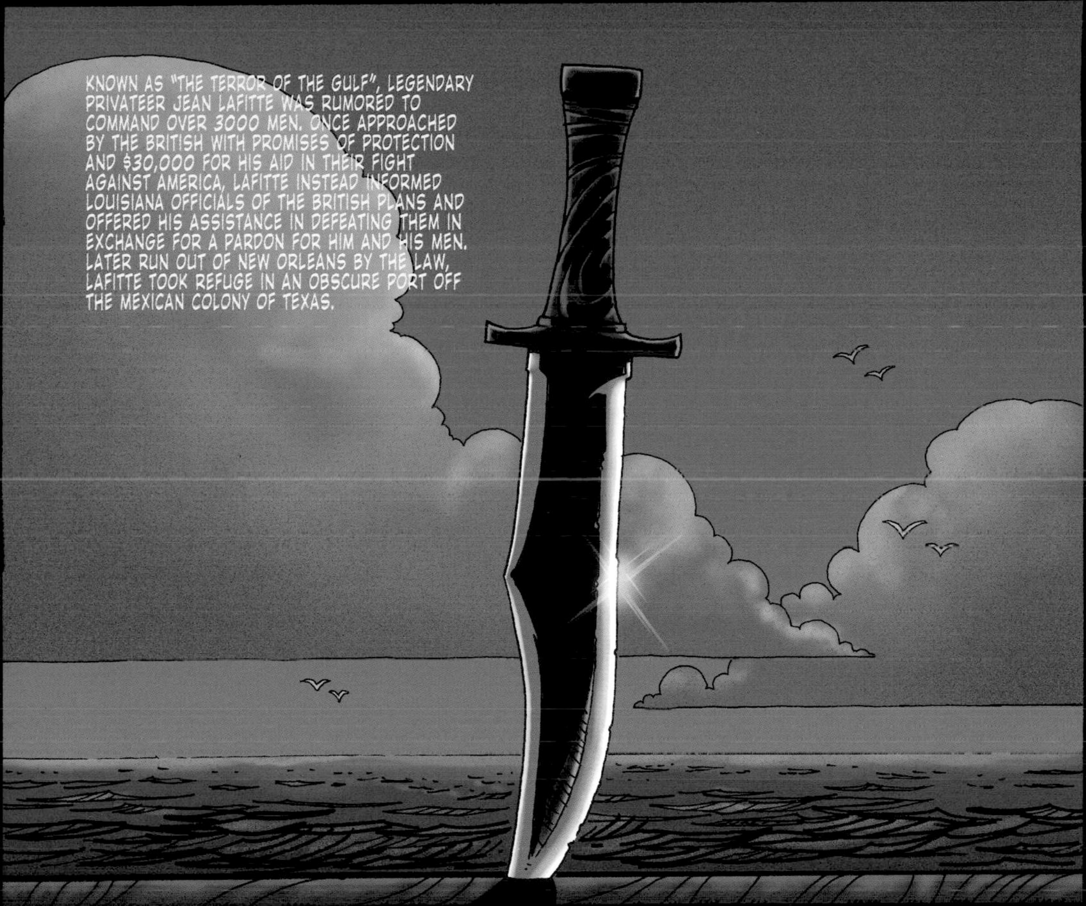
KNOWN AS "THE TERROR OF THE GULF", LEGENDARY PRIVATEER JEAN LAFITTE WAS RUMORED TO COMMAND OVER 3000 MEN. ONCE APPROACHED BY THE BRITISH WITH PROMISES OF PROTECTION AND $30,000 FOR HIS AID IN THEIR FIGHT AGAINST AMERICA, LAFITTE INSTEAD INFORMED LOUISIANA OFFICIALS OF THE BRITISH PLANS AND OFFERED HIS ASSISTANCE IN DEFEATING THEM IN EXCHANGE FOR A PARDON FOR HIM AND HIS MEN. LATER RUN OUT OF NEW ORLEANS BY THE LAW, LAFITTE TOOK REFUGE IN AN OBSCURE PORT OFF THE MEXICAN COLONY OF TEXAS.

BOWIE AND LAFITTE WERE KNOWN THE WORLD OVER. THEY WERE HEROES. THEY WERE LEGENDS. THEY WERE FRIENDS.

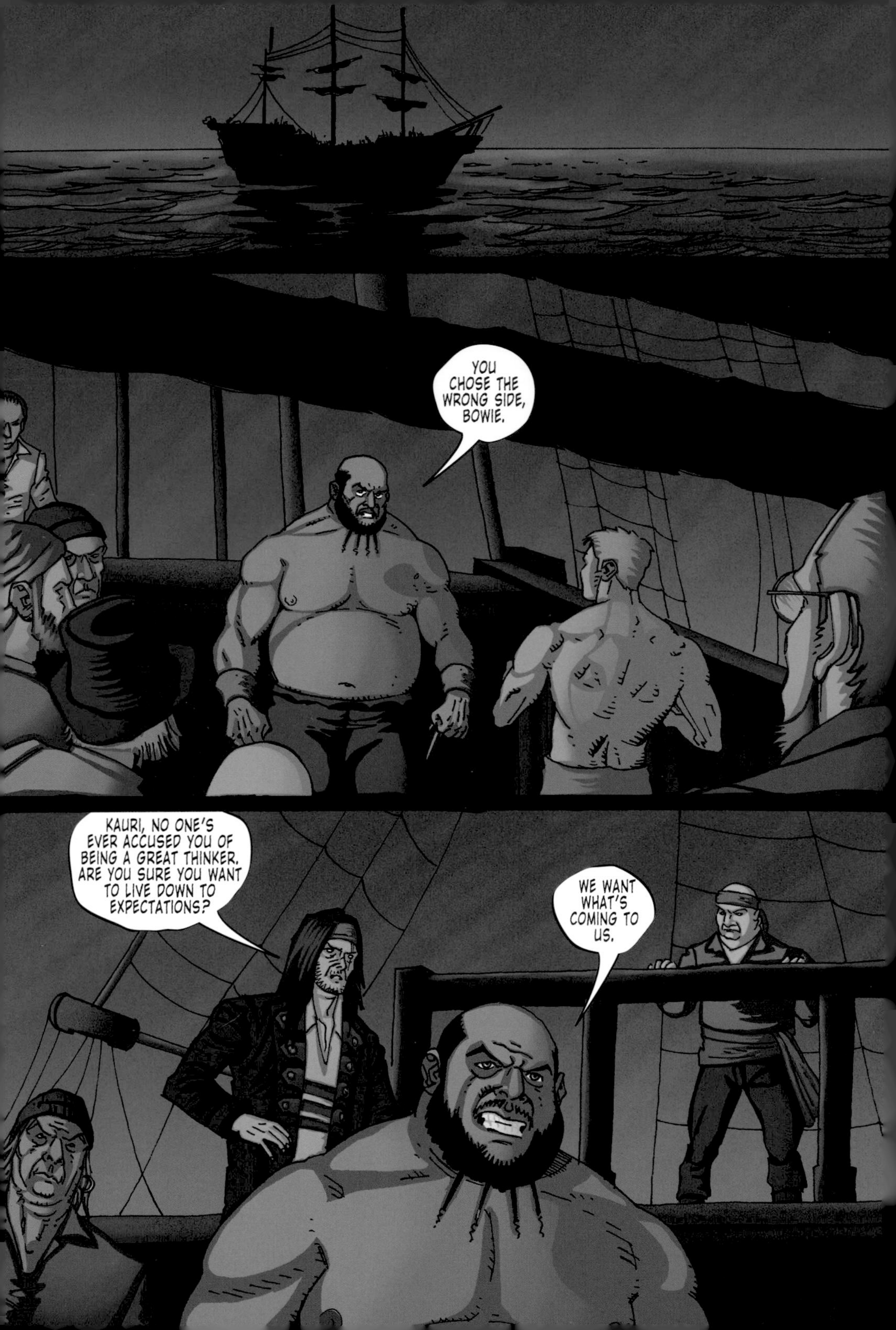

YOU CHOSE THE WRONG SIDE, BOWIE.
KAURI, NO ONE'S EVER ACCUSED YOU OF BEING A GREAT THINKER. ARE YOU SURE YOU WANT TO LIVE DOWN TO EXPECTATIONS?
WE WANT WHAT'S COMING TO US.

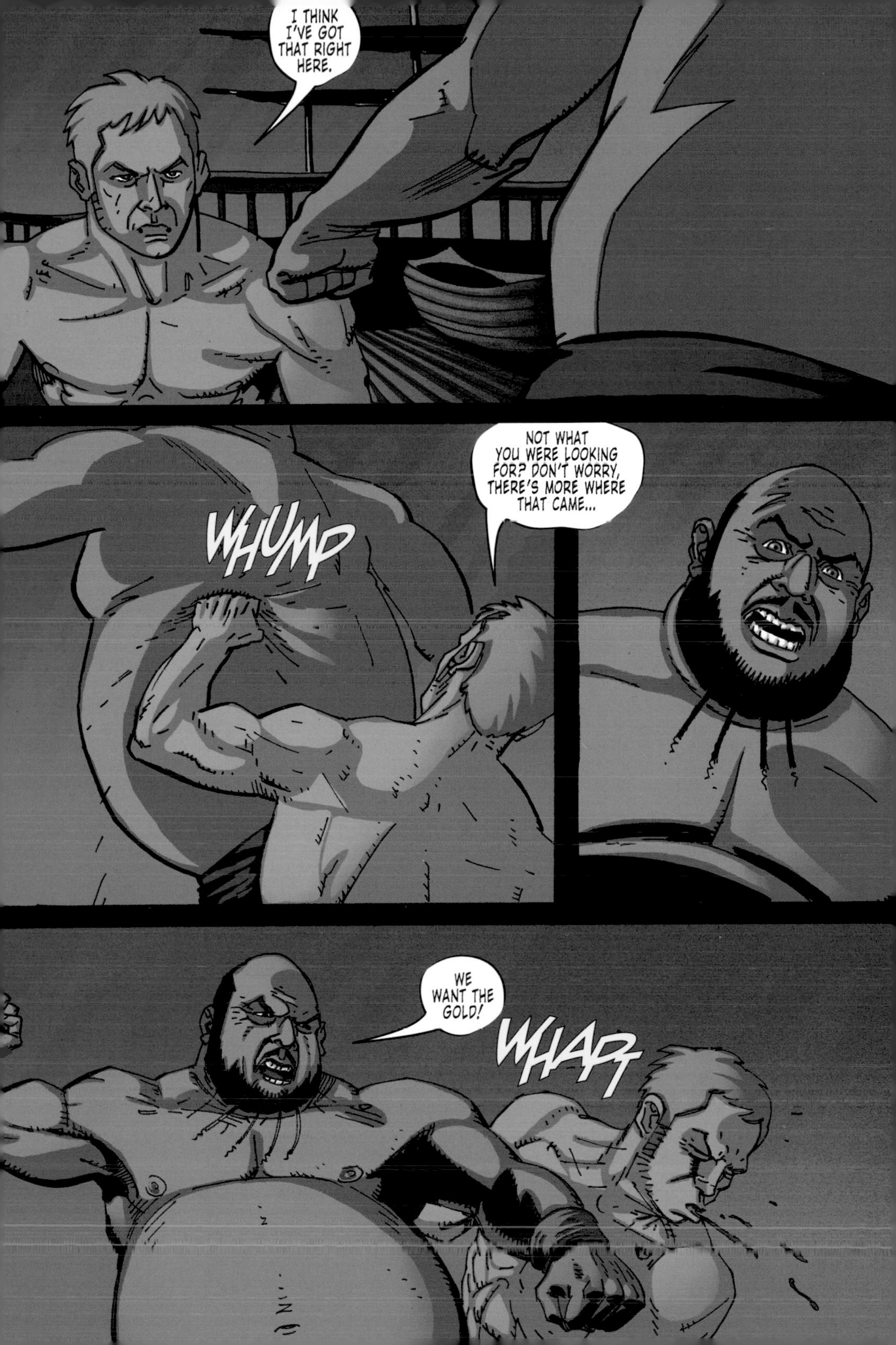
I THINK I'VE GOT THAT RIGHT HERE.
WHUMP
NOT WHAT YOU WERE LOOKING FOR? DON'T WORRY, THERE'S MORE WHERE THAT CAME...
WE WANT THE GOLD!
WHAP

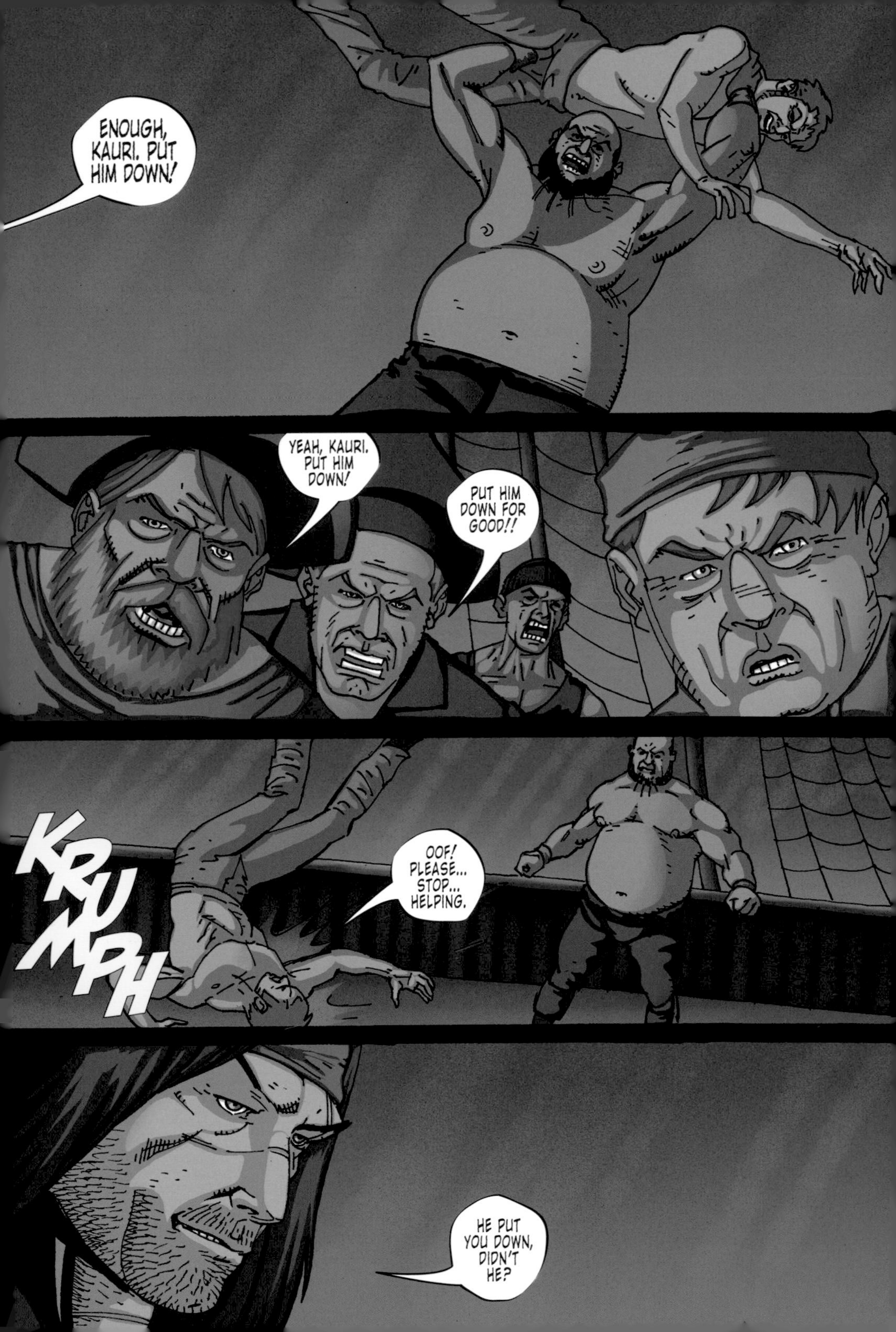
ENOUGH, KAURI. PUT HIM DOWN!
YEAH, KAURI. PUT HIM DOWN!
PUT HIM DOWN FOR GOOD!!
KRUMPH
OOF! PLEASE... STOP... HELPING.
HE PUT YOU DOWN, DIDN'T HE?

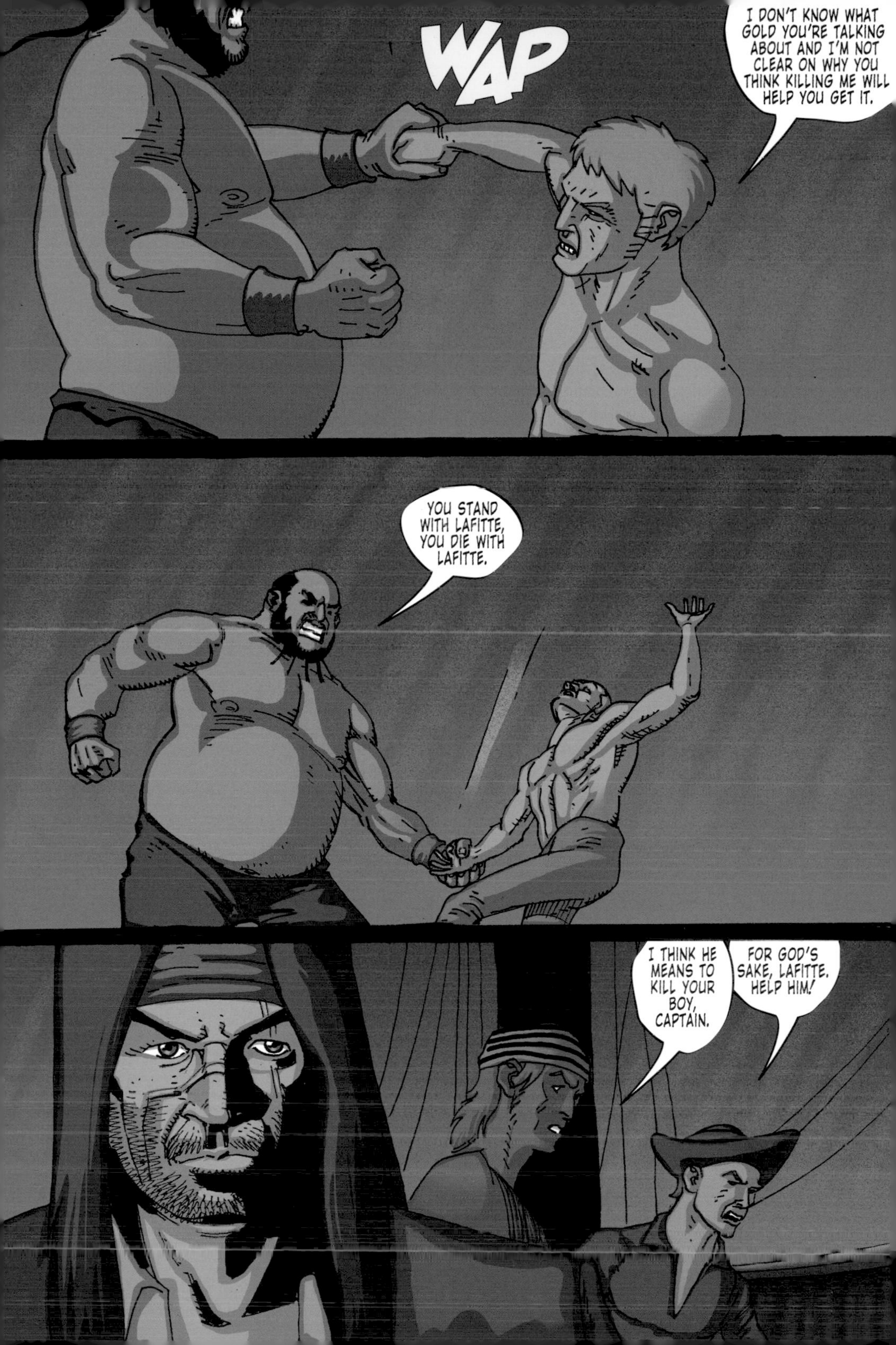
WAP
I DON'T KNOW WHAT GOLD YOU'RE TALKING ABOUT AND I'M NOT CLEAR ON WHY YOU THINK KILLING ME WILL HELP YOU GET IT.
YOU STAND WITH LAFITTE, YOU DIE WITH LAFITTE.
I THINK HE MEANS TO KILL YOUR BOY, CAPTAIN.
FOR GOD'S SAKE, LAFITTE. HELP HIM!

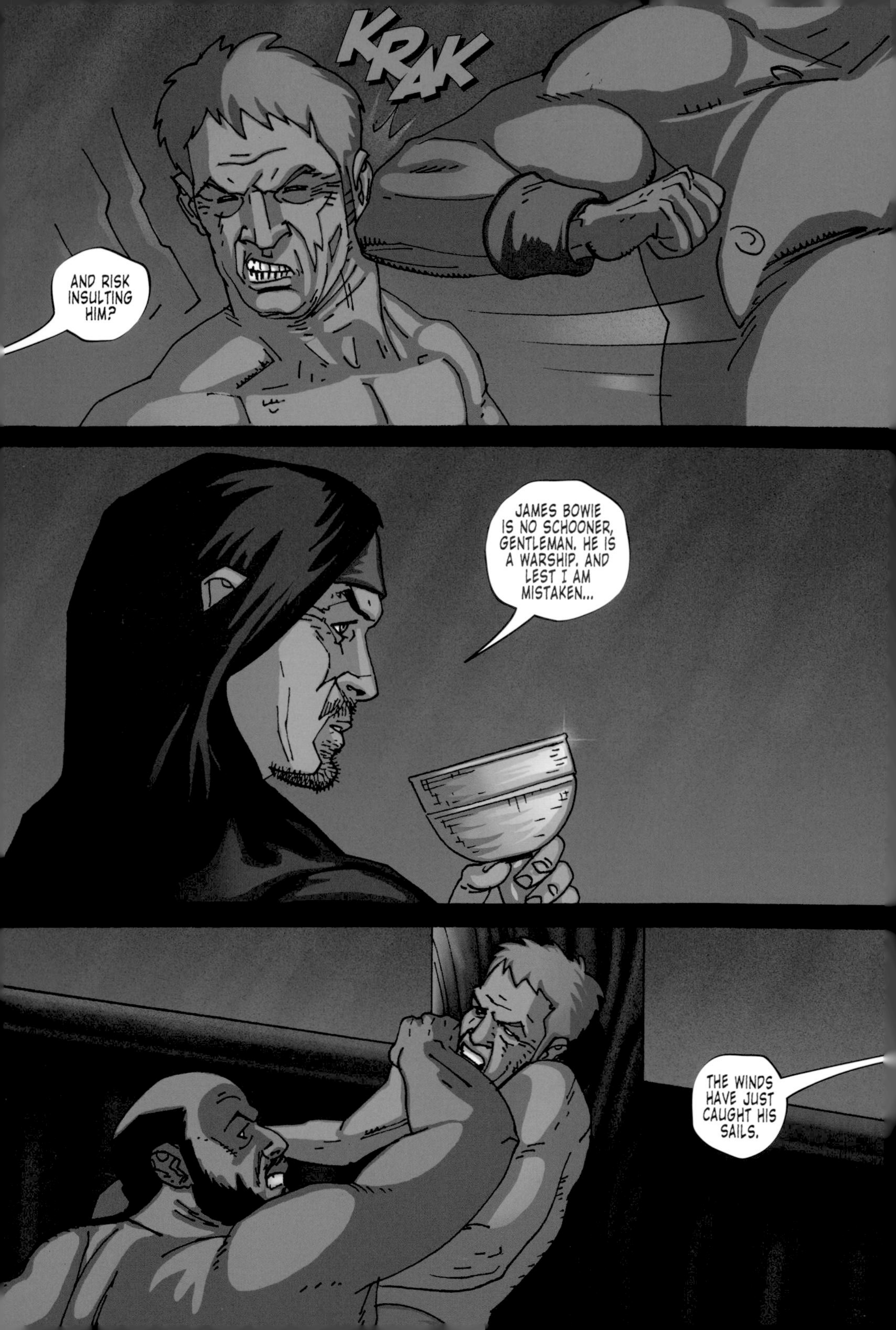
KRAK
AND RISK INSULTING HIM?
JAMES BOWIE IS NO SCHOONER, GENTLEMAN. HE IS A WARSHIP. AND LEST I AM MISTAKEN...
THE WINDS HAVE JUST CAUGHT HIS SAILS.

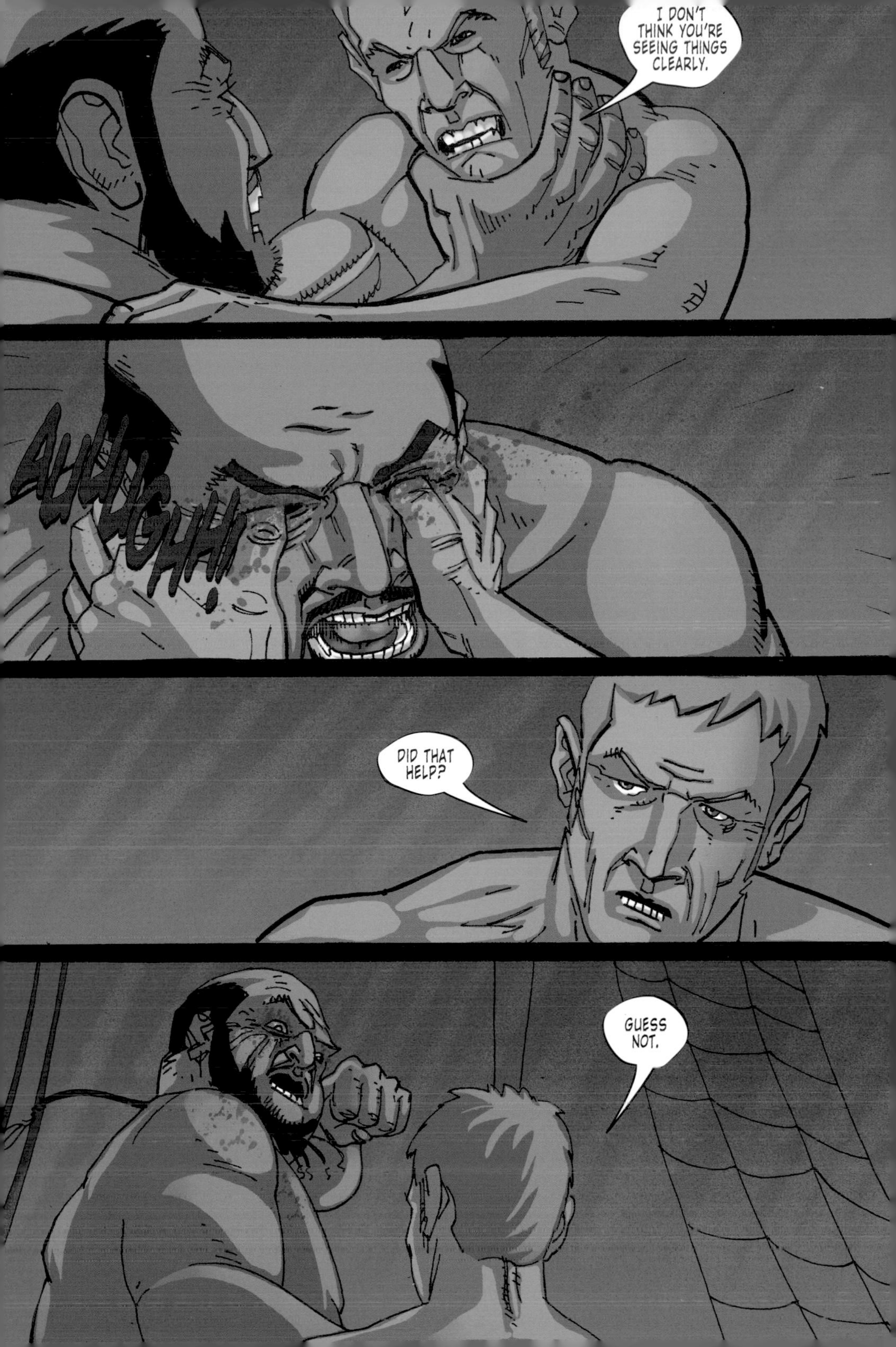
I DON'T THINK YOU'RE SEEING THINGS CLEARLY.
AUUUGHH!!
DID THAT HELP?
GUESS NOT.

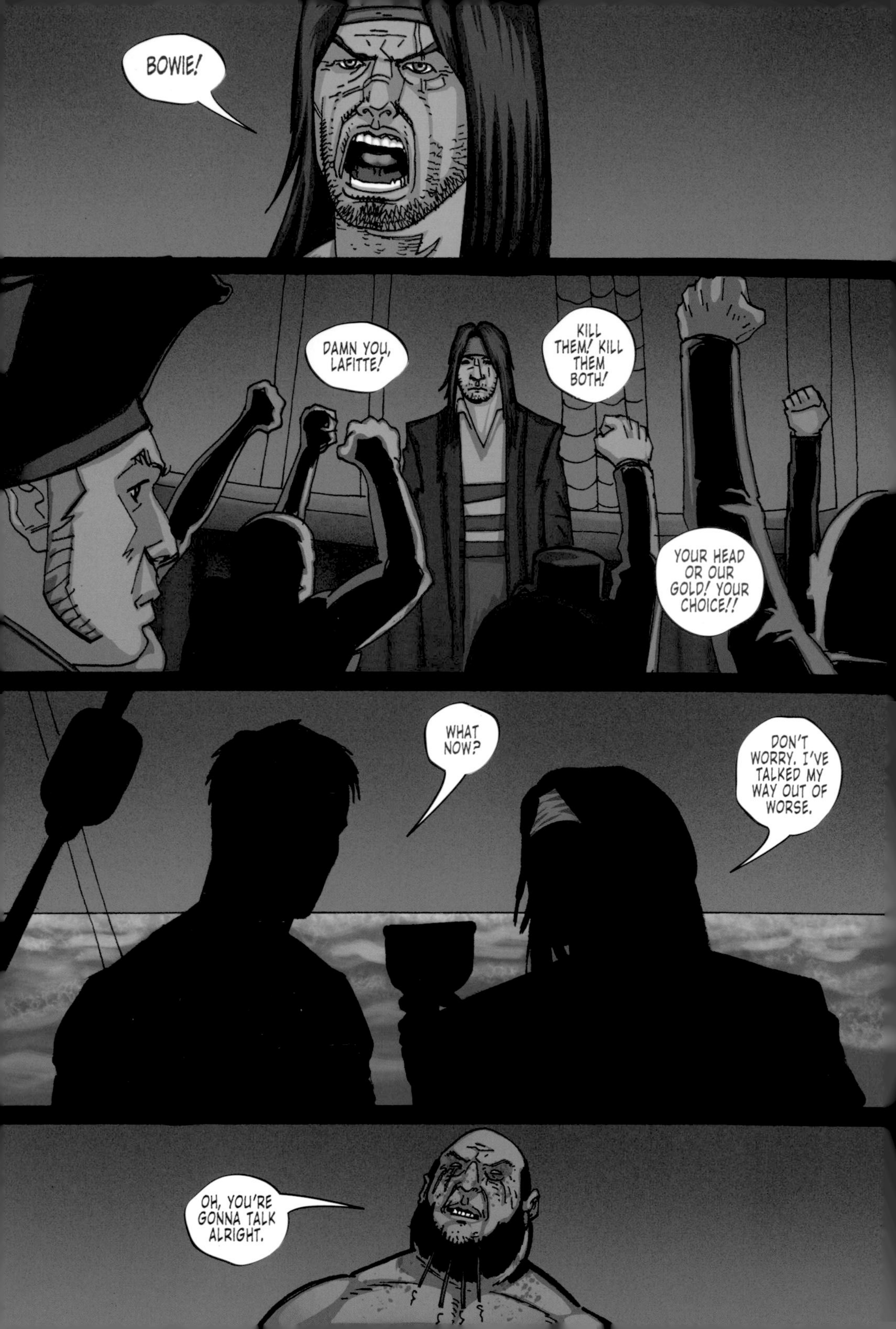
BOWIE!
DAMN YOU, LAFITTE!
KILL THEM! KILL THEM BOTH!
YOUR HEAD OR OUR GOLD! YOUR CHOICE!!
WHAT NOW?
DON'T WORRY. I'VE TALKED MY WAY OUT OF WORSE.
OH, YOU'RE GONNA TALK ALRIGHT.

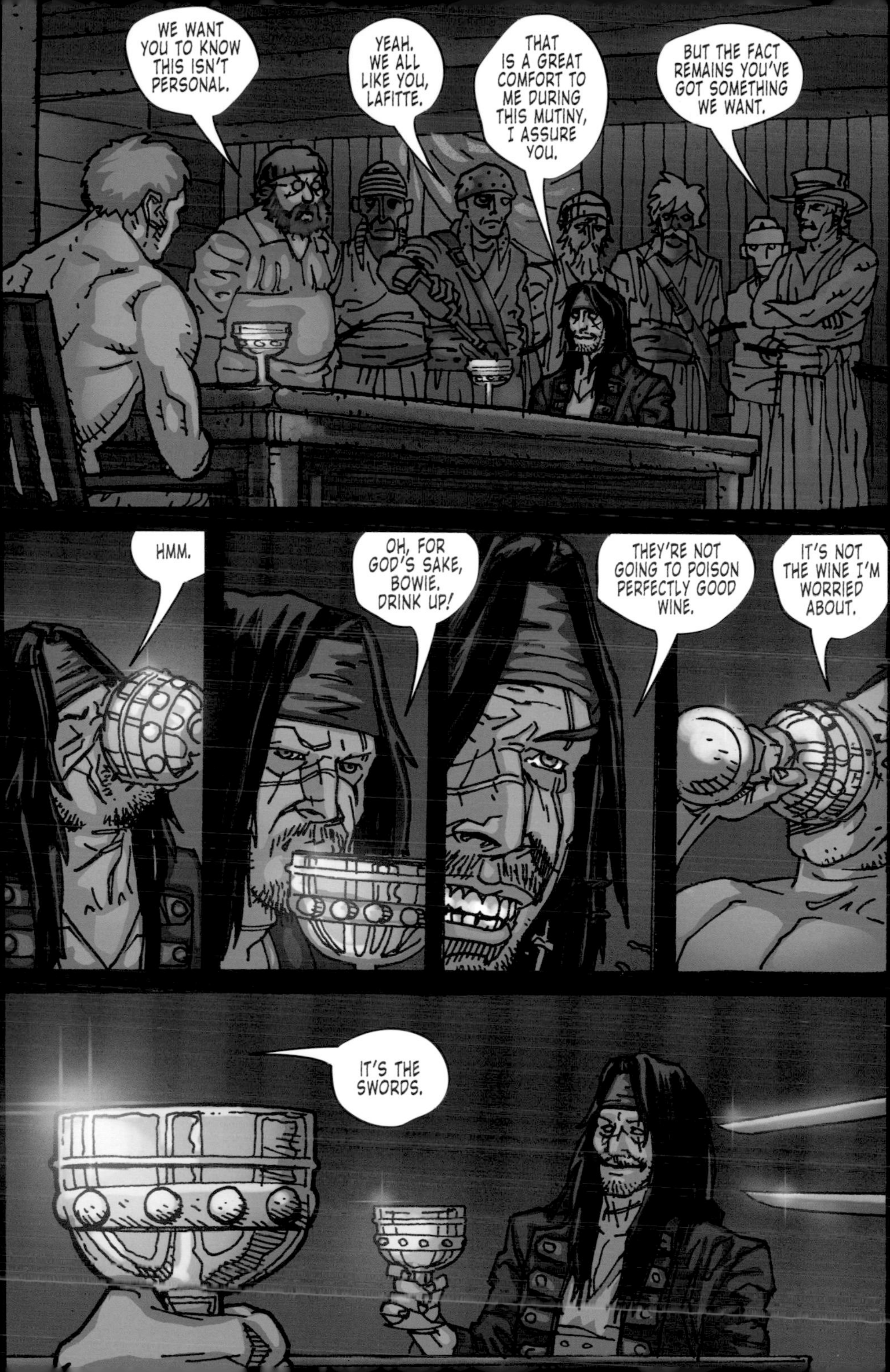
WE WANT YOU TO KNOW THIS ISN'T PERSONAL.
YEAH. WE ALL LIKE YOU, LAFITTE.
THAT IS A GREAT COMFORT TO ME DURING THIS MUTINY, I ASSURE YOU.
BUT THE FACT REMAINS YOU'VE GOT SOMETHING WE WANT.
HMM.
OH, FOR GOD'S SAKE, BOWIE. DRINK UP!
THEY'RE NOT GOING TO POISON PERFECTLY GOOD WINE.
IT'S NOT THE WINE I'M WORRIED ABOUT.
IT'S THE SWORDS.

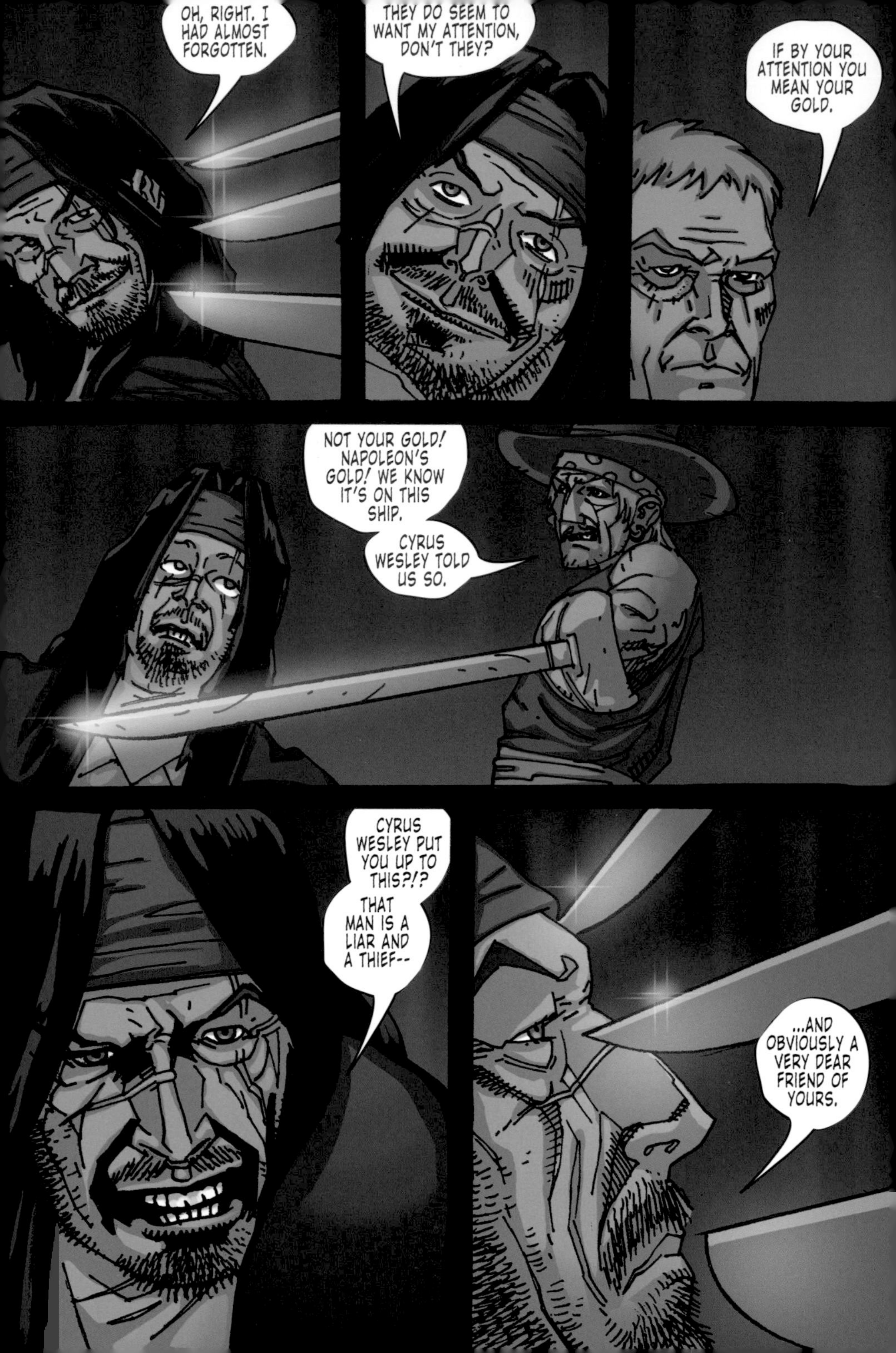
OH, RIGHT. I HAD ALMOST FORGOTTEN.
THEY DO SEEM TO WANT MY ATTENTION, DON'T THEY?
IF BY YOUR ATTENTION YOU MEAN YOUR GOLD.
NOT YOUR GOLD! NAPOLEON'S GOLD! WE KNOW IT'S ON THIS SHIP.
CYRUS WESLEY TOLD US SO.
CYRUS WESLEY PUT YOU UP TO THIS?!?
THAT MAN IS A LIAR AND A THIEF--
...AND OBVIOUSLY A VERY DEAR FRIEND OF YOURS.

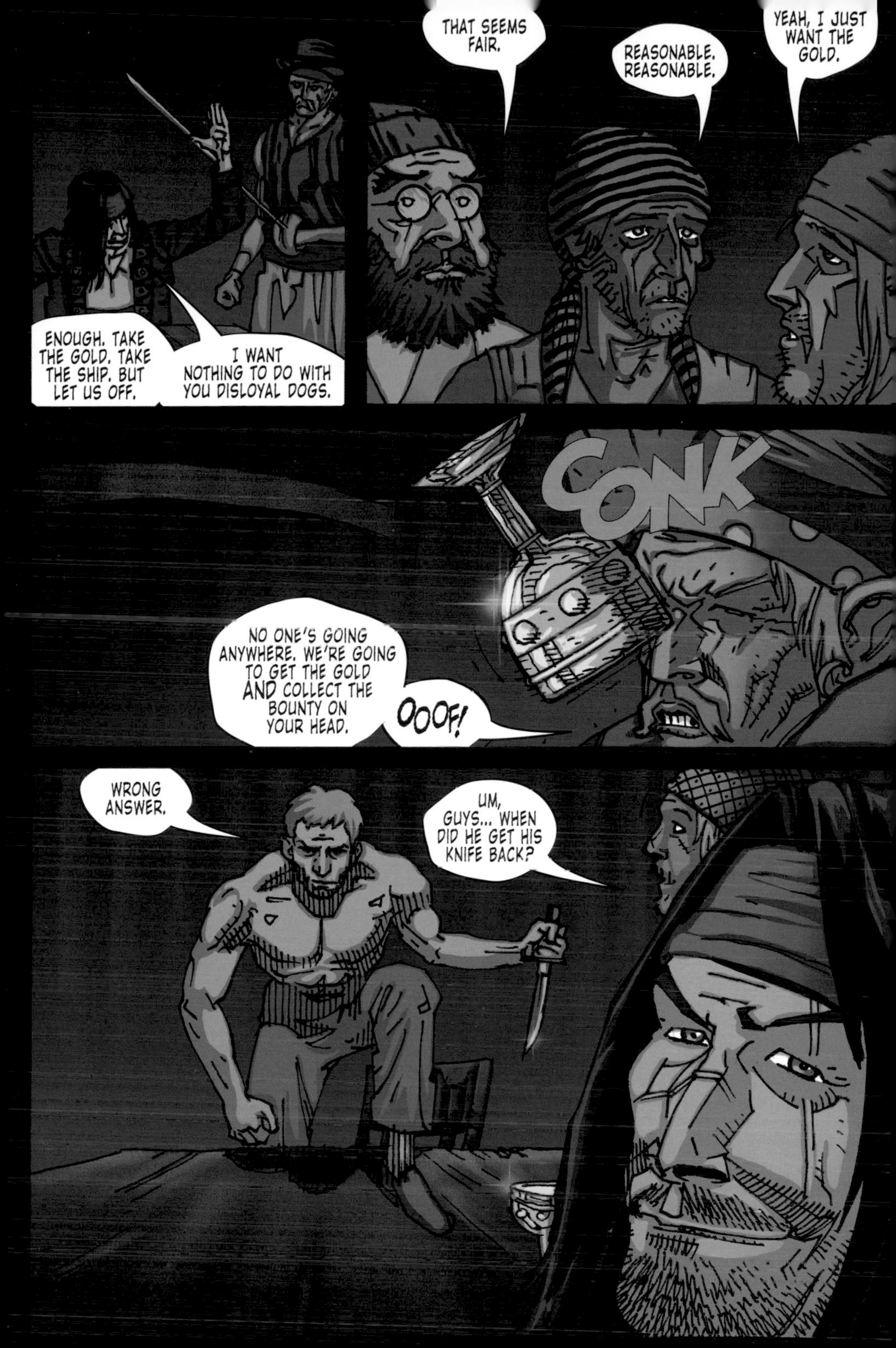
ENOUGH. TAKE THE GOLD. TAKE THE SHIP. BUT LET US OFF.
I WANT NOTHING TO DO WITH YOU DISLOYAL DOGS.
THAT SEEMS FAIR.
REASONABLE. REASONABLE.
YEAH, I JUST WANT THE GOLD.
CONK
NO ONE'S GOING ANYWHERE. WE'RE GOING TO GET THE GOLD AND COLLECT THE BOUNTY ON YOUR HEAD.
OOOF!
WRONG ANSWER.
UM, GUYS... WHEN DID HE GET HIS KNIFE BACK?

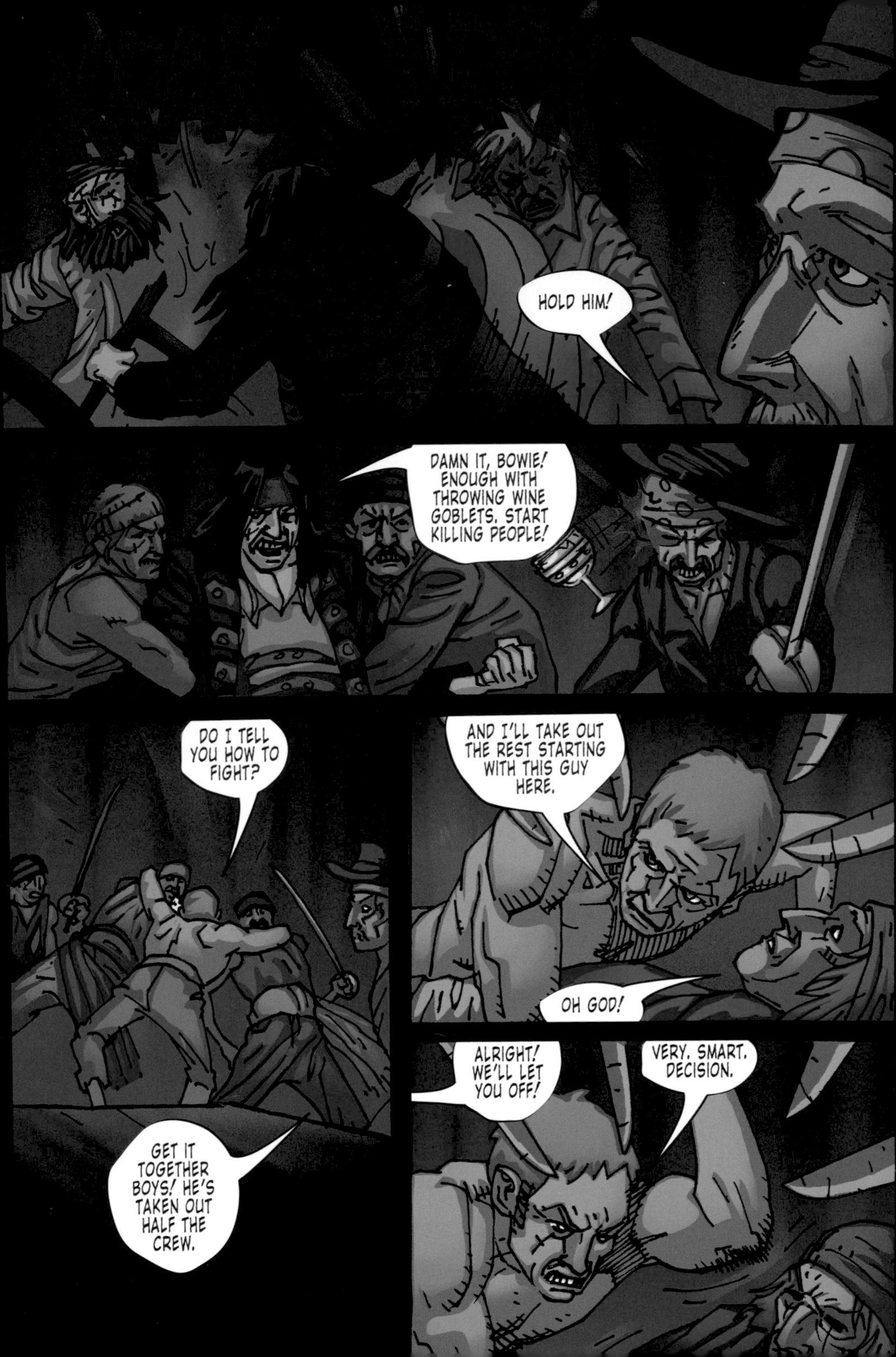
HOLD HIM!
DAMN IT, BOWIE! ENOUGH WITH THROWING WINE GOBLETS. START KILLING PEOPLE!
DO I TELL YOU HOW TO FIGHT?
GET IT TOGETHER BOYS! HE'S TAKEN OUT HALF THE CREW.
AND I'LL TAKE OUT THE REST STARTING WITH THIS GUY HERE.
OH GOD!
ALRIGHT! WE'LL LET YOU OFF!
VERY. SMART. DECISION.

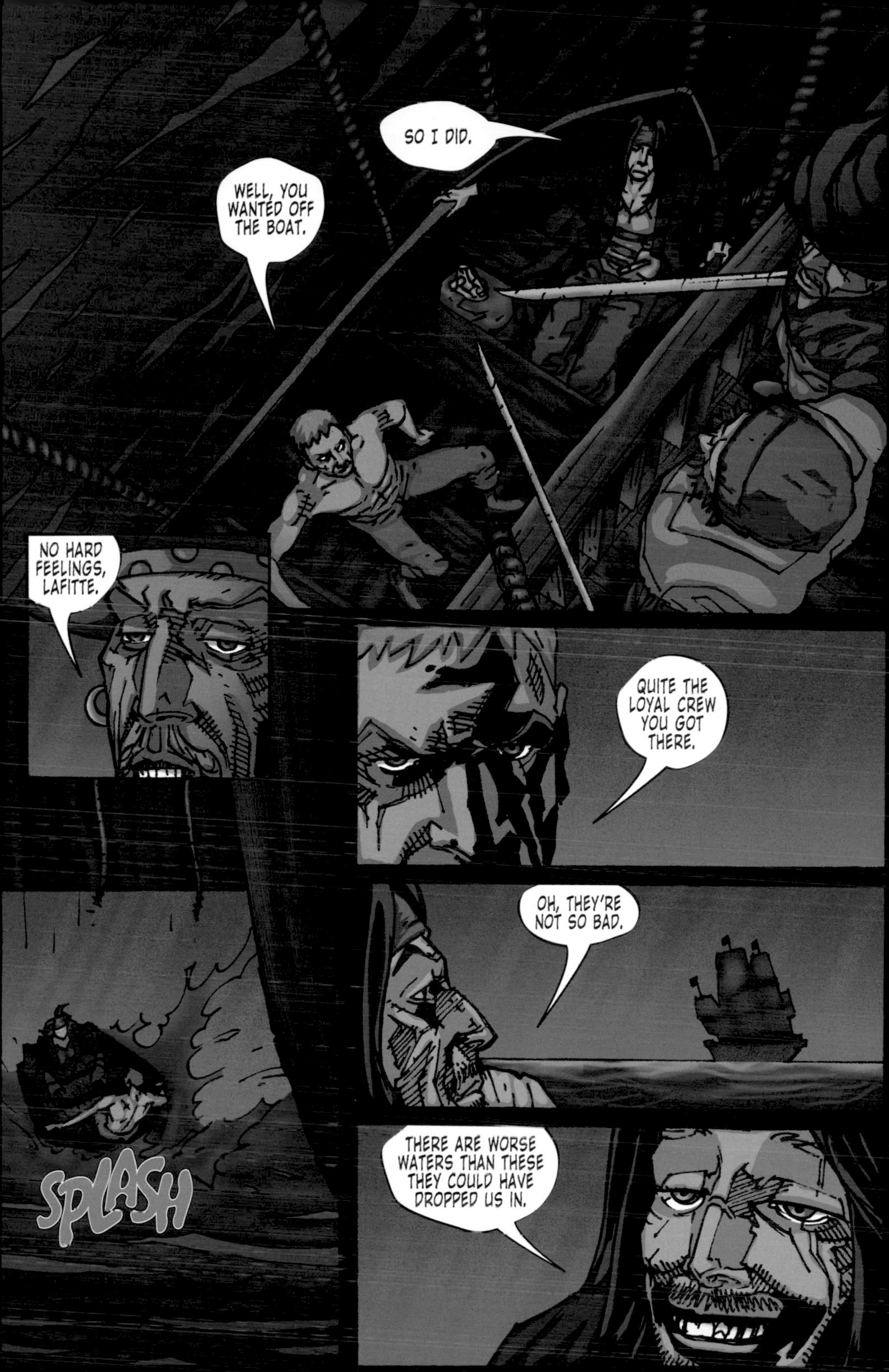
SO I DID.
WELL, YOU WANTED OFF THE BOAT.
NO HARD FEELINGS, LAFITTE.
QUITE THE LOYAL CREW YOU GOT THERE.
SPLASH
OH, THEY'RE NOT SO BAD.
THERE ARE WORSE WATERS THAN THESE THEY COULD HAVE DROPPED US IN.

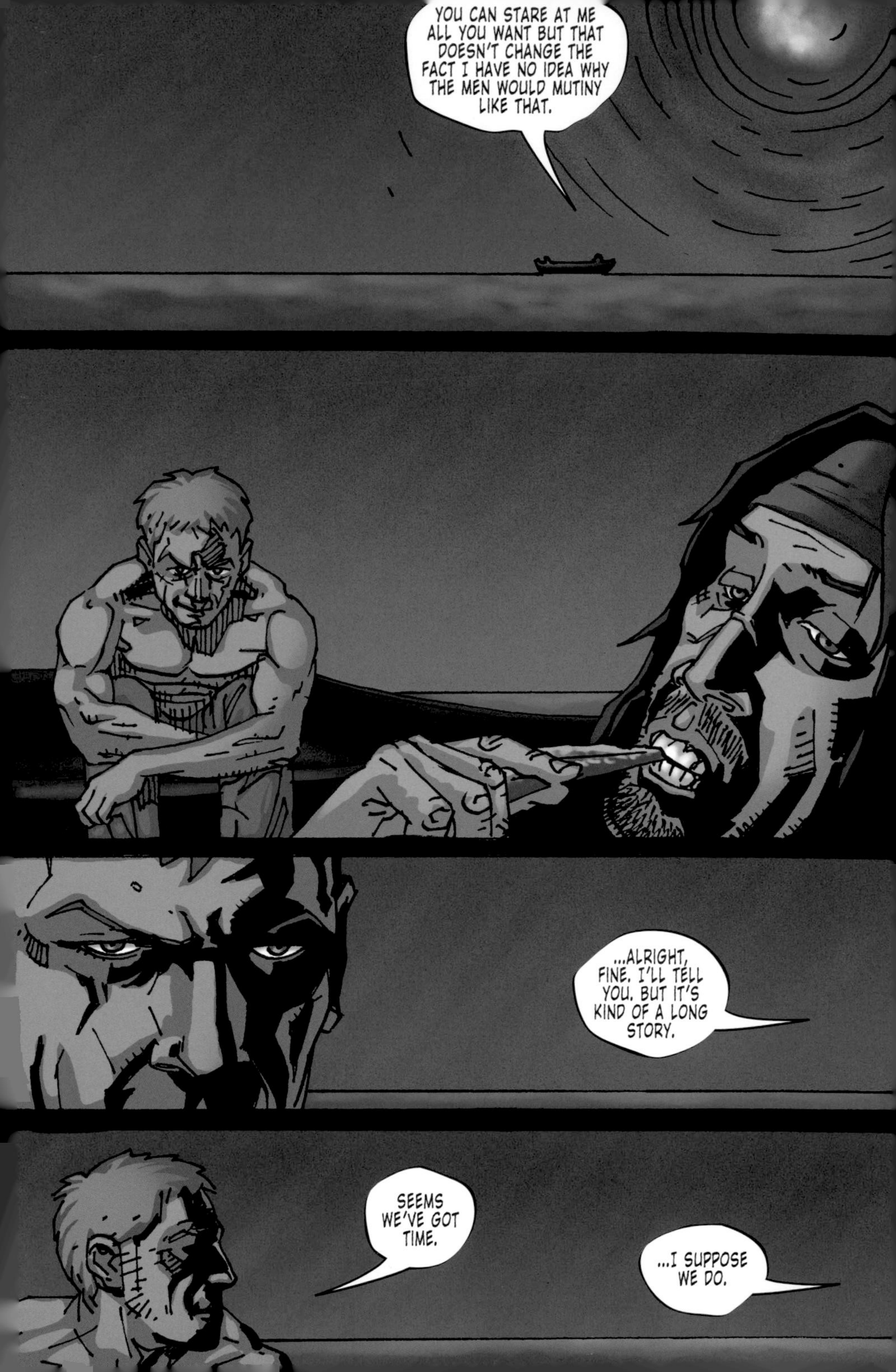
YOU CAN STARE AT ME ALL YOU WANT BUT THAT DOESN'T CHANGE THE FACT I HAVE NO IDEA WHY THE MEN WOULD MUTINY LIKE THAT.
...ALRIGHT, FINE. I'LL TELL YOU. BUT IT'S KIND OF A LONG STORY.
SEEMS WE'VE GOT TIME.
...I SUPPOSE WE DO.

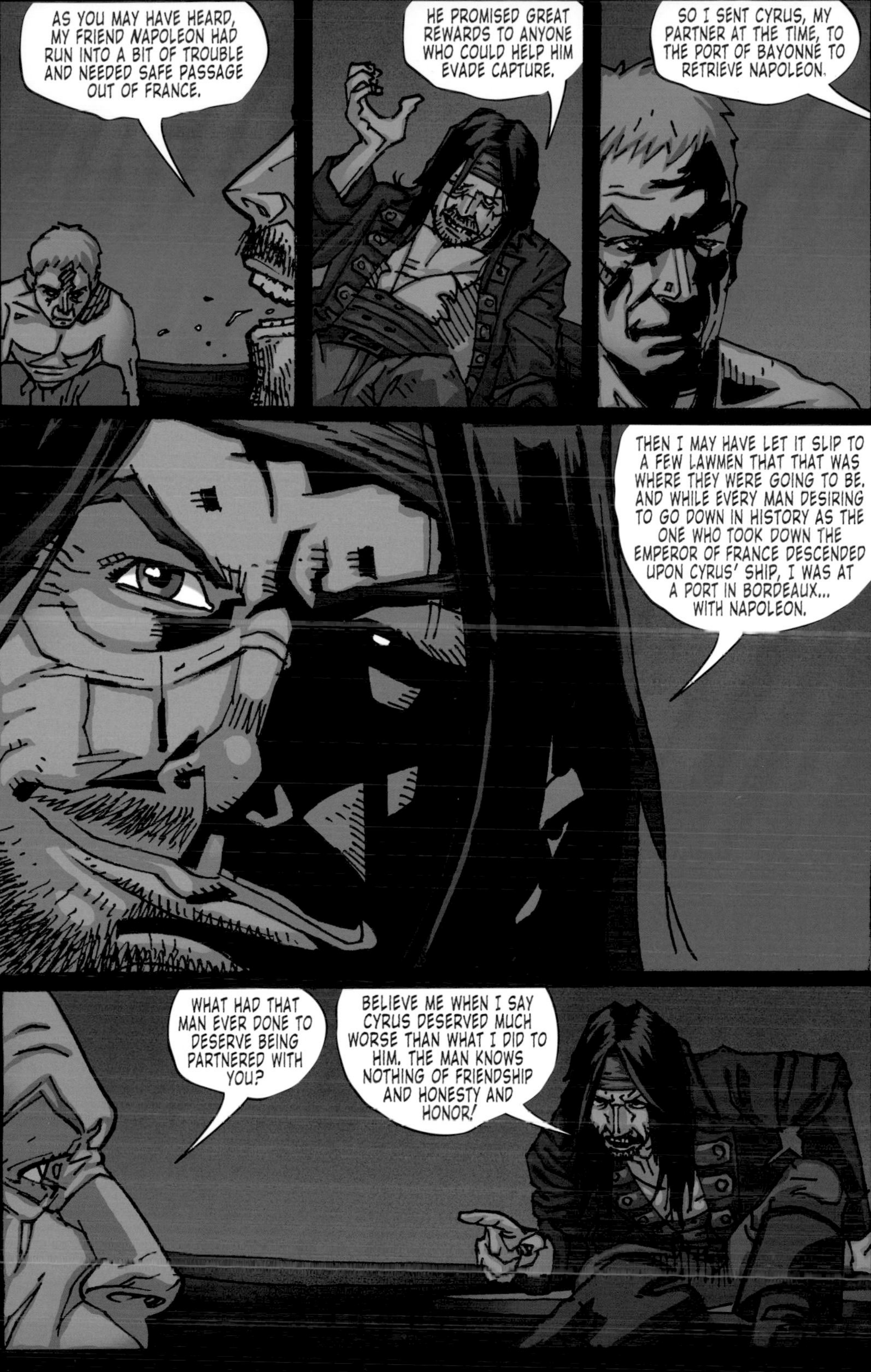
AS YOU MAY HAVE HEARD, MY FRIEND NAPOLEON HAD RUN INTO A BIT OF TROUBLE AND NEEDED SAFE PASSAGE OUT OF FRANCE.
HE PROMISED GREAT REWARDS TO ANYONE WHO COULD HELP HIM EVADE CAPTURE.
SO I SENT CYRUS, MY PARTNER AT THE TIME, TO THE PORT OF BAYONNE TO RETRIEVE NAPOLEON.
THEN I MAY HAVE LET IT SLIP TO A FEW LAWMEN THAT THAT WAS WHERE THEY WERE GOING TO BE. AND WHILE EVERY MAN DESIRING TO GO DOWN IN HISTORY AS THE ONE WHO TOOK DOWN THE EMPEROR OF FRANCE DESCENDED UPON CYRUS' SHIP, I WAS AT A PORT IN BORDEAUX... WITH NAPOLEON.
WHAT HAD THAT MAN EVER DONE TO DESERVE BEING PARTNERED WITH YOU?
BELIEVE ME WHEN I SAY CYRUS DESERVED MUCH WORSE THAN WHAT I DID TO HIM. THE MAN KNOWS NOTHING OF FRIENDSHIP AND HONESTY AND HONOR!

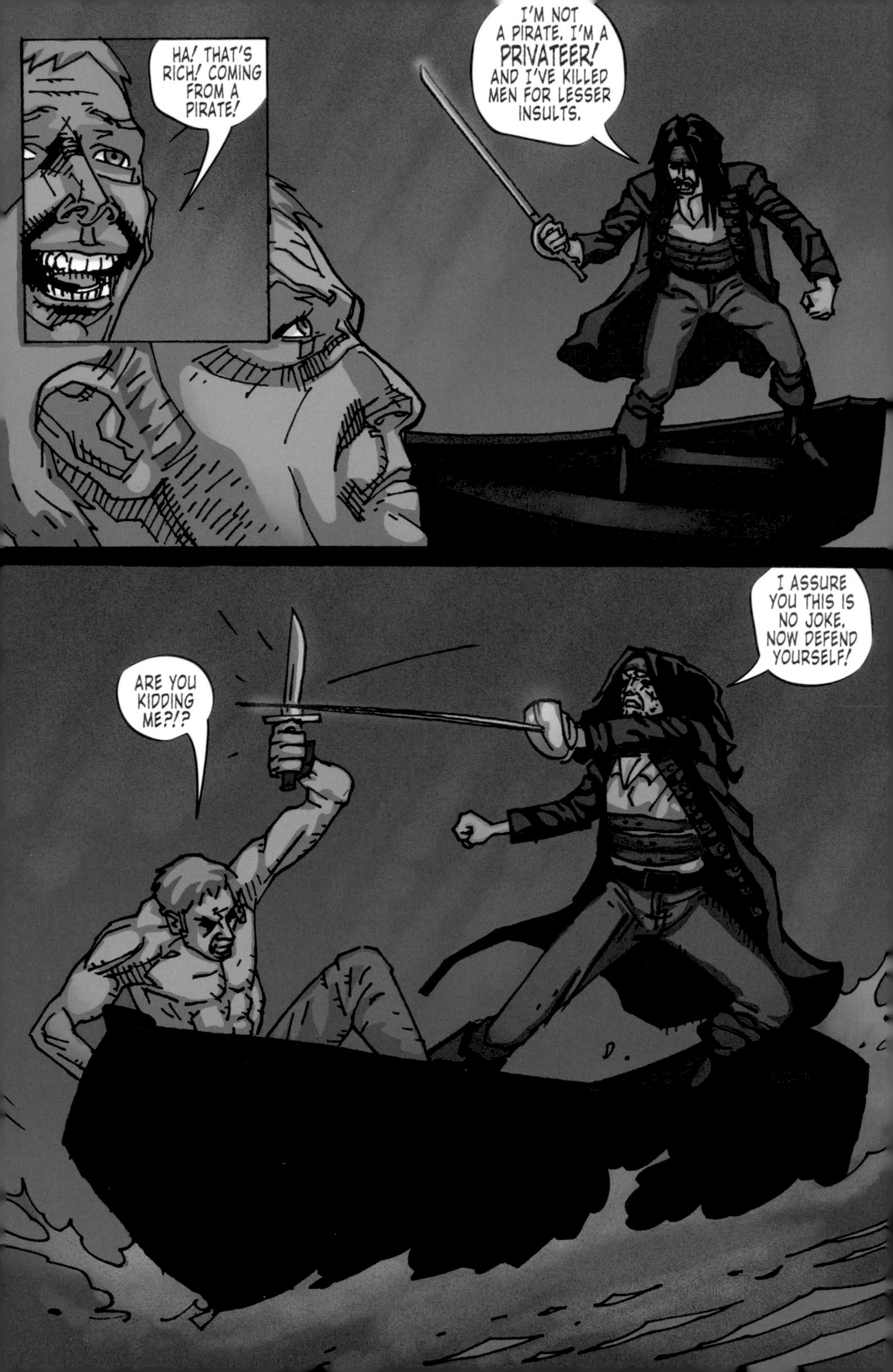
HA! THAT'S RICH! COMING FROM A PIRATE!
I'M NOT A PIRATE. I'M A PRIVATEER! AND I'VE KILLED MEN FOR LESSER INSULTS.
ARE YOU KIDDING ME?!?
I ASSURE YOU THIS IS NO JOKE. NOW DEFEND YOURSELF!

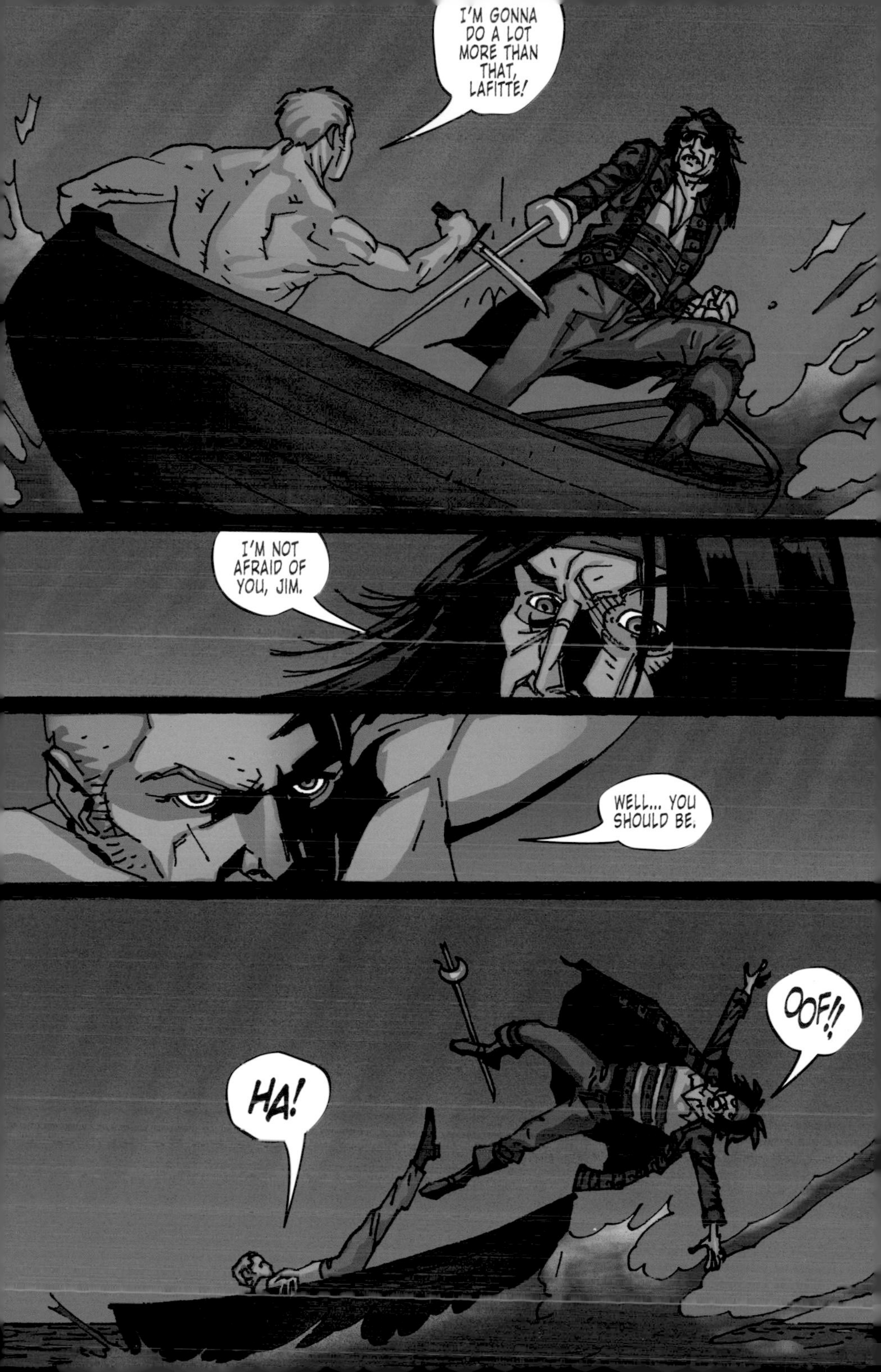
I'M GONNA DO A LOT MORE THAN THAT, LAFITTE!
I'M NOT AFRAID OF YOU, JIM.
WELL... YOU SHOULD BE.
HA!
OOF!!

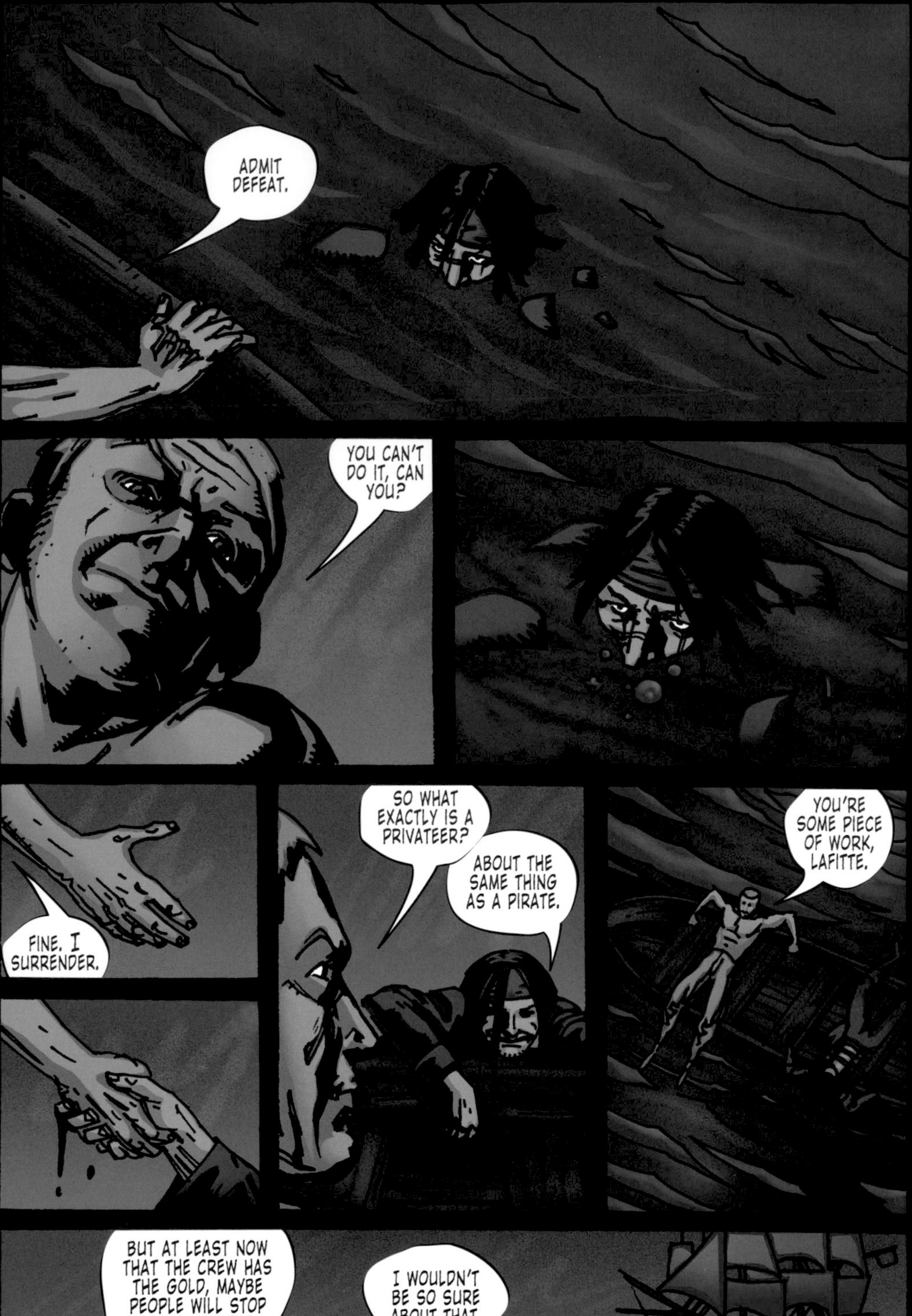
ADMIT DEFEAT.
YOU CAN'T DO IT, CAN YOU?
FINE. I SURRENDER.
SO WHAT EXACTLY IS A PRIVATEER?
ABOUT THE SAME THING AS A PIRATE.
YOU'RE SOME PIECE OF WORK, LAFITTE.
BUT AT LEAST NOW THAT THE CREW HAS THE GOLD, MAYBE PEOPLE WILL STOP TRYING TO KILL YOU.
I WOULDN'T BE SO SURE ABOUT THAT.

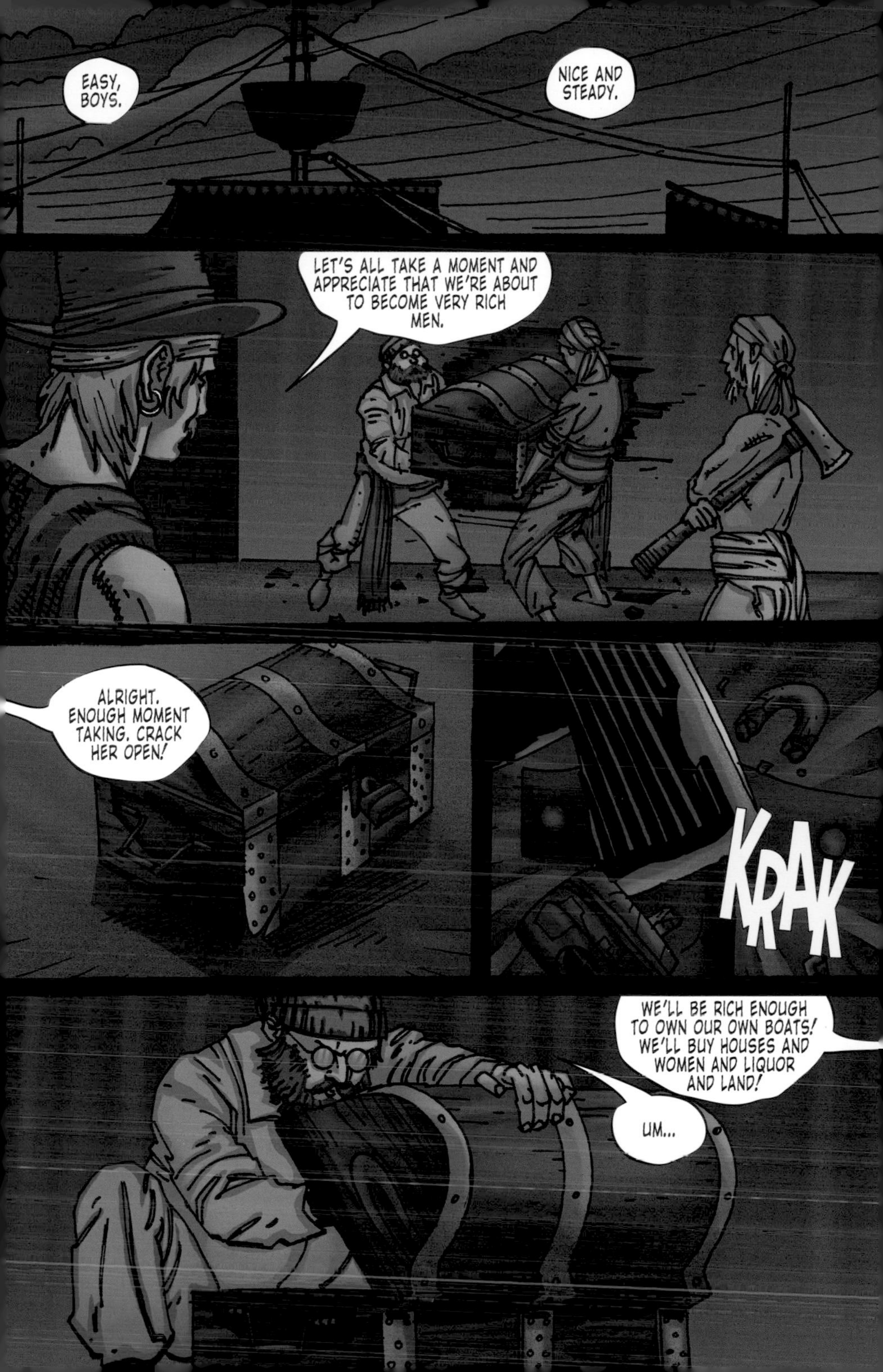
EASY, BOYS.
NICE AND STEADY.
LET'S ALL TAKE A MOMENT AND APPRECIATE THAT WE'RE ABOUT TO BECOME VERY RICH MEN.
ALRIGHT. ENOUGH MOMENT TAKING. CRACK HER OPEN!
KRAK
WE'LL BE RICH ENOUGH TO OWN OUR OWN BOATS! WE'LL BUY HOUSES AND WOMEN AND LIQUOR AND LAND!
UM...

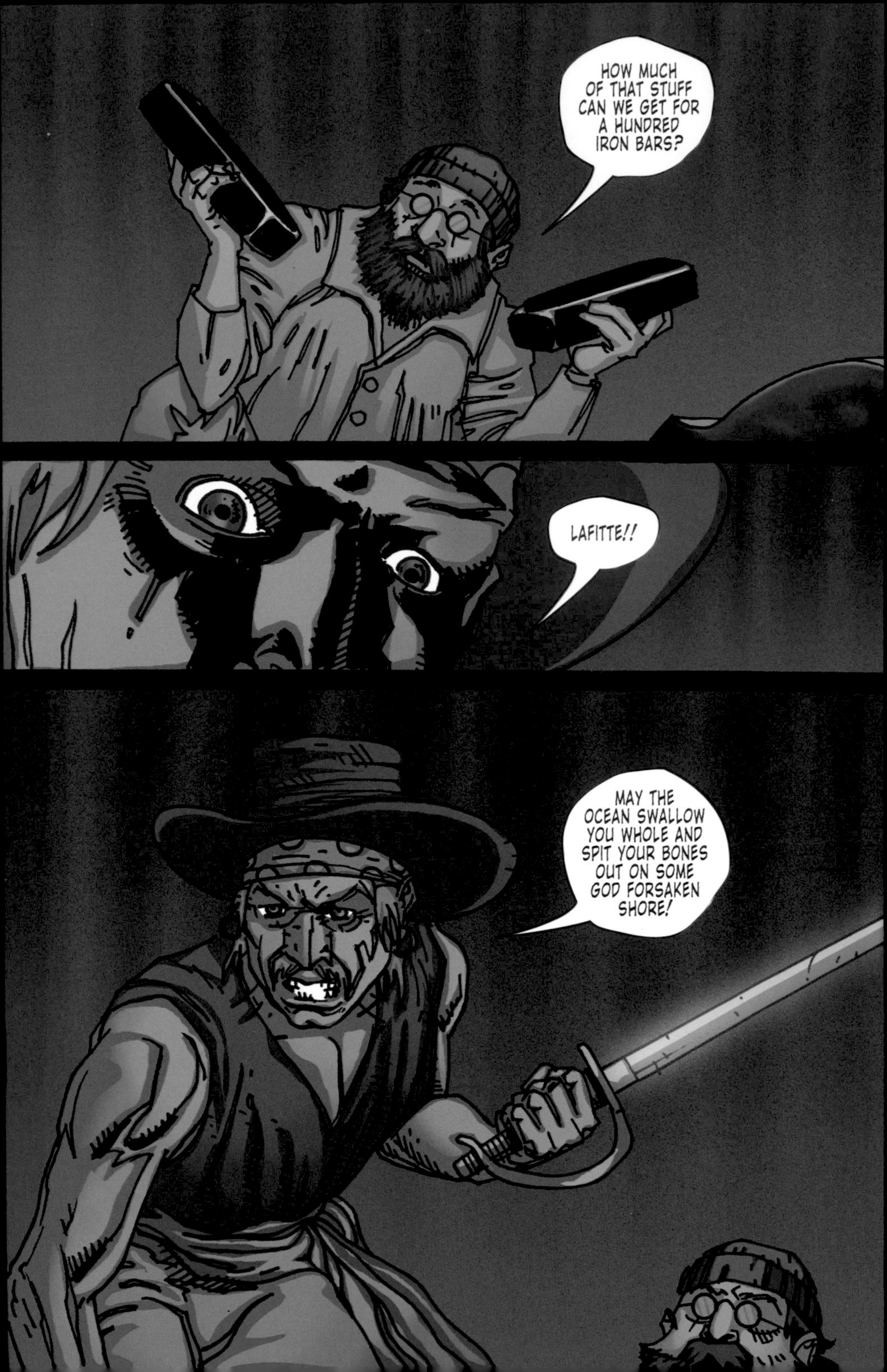
HOW MUCH OF THAT STUFF CAN WE GET FOR A HUNDRED IRON BARS?
LAFITTE!!
MAY THE OCEAN SWALLOW YOU WHOLE AND SPIT YOUR BONES OUT ON SOME GOD FORSAKEN SHORE!

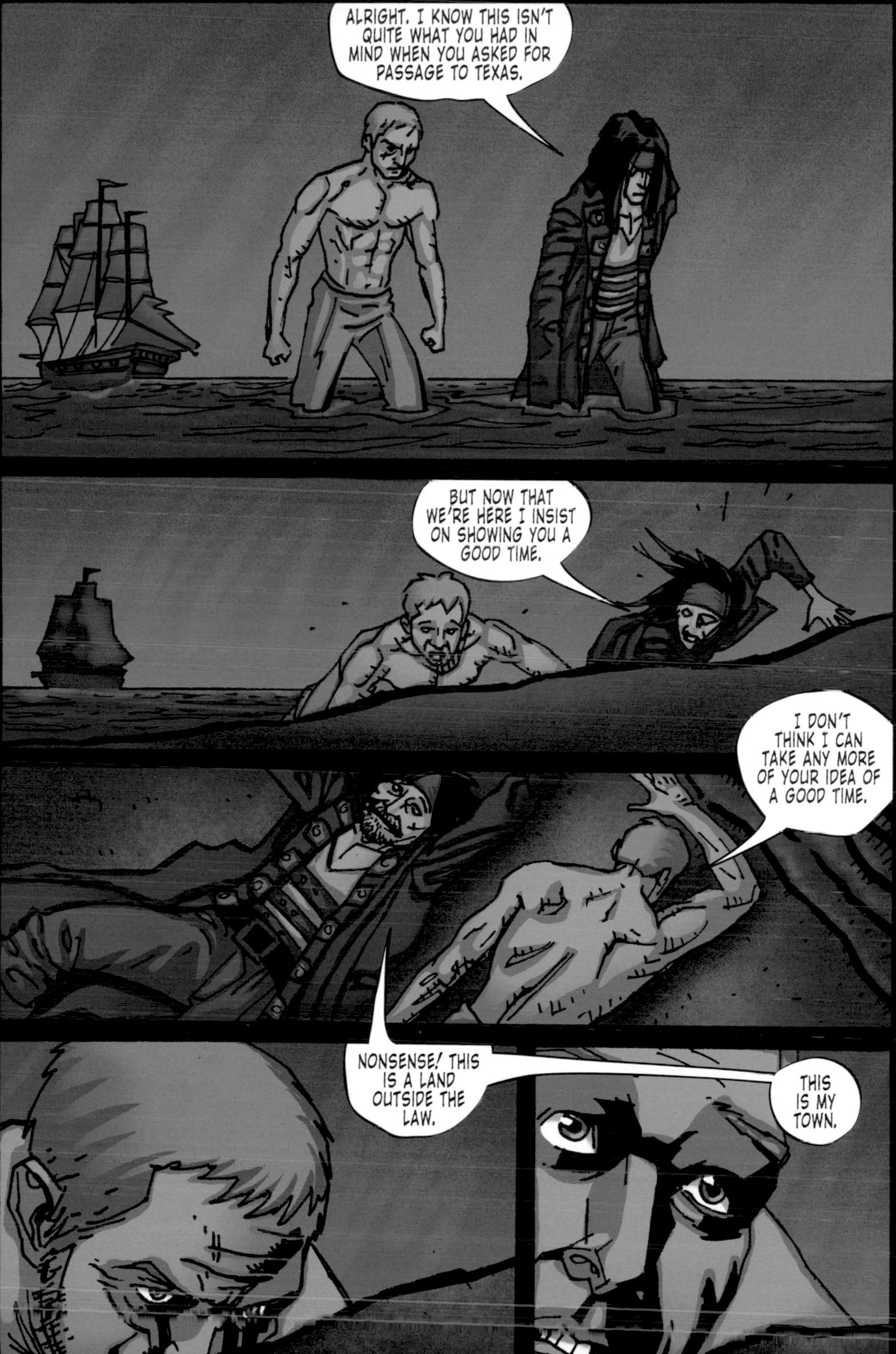
ALRIGHT. I KNOW THIS ISN'T QUITE WHAT YOU HAD IN MIND WHEN YOU ASKED FOR PASSAGE TO TEXAS.
BUT NOW THAT WE'RE HERE I INSIST ON SHOWING YOU A GOOD TIME.
I DON'T THINK I CAN TAKE ANY MORE OF YOUR IDEA OF A GOOD TIME.
NONSENSE! THIS IS A LAND OUTSIDE THE LAW.
THIS IS MY TOWN.

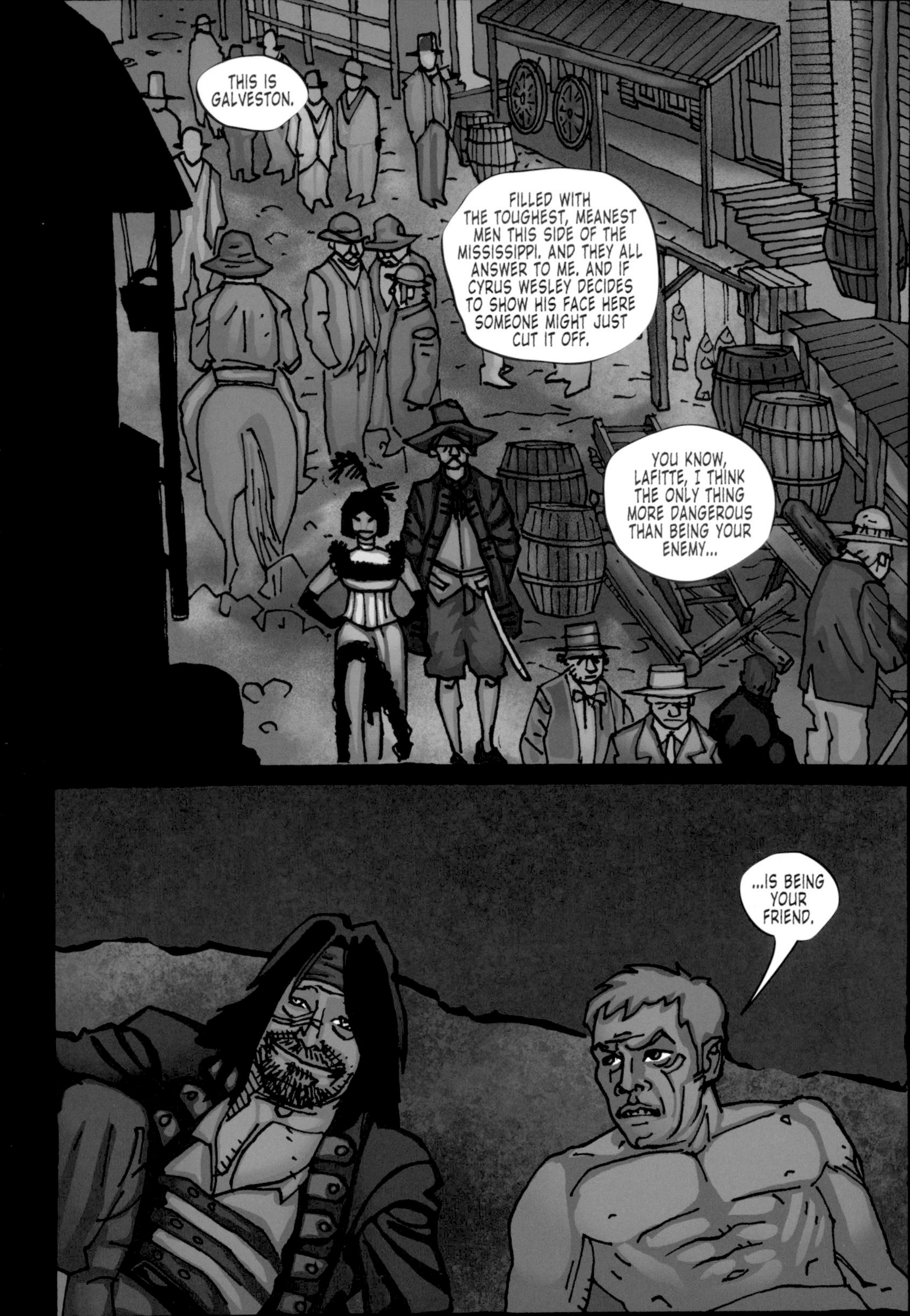

THIS IS GALVESTON.
FILLED WITH THE TOUGHEST, MEANEST MEN THIS SIDE OF THE MISSISSIPPI. AND THEY ALL ANSWER TO ME. AND IF CYRUS WESLEY DECIDES TO SHOW HIS FACE HERE SOMEONE MIGHT JUST CUT IT OFF.
YOU KNOW, LAFITTE, I THINK THE ONLY THING MORE DANGEROUS THAN BEING YOUR ENEMY...
...IS BEING YOUR FRIEND.

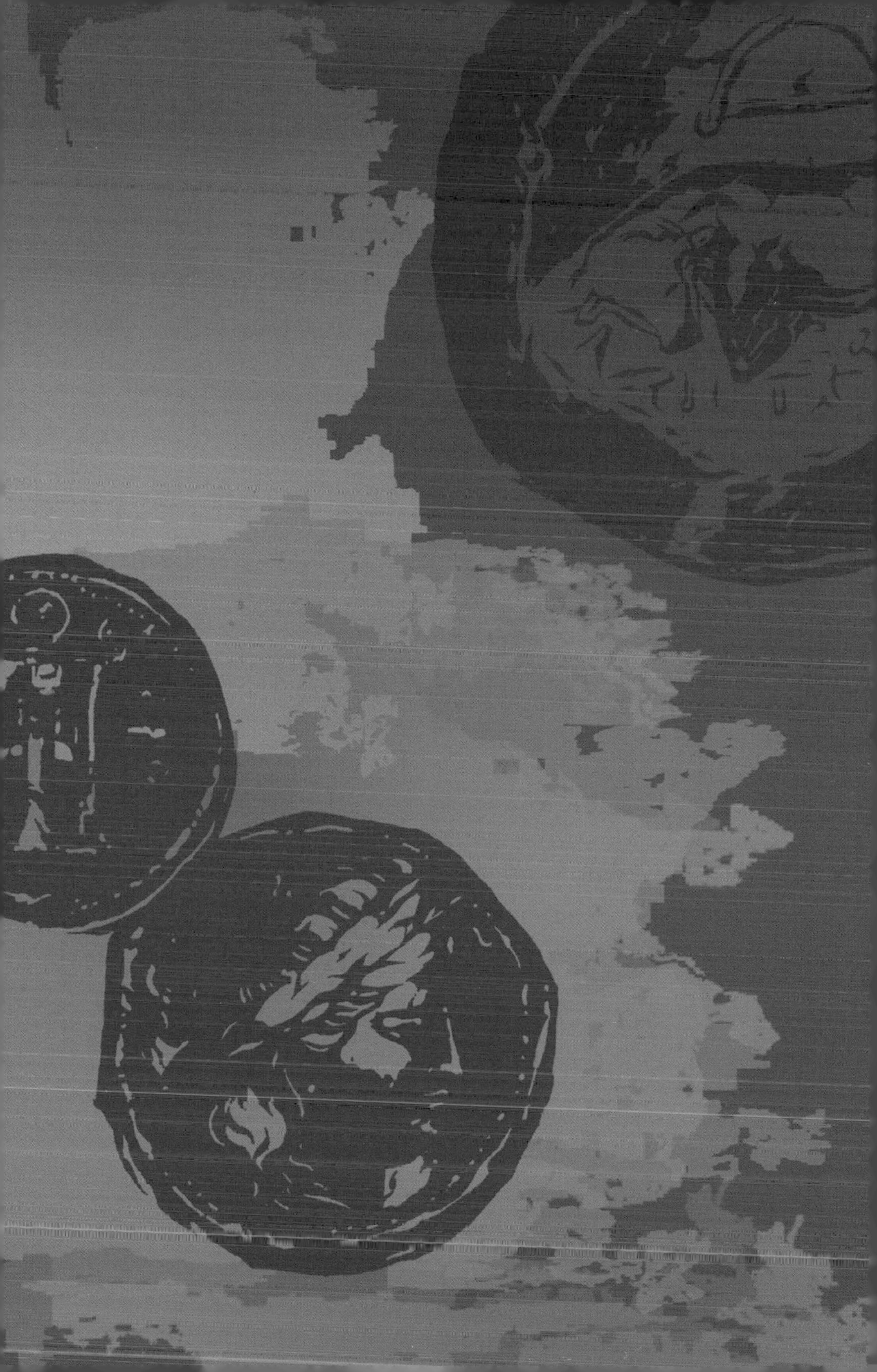

CHAPTER II

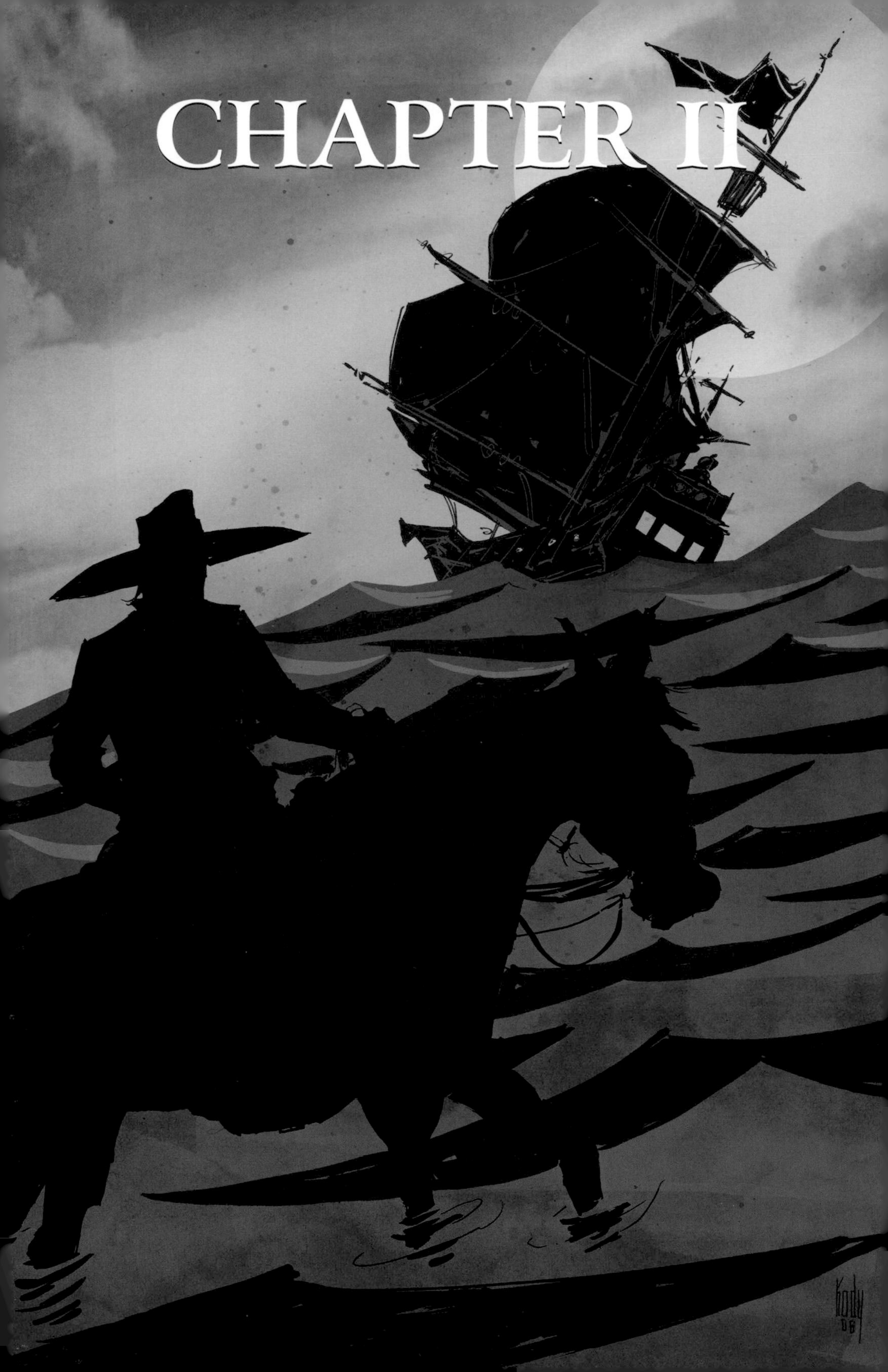

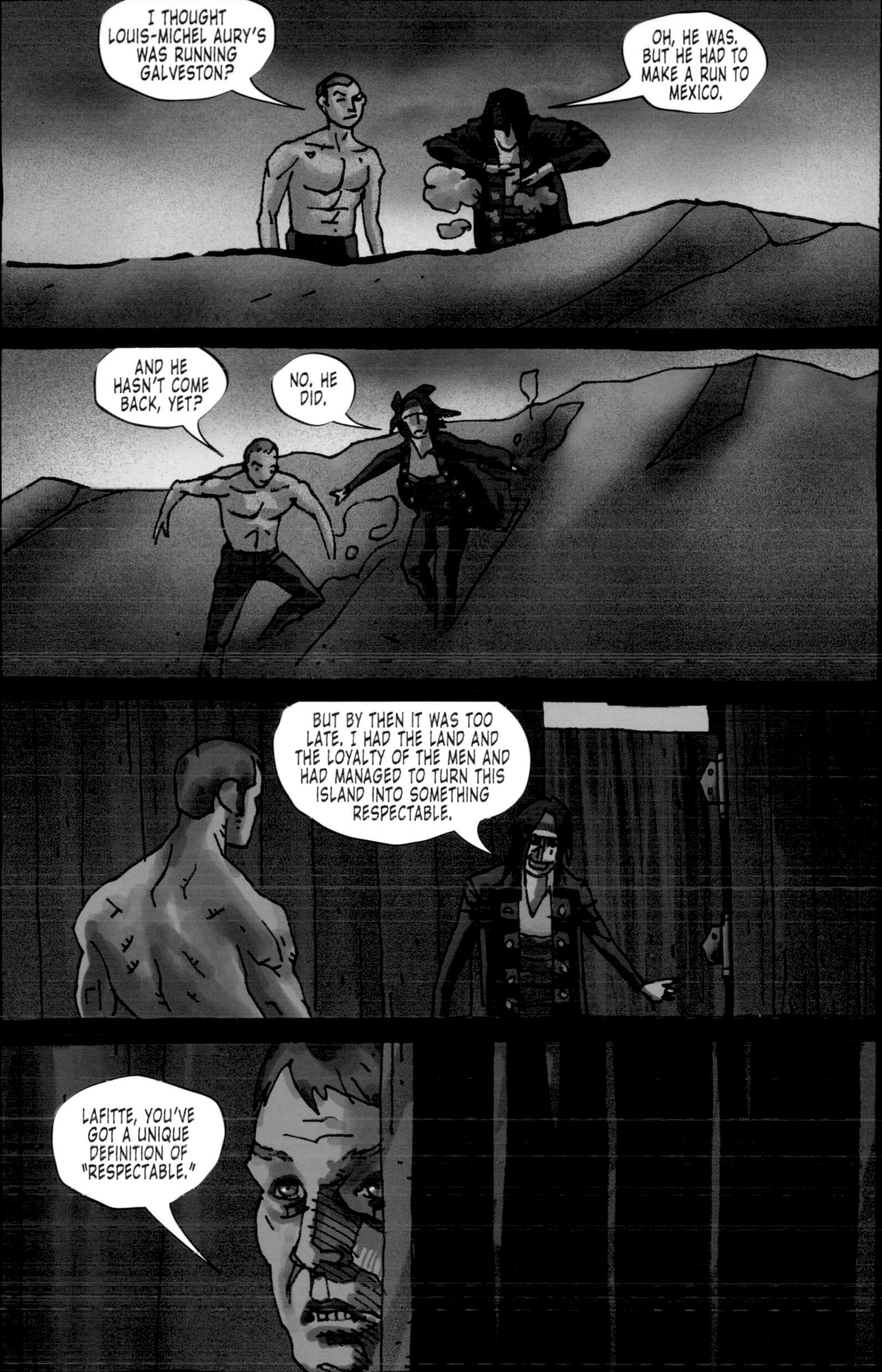

I THOUGHT LOUIS-MICHEL AURY'S WAS RUNNING GALVESTON?
OH, HE WAS. BUT HE HAD TO MAKE A RUN TO MEXICO.
AND HE HASN'T COME BACK, YET?
NO. HE DID.
BUT BY THEN IT WAS TOO LATE. I HAD THE LAND AND THE LOYALTY OF THE MEN AND HAD MANAGED TO TURN THIS ISLAND INTO SOMETHING RESPECTABLE.
LAFITTE, YOU'VE GOT A UNIQUE DEFINITION OF "RESPECTABLE."

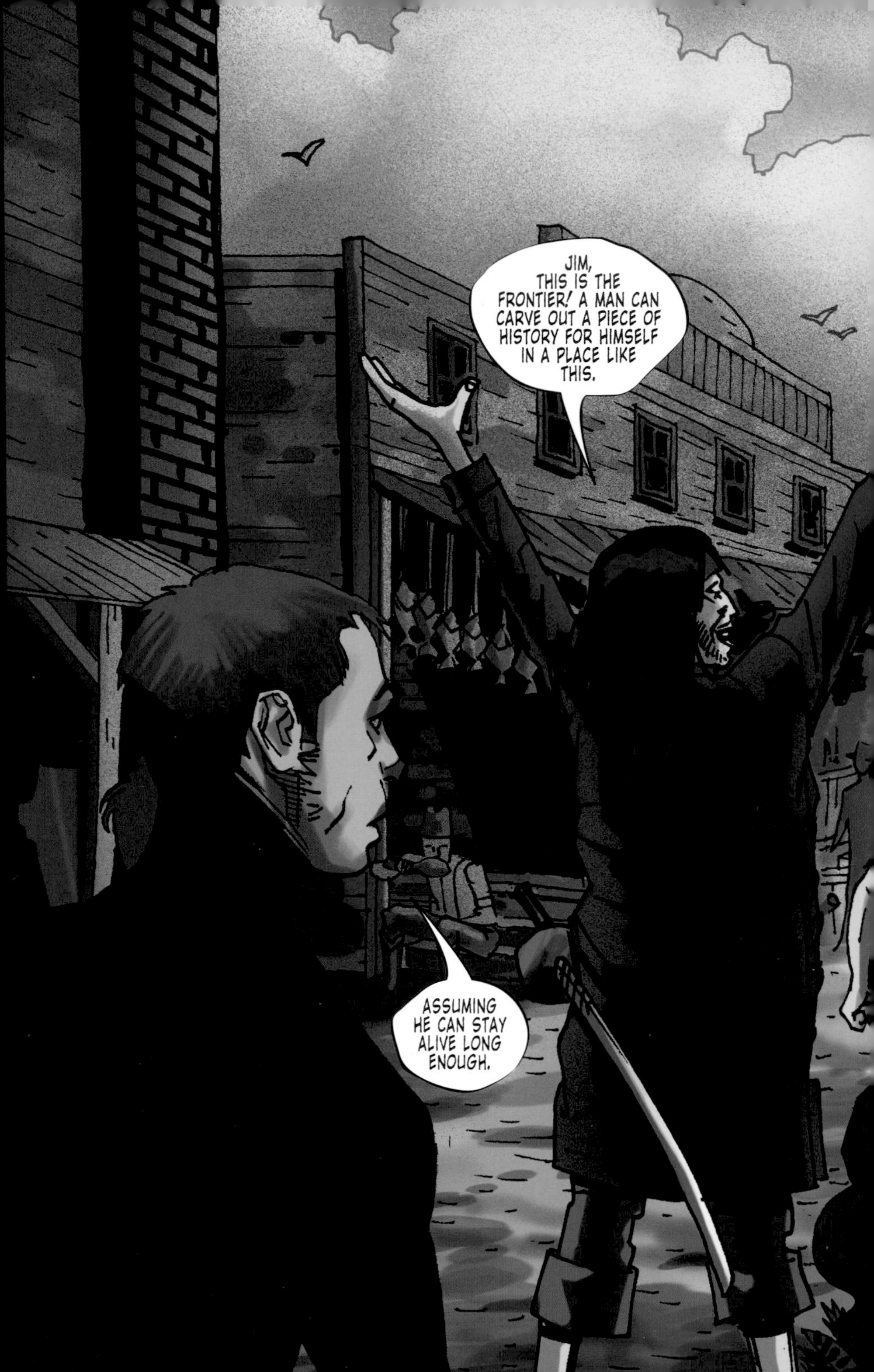
JIM, THIS IS THE FRONTIER! A MAN CAN CARVE OUT A PIECE OF HISTORY FOR HIMSELF IN A PLACE LIKE THIS.
ASSUMING HE CAN STAY ALIVE LONG ENOUGH.

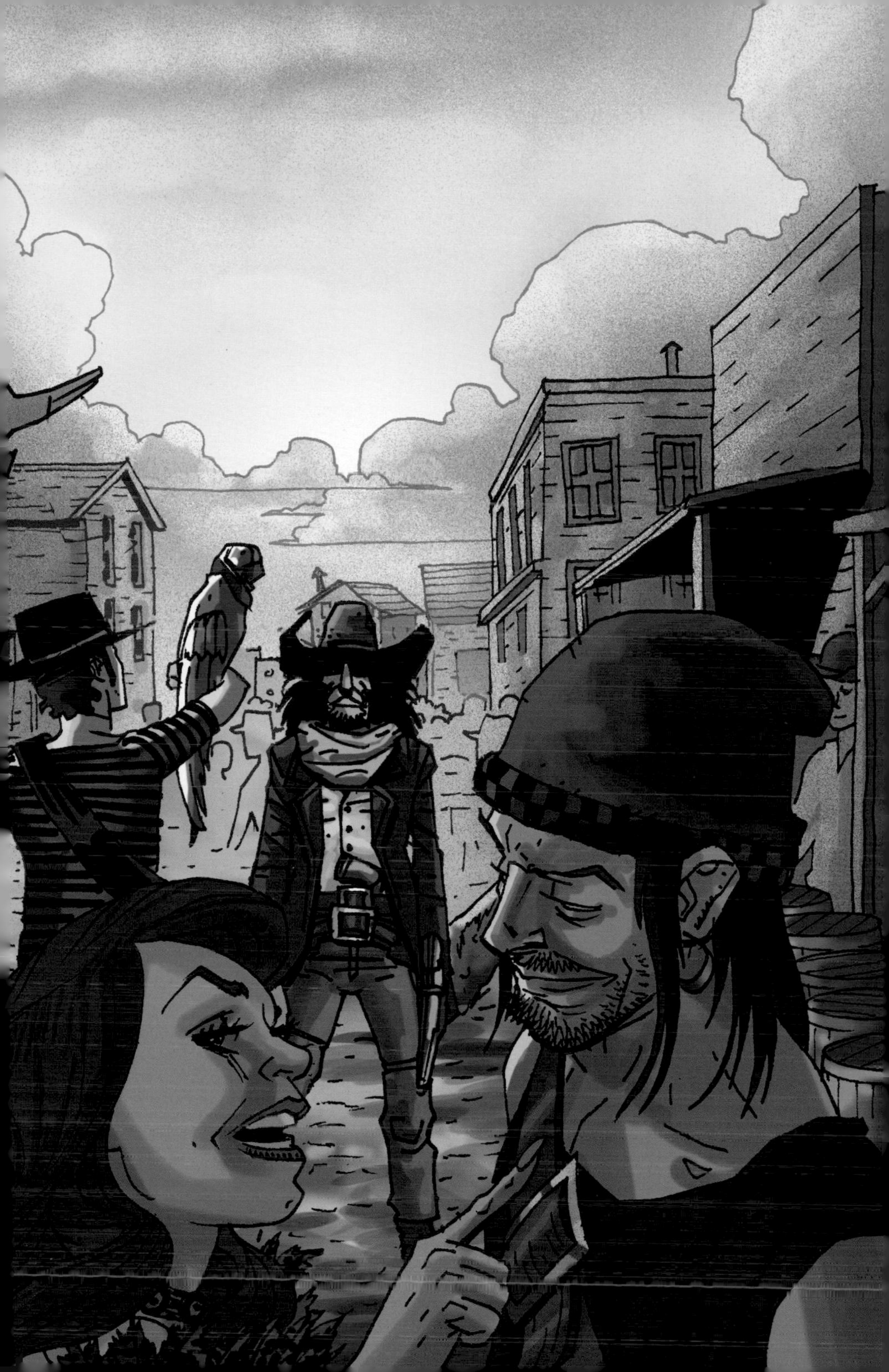

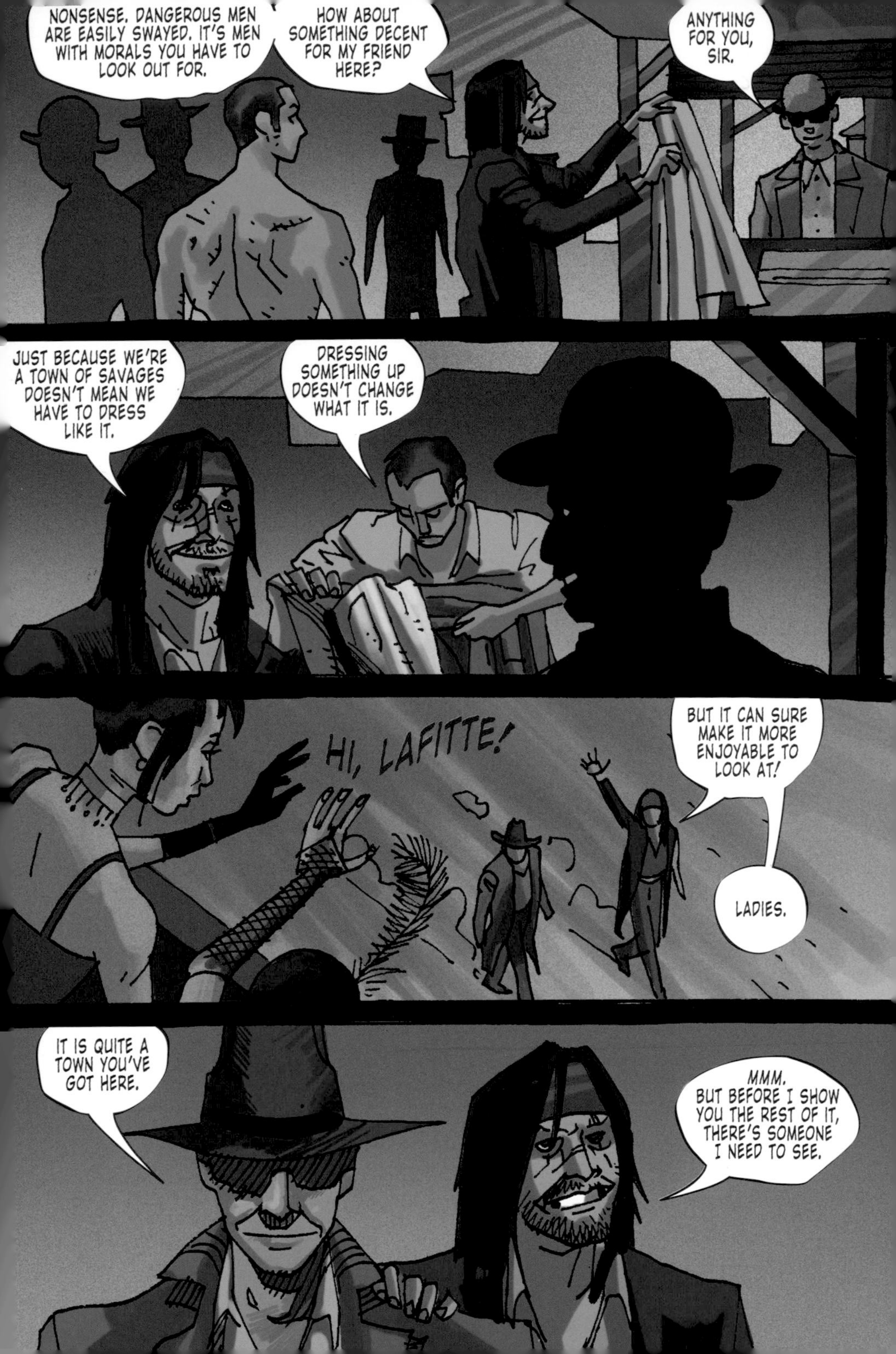
NONSENSE. DANGEROUS MEN ARE EASILY SWAYED. IT'S MEN WITH MORALS YOU HAVE TO LOOK OUT FOR.
HOW ABOUT SOMETHING DECENT FOR MY FRIEND HERE?
ANYTHING FOR YOU, SIR.
JUST BECAUSE WE'RE A TOWN OF SAVAGES DOESN'T MEAN WE HAVE TO DRESS LIKE IT.
DRESSING SOMETHING UP DOESN'T CHANGE WHAT IT IS.
HI, LAFITTE!
BUT IT CAN SURE MAKE IT MORE ENJOYABLE TO LOOK AT!
LADIES.
IT IS QUITE A TOWN YOU'VE GOT HERE.
MMM. BUT BEFORE I SHOW YOU THE REST OF IT, THERE'S SOMEONE I NEED TO SEE.

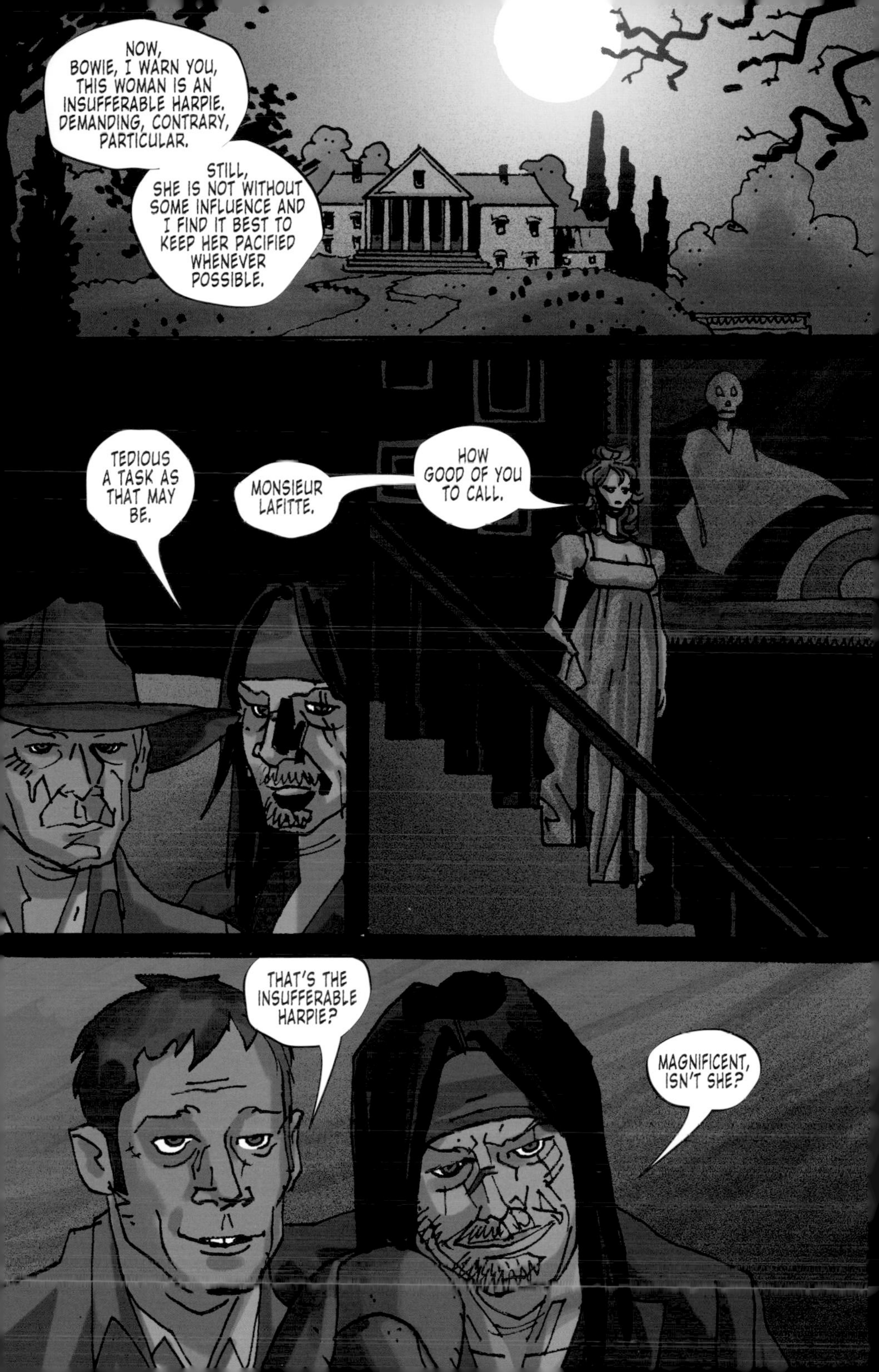
NOW, BOWIE, I WARN YOU, THIS WOMAN IS AN INSUFFERABLE HARPIE. DEMANDING, CONTRARY, PARTICULAR.
STILL, SHE IS NOT WITHOUT SOME INFLUENCE AND I FIND IT BEST TO KEEP HER PACIFIED WHENEVER POSSIBLE.
TEDIOUS A TASK AS THAT MAY BE.
MONSIEUR LAFITTE.
HOW GOOD OF YOU TO CALL.
THAT'S THE INSUFFERABLE HARPIE?
MAGNIFICENT, ISN'T SHE?

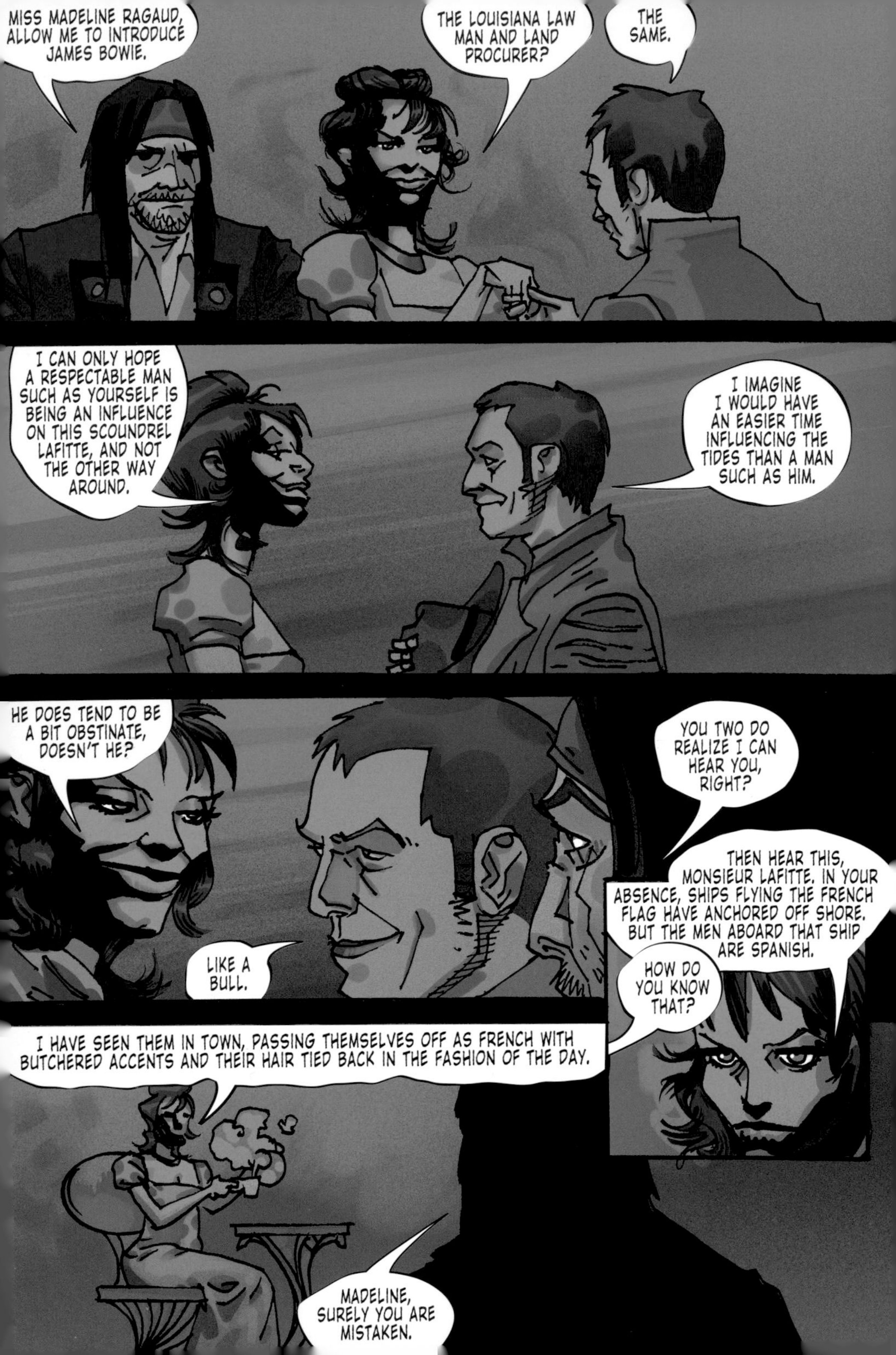
MISS MADELINE RAGAUD, ALLOW ME TO INTRODUCE JAMES BOWIE.
THE LOUISIANA LAW MAN AND LAND PROCURER?
THE SAME.
I CAN ONLY HOPE A RESPECTABLE MAN SUCH AS YOURSELF IS BEING AN INFLUENCE ON THIS SCOUNDREL LAFITTE, AND NOT THE OTHER WAY AROUND.
I IMAGINE I WOULD HAVE AN EASIER TIME INFLUENCING THE TIDES THAN A MAN SUCH AS HIM.
HE DOES TEND TO BE A BIT OBSTINATE, DOESN'T HE?
LIKE A BULL.
YOU TWO DO REALIZE I CAN HEAR YOU, RIGHT?
THEN HEAR THIS, MONSIEUR LAFITTE. IN YOUR ABSENCE, SHIPS FLYING THE FRENCH FLAG HAVE ANCHORED OFF SHORE. BUT THE MEN ABOARD THAT SHIP ARE SPANISH.
HOW DO YOU KNOW THAT?
I HAVE SEEN THEM IN TOWN, PASSING THEMSELVES OFF AS FRENCH WITH BUTCHERED ACCENTS AND THEIR HAIR TIED BACK IN THE FASHION OF THE DAY.
MADELINE, SURELY YOU ARE MISTAKEN.

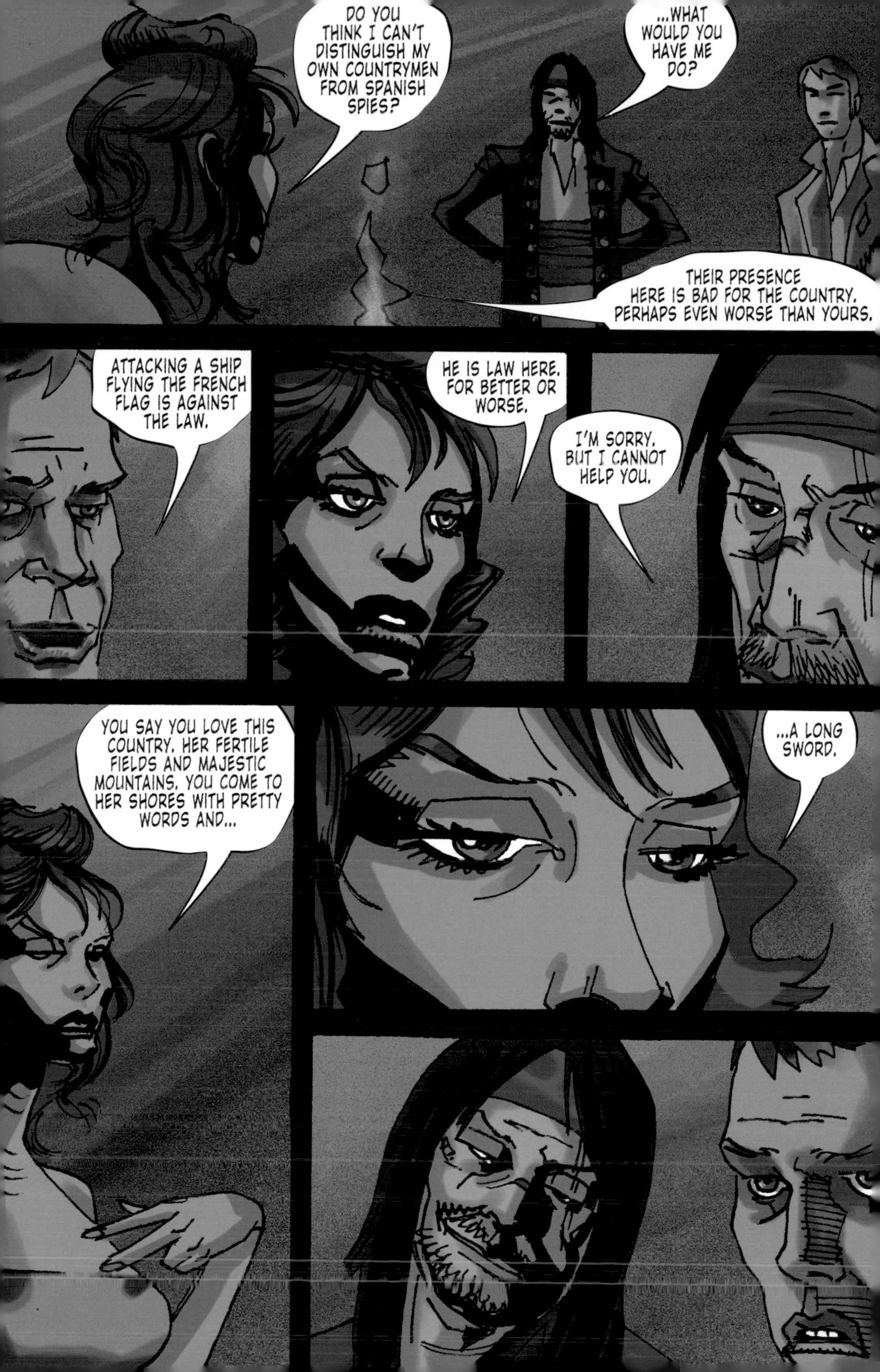
DO YOU THINK I CAN'T DISTINGUISH MY OWN COUNTRYMEN FROM SPANISH SPIES?
...WHAT WOULD YOU HAVE ME DO?
THEIR PRESENCE HERE IS BAD FOR THE COUNTRY. PERHAPS EVEN WORSE THAN YOURS.
ATTACKING A SHIP FLYING THE FRENCH FLAG IS AGAINST THE LAW.
HE IS LAW HERE. FOR BETTER OR WORSE.
I'M SORRY. BUT I CANNOT HELP YOU.
YOU SAY YOU LOVE THIS COUNTRY. HER FERTILE FIELDS AND MAJESTIC MOUNTAINS. YOU COME TO HER SHORES WITH PRETTY WORDS AND...
...A LONG SWORD.

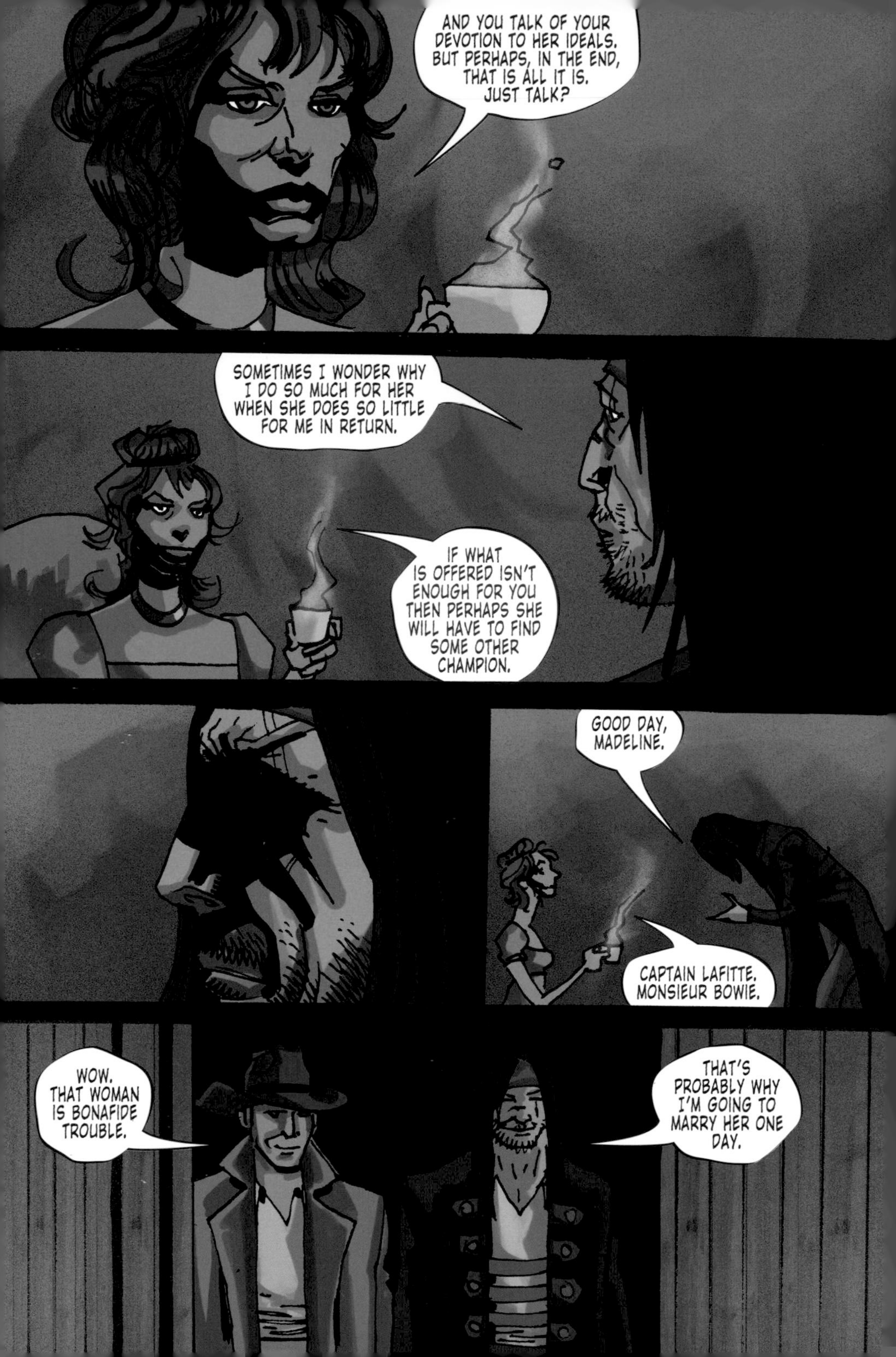
AND YOU TALK OF YOUR DEVOTION TO HER IDEALS. BUT PERHAPS, IN THE END, THAT IS ALL IT IS. JUST TALK?
SOMETIMES I WONDER WHY I DO SO MUCH FOR HER WHEN SHE DOES SO LITTLE FOR ME IN RETURN.
IF WHAT IS OFFERED ISN'T ENOUGH FOR YOU THEN PERHAPS SHE WILL HAVE TO FIND SOME OTHER CHAMPION.
GOOD DAY, MADELINE.
CAPTAIN LAFITTE. MONSIEUR BOWIE.
WOW. THAT WOMAN IS BONAFIDE TROUBLE.
THAT'S PROBABLY WHY I'M GOING TO MARRY HER ONE DAY.

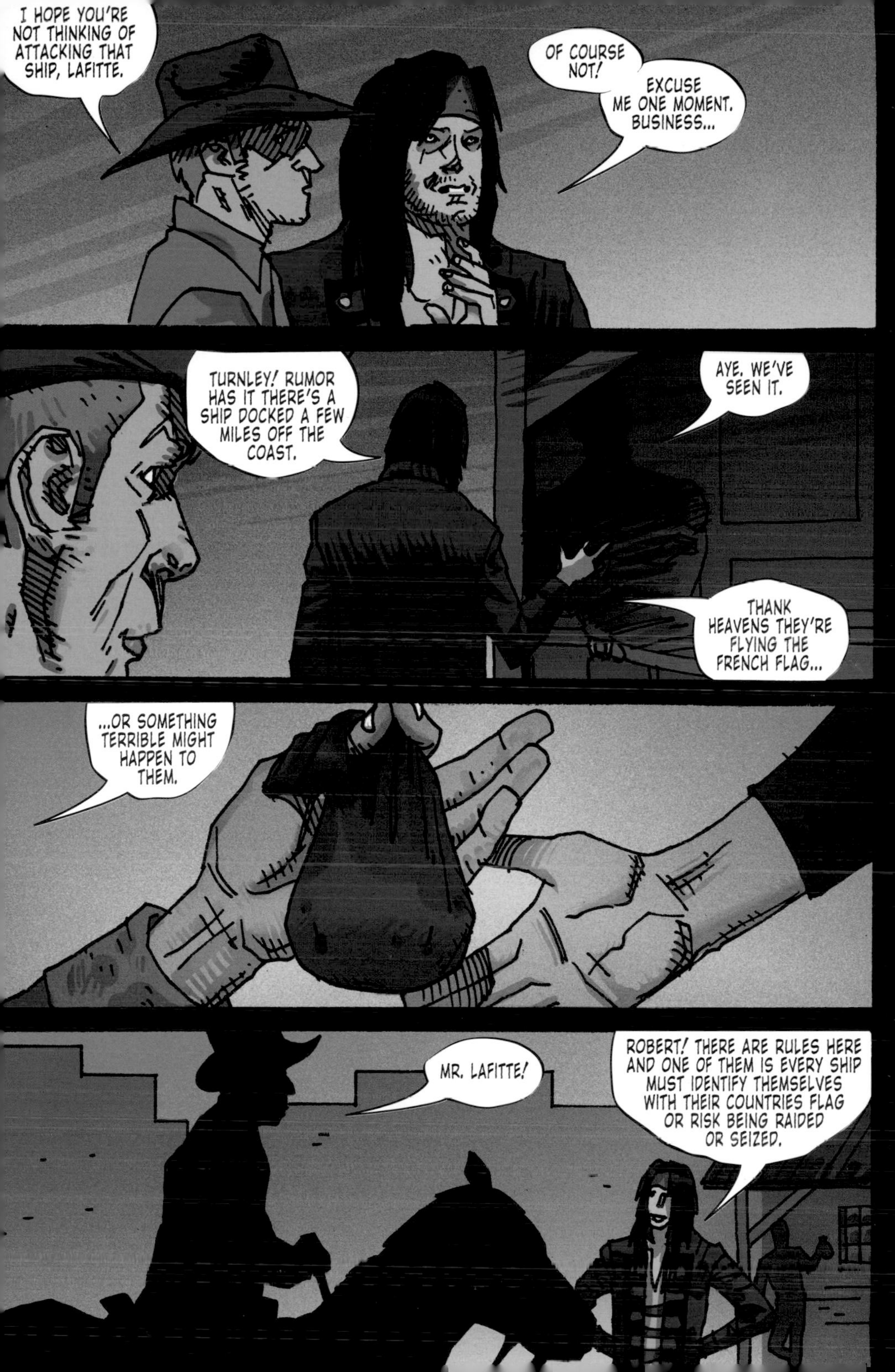
I HOPE YOU'RE NOT THINKING OF ATTACKING THAT SHIP, LAFITTE.
OF COURSE NOT!
EXCUSE ME ONE MOMENT. BUSINESS...
TURNLEY! RUMOR HAS IT THERE'S A SHIP DOCKED A FEW MILES OFF THE COAST.
AYE. WE'VE SEEN IT.
THANK HEAVENS THEY'RE FLYING THE FRENCH FLAG...
...OR SOMETHING TERRIBLE MIGHT HAPPEN TO THEM.
MR. LAFITTE!
ROBERT! THERE ARE RULES HERE AND ONE OF THEM IS EVERY SHIP MUST IDENTIFY THEMSELVES WITH THEIR COUNTRIES FLAG OR RISK BEING RAIDED OR SEIZED.

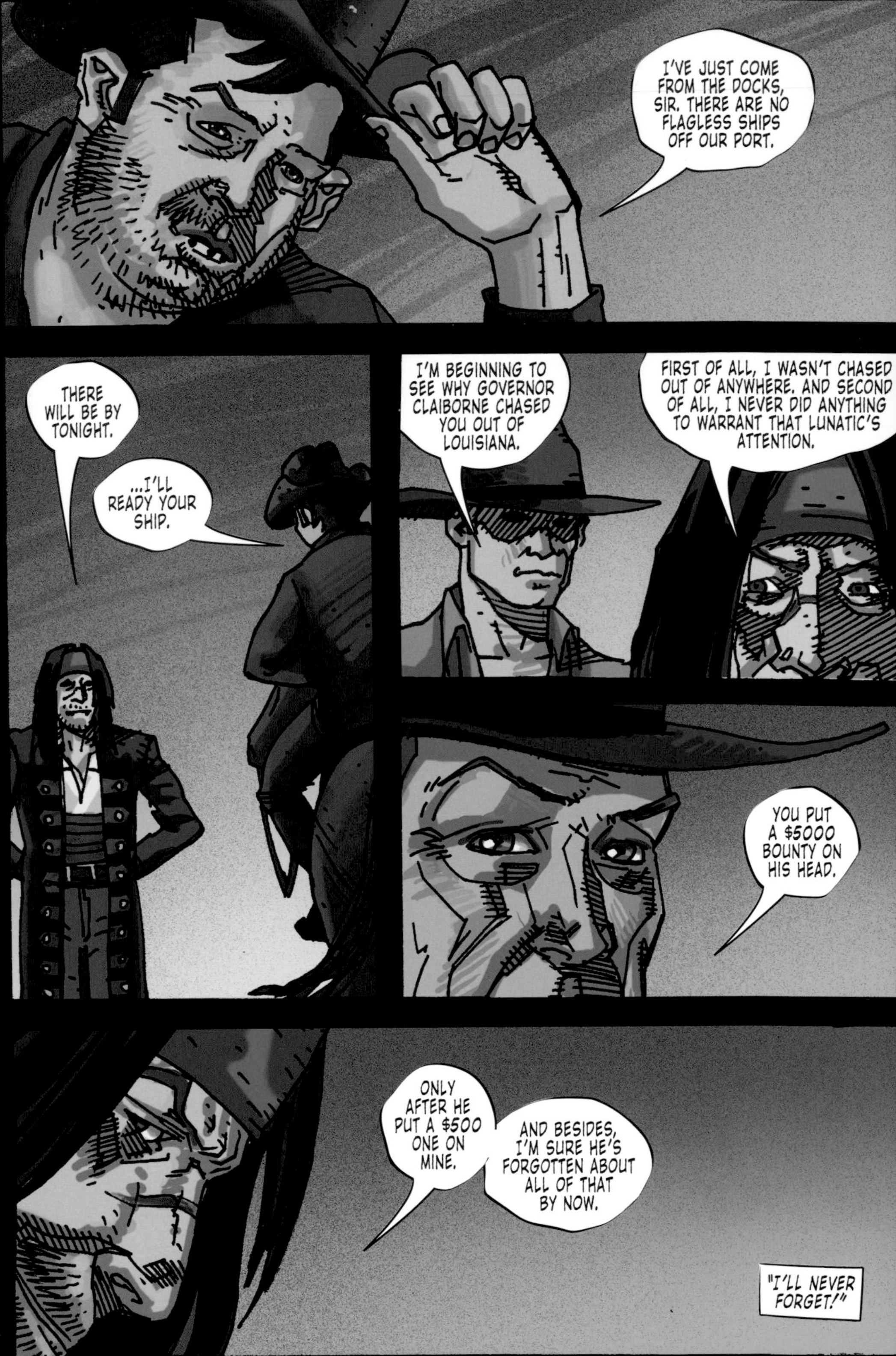
I'VE JUST COME FROM THE DOCKS, SIR. THERE ARE NO FLAGLESS SHIPS OFF OUR PORT.
THERE WILL BE BY TONIGHT.
...I'LL READY YOUR SHIP.
I'M BEGINNING TO SEE WHY GOVERNOR CLAIBORNE CHASED YOU OUT OF LOUISIANA.
FIRST OF ALL, I WASN'T CHASED OUT OF ANYWHERE. AND SECOND OF ALL, I NEVER DID ANYTHING TO WARRANT THAT LUNATIC'S ATTENTION.
YOU PUT A $5000 BOUNTY ON HIS HEAD.
ONLY AFTER HE PUT A $500 ONE ON MINE.
AND BESIDES, I'M SURE HE'S FORGOTTEN ABOUT ALL OF THAT BY NOW.
"I'LL NEVER FORGET!"

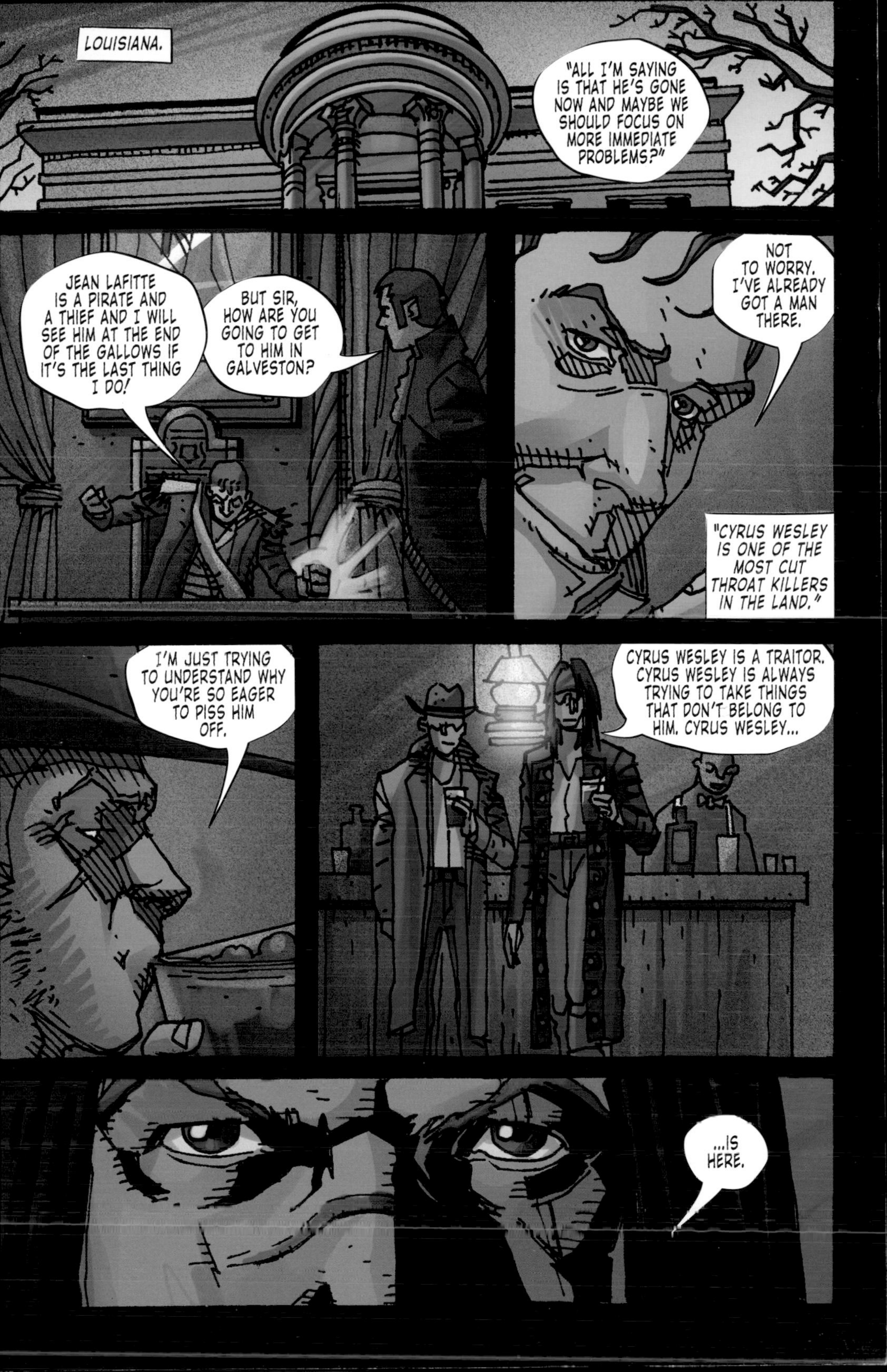
LOUISIANA.
"ALL I'M SAYING IS THAT HE'S GONE NOW AND MAYBE WE SHOULD FOCUS ON MORE IMMEDIATE PROBLEMS?"
JEAN LAFITTE IS A PIRATE AND A THIEF AND I WILL SEE HIM AT THE END OF THE GALLOWS IF IT'S THE LAST THING I DO!
BUT SIR, HOW ARE YOU GOING TO GET TO HIM IN GALVESTON?
NOT TO WORRY. I'VE ALREADY GOT A MAN THERE.
"CYRUS WESLEY IS ONE OF THE MOST CUT THROAT KILLERS IN THE LAND."
I'M JUST TRYING TO UNDERSTAND WHY YOU'RE SO EAGER TO PISS HIM OFF.
CYRUS WESLEY IS A TRAITOR. CYRUS WESLEY IS ALWAYS TRYING TO TAKE THINGS THAT DON'T BELONG TO HIM. CYRUS WESLEY...
...IS HERE.

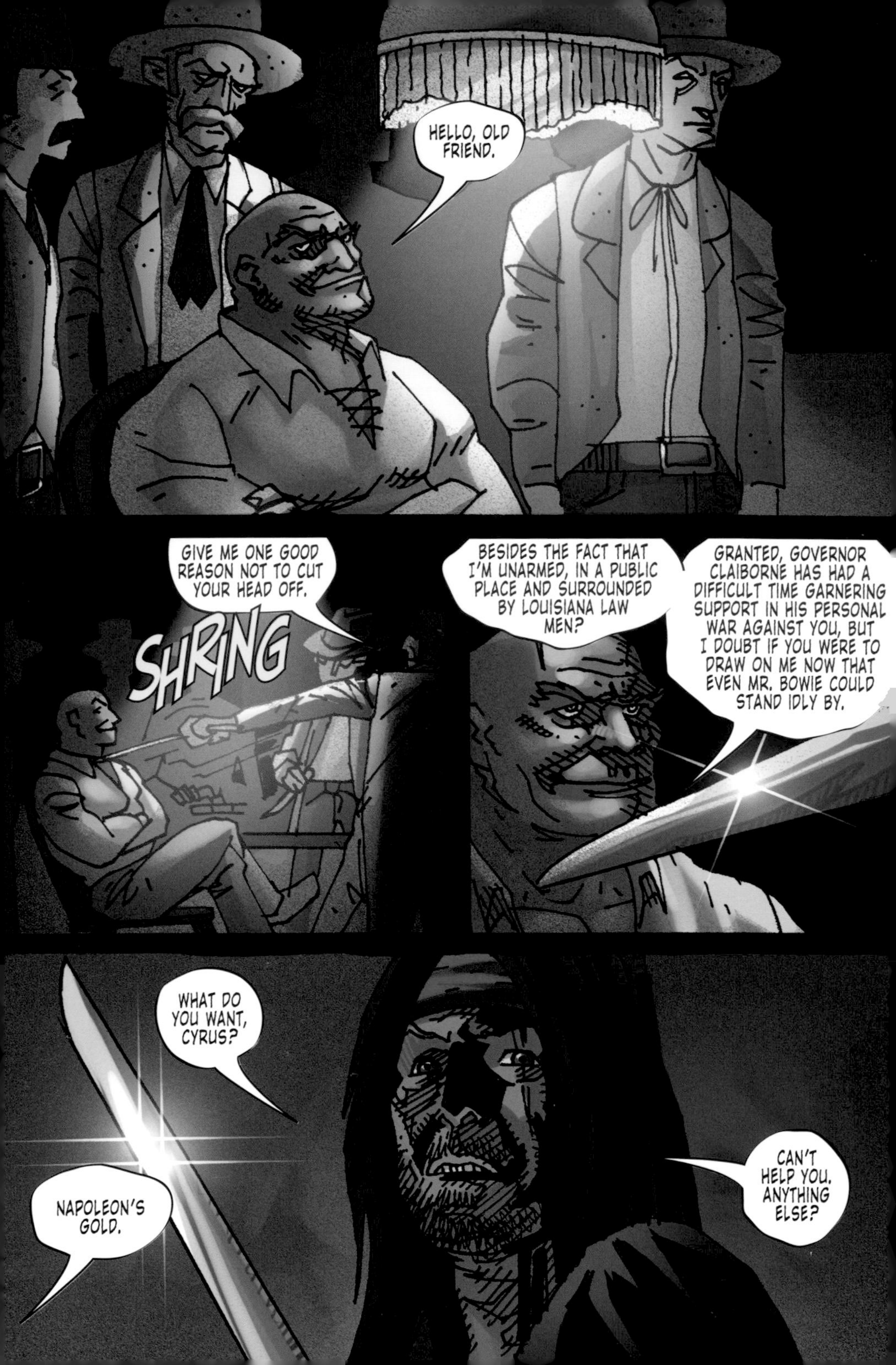
HELLO, OLD FRIEND.
GIVE ME ONE GOOD REASON NOT TO CUT YOUR HEAD OFF.
SHRING
BESIDES THE FACT THAT I'M UNARMED, IN A PUBLIC PLACE AND SURROUNDED BY LOUISIANA LAW MEN?
GRANTED, GOVERNOR CLAIBORNE HAS HAD A DIFFICULT TIME GARNERING SUPPORT IN HIS PERSONAL WAR AGAINST YOU, BUT I DOUBT IF YOU WERE TO DRAW ON ME NOW THAT EVEN MR. BOWIE COULD STAND IDLY BY.
WHAT DO YOU WANT, CYRUS?
NAPOLEON'S GOLD.
CAN'T HELP YOU. ANYTHING ELSE?

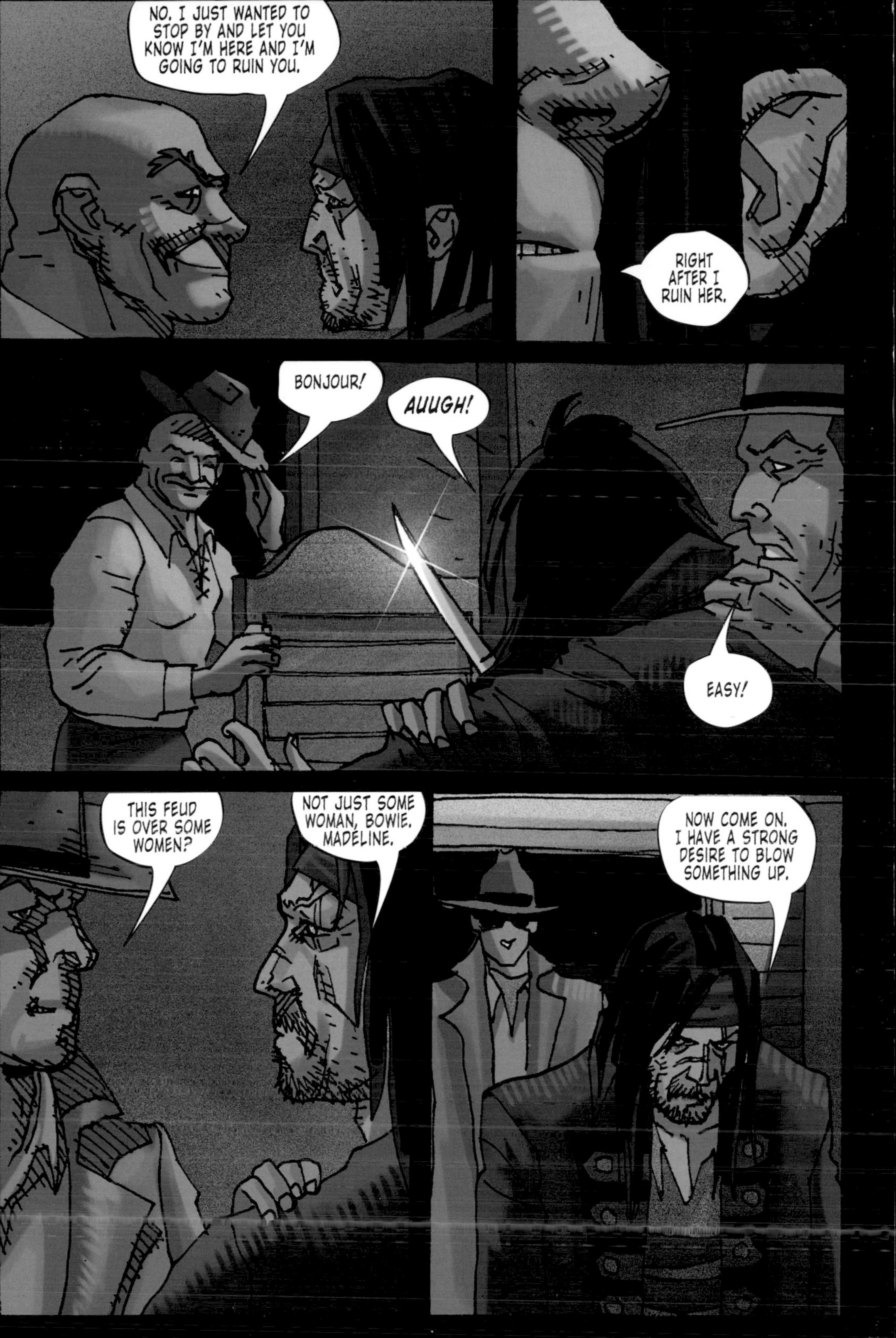
NO. I JUST WANTED TO STOP BY AND LET YOU KNOW I'M HERE AND I'M GOING TO RUIN YOU.
RIGHT AFTER I RUIN HER.
BONJOUR!
AUUGH!
EASY!
THIS FEUD IS OVER SOME WOMEN?
NOT JUST SOME WOMAN, BOWIE. MADELINE.
NOW COME ON. I HAVE A STRONG DESIRE TO BLOW SOMETHING UP.

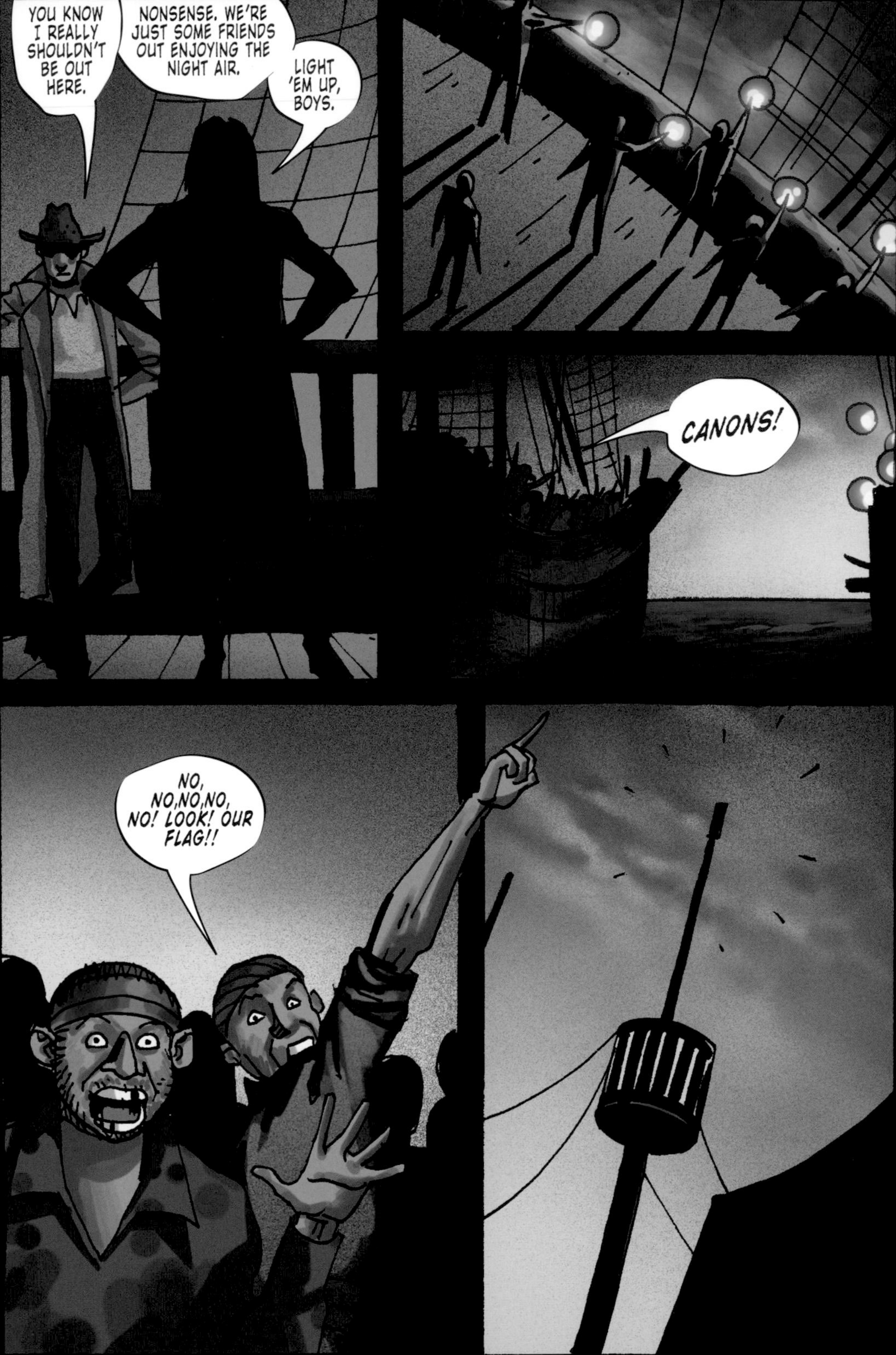
YOU KNOW I REALLY SHOULDN'T BE OUT HERE.
NONSENSE. WE'RE JUST SOME FRIENDS OUT ENJOYING THE NIGHT AIR.
LIGHT 'EM UP, BOYS.
CANONS!
NO, NO,NO,NO, NO! LOOK! OUR FLAG!!

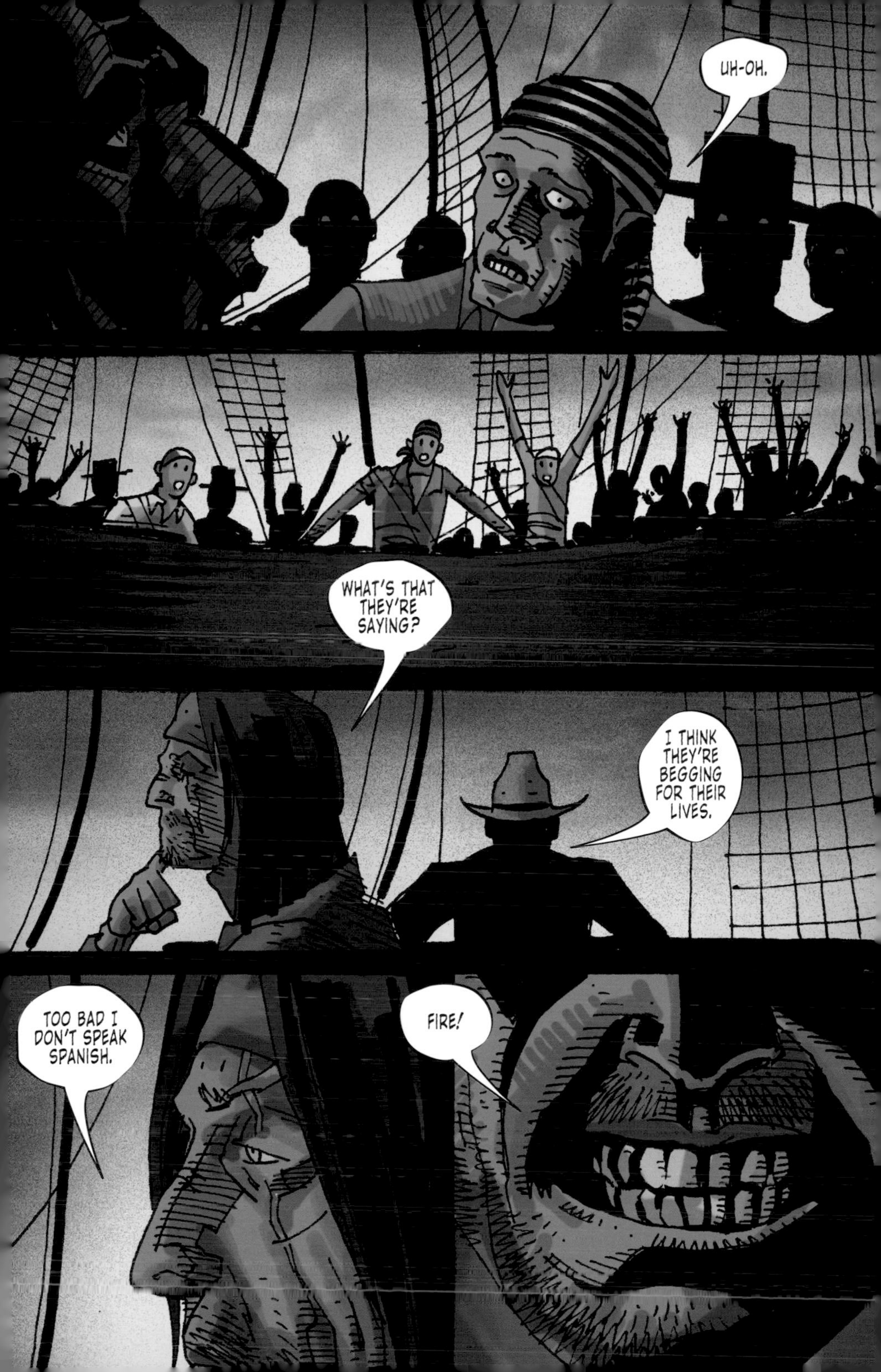
UH-OH.
WHAT'S THAT THEY'RE SAYING?
I THINK THEY'RE BEGGING FOR THEIR LIVES.
TOO BAD I DON'T SPEAK SPANISH.
FIRE!

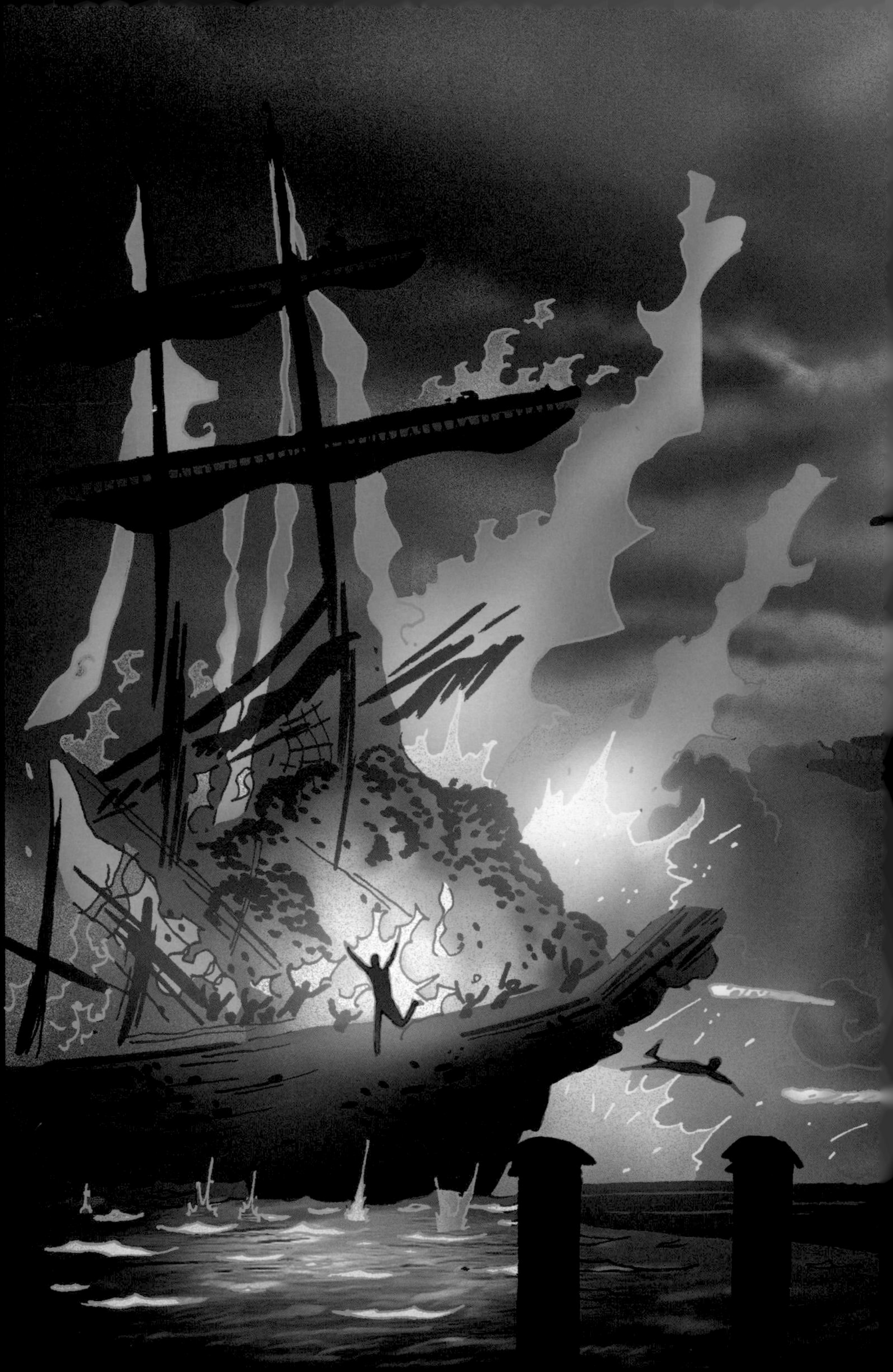

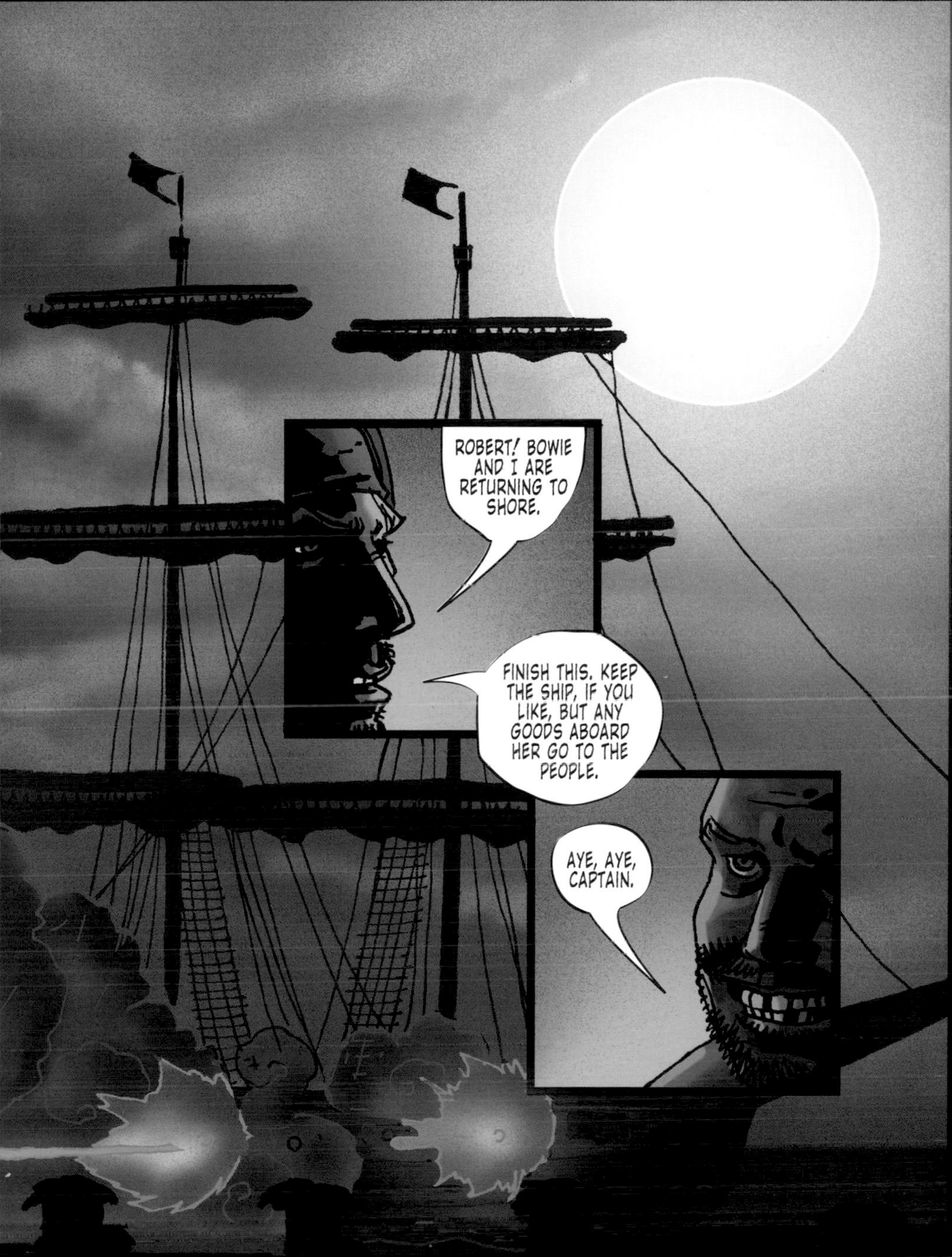
ROBERT! BOWIE AND I ARE RETURNING TO SHORE.
FINISH THIS. KEEP THE SHIP, IF YOU LIKE, BUT ANY GOODS ABOARD HER GO TO THE PEOPLE.
AYE, AYE, CAPTAIN.

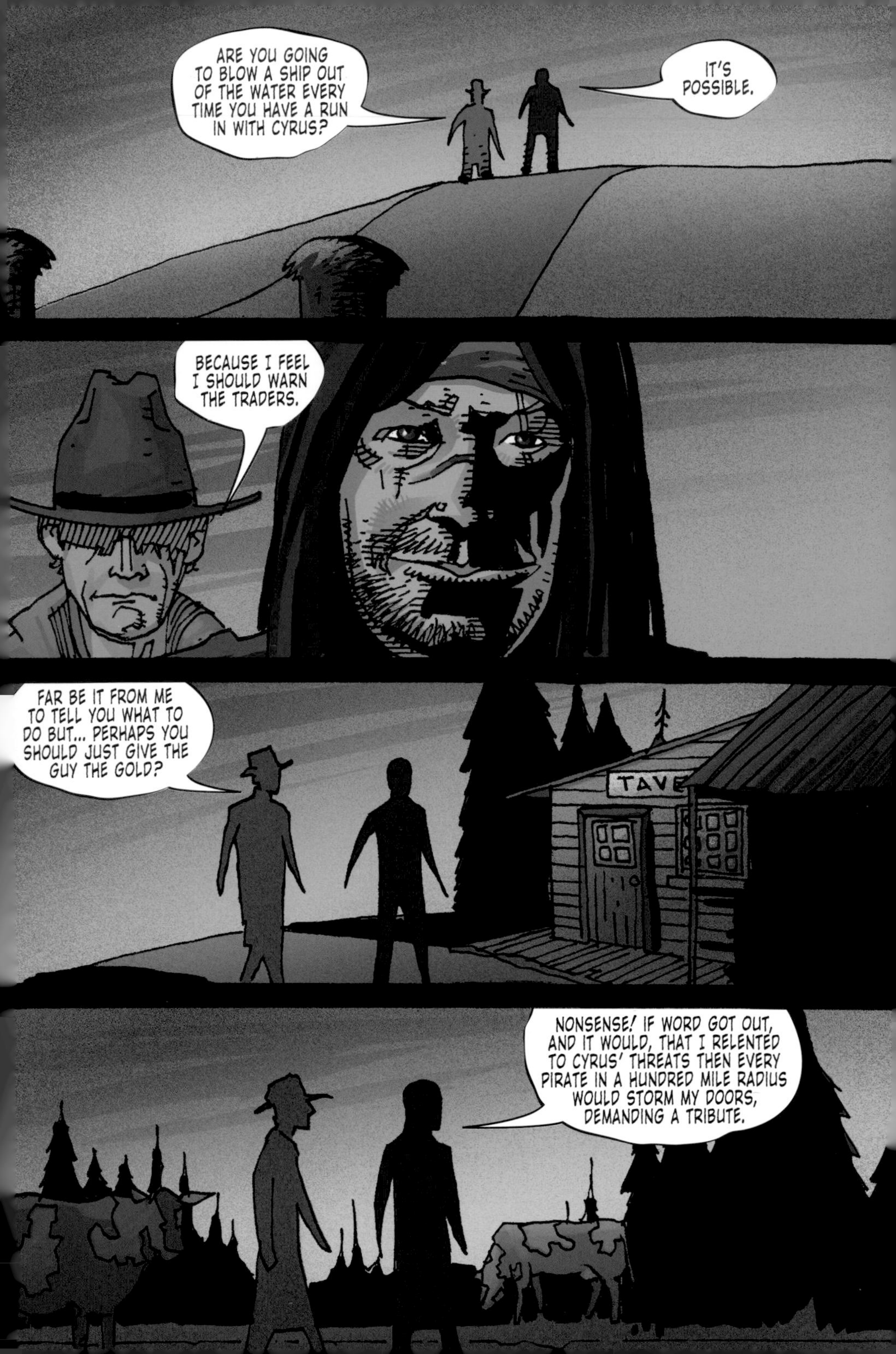
ARE YOU GOING TO BLOW A SHIP OUT OF THE WATER EVERY TIME YOU HAVE A RUN IN WITH CYRUS?
IT'S POSSIBLE.
BECAUSE I FEEL I SHOULD WARN THE TRADERS.
FAR BE IT FROM ME TO TELL YOU WHAT TO DO BUT... PERHAPS YOU SHOULD JUST GIVE THE GUY THE GOLD?
TAVE
NONSENSE! IF WORD GOT OUT, AND IT WOULD, THAT I RELENTED TO CYRUS' THREATS THEN EVERY PIRATE IN A HUNDRED MILE RADIUS WOULD STORM MY DOORS, DEMANDING A TRIBUTE.

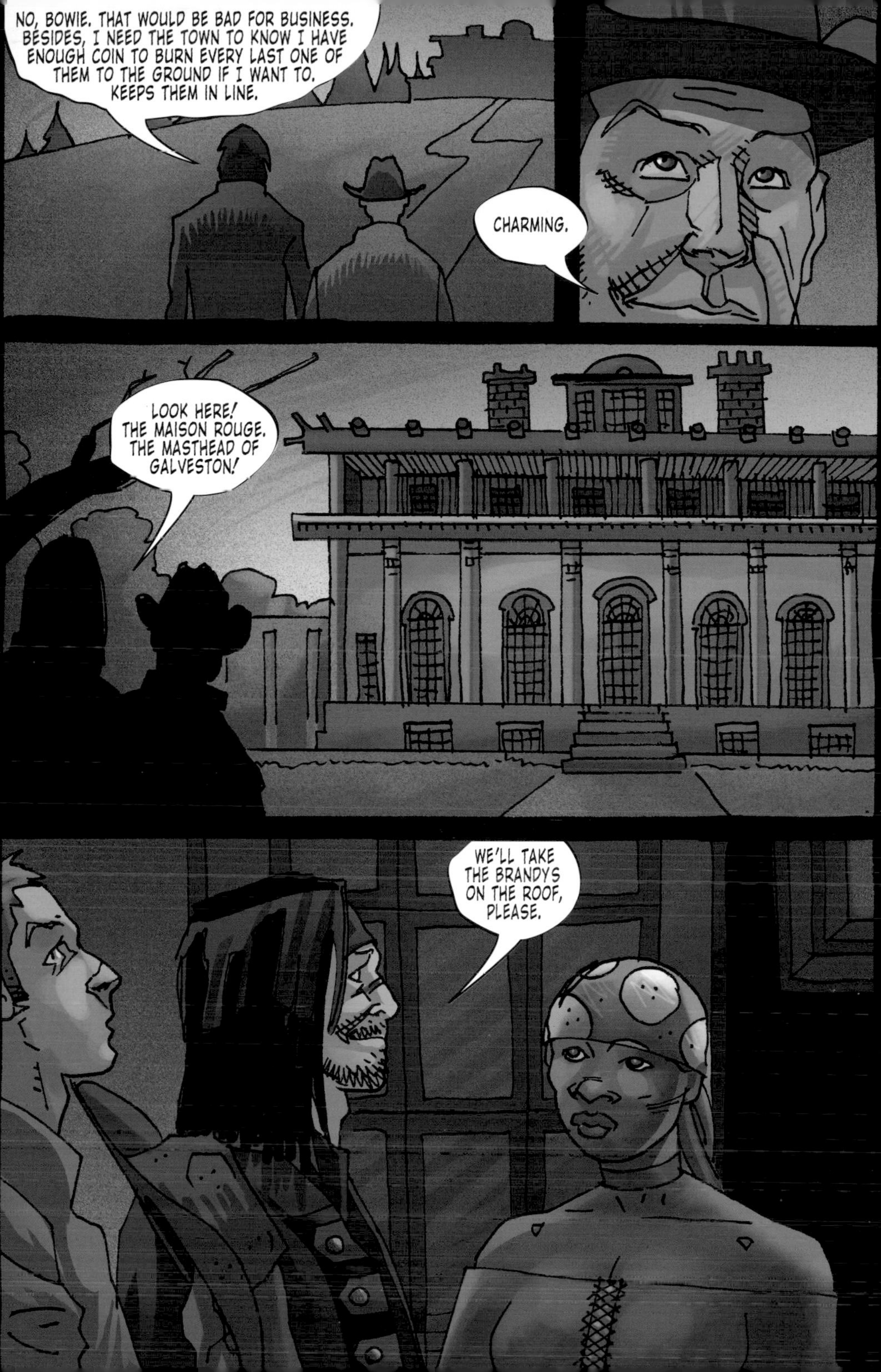
NO, BOWIE. THAT WOULD BE BAD FOR BUSINESS. BESIDES, I NEED THE TOWN TO KNOW I HAVE ENOUGH COIN TO BURN EVERY LAST ONE OF THEM TO THE GROUND IF I WANT TO. KEEPS THEM IN LINE.
CHARMING.
LOOK HERE! THE MAISON ROUGE. THE MASTHEAD OF GALVESTON!
WE'LL TAKE THE BRANDYS ON THE ROOF, PLEASE.

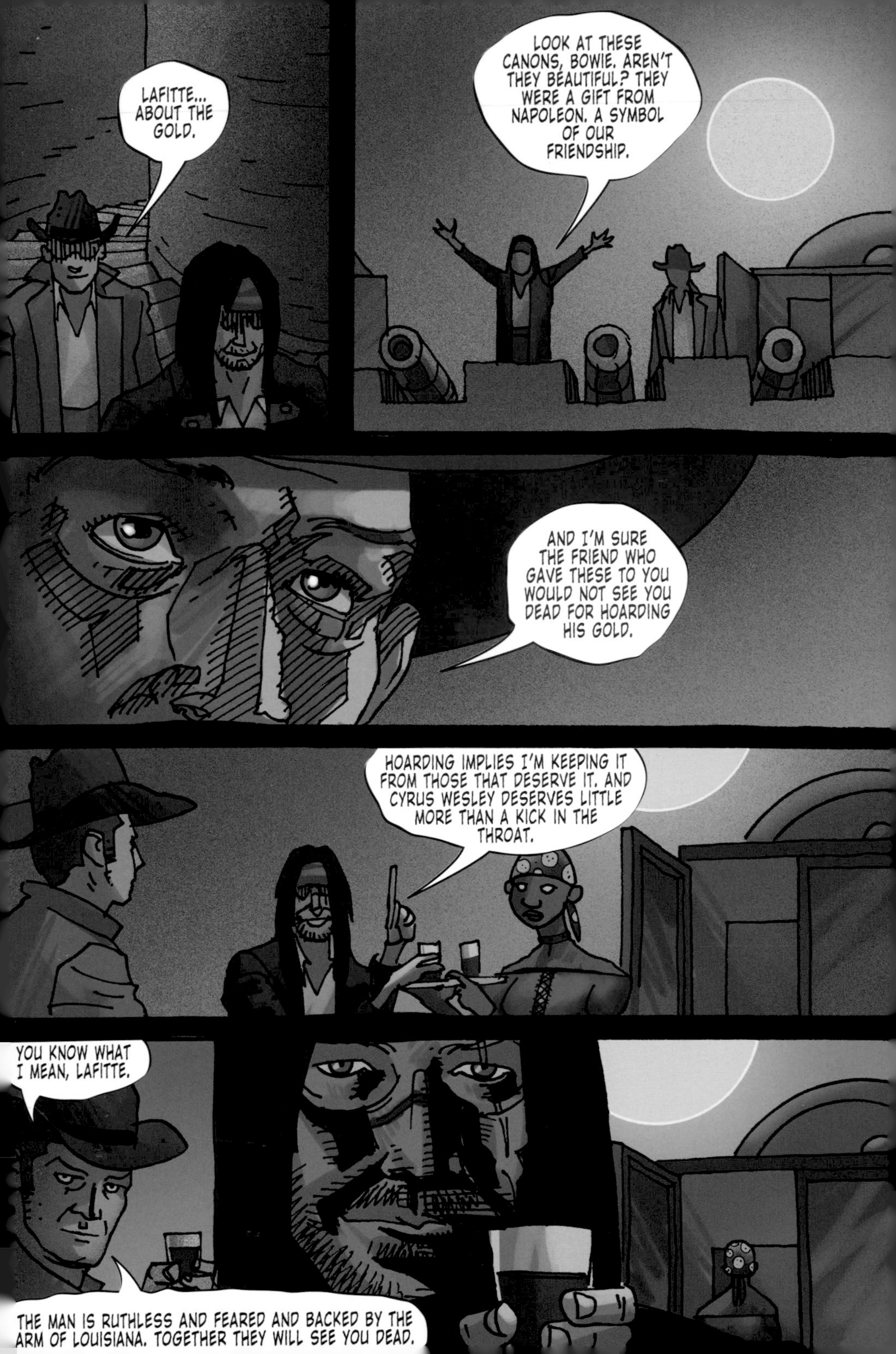
LAFITTE... ABOUT THE GOLD.
LOOK AT THESE CANONS, BOWIE. AREN'T THEY BEAUTIFUL? THEY WERE A GIFT FROM NAPOLEON. A SYMBOL OF OUR FRIENDSHIP.
AND I'M SURE THE FRIEND WHO GAVE THESE TO YOU WOULD NOT SEE YOU DEAD FOR HOARDING HIS GOLD.
HOARDING IMPLIES I'M KEEPING IT FROM THOSE THAT DESERVE IT. AND CYRUS WESLEY DESERVES LITTLE MORE THAN A KICK IN THE THROAT.
YOU KNOW WHAT I MEAN, LAFITTE.
THE MAN IS RUTHLESS AND FEARED AND BACKED BY THE ARM OF LOUISIANA. TOGETHER THEY WILL SEE YOU DEAD.

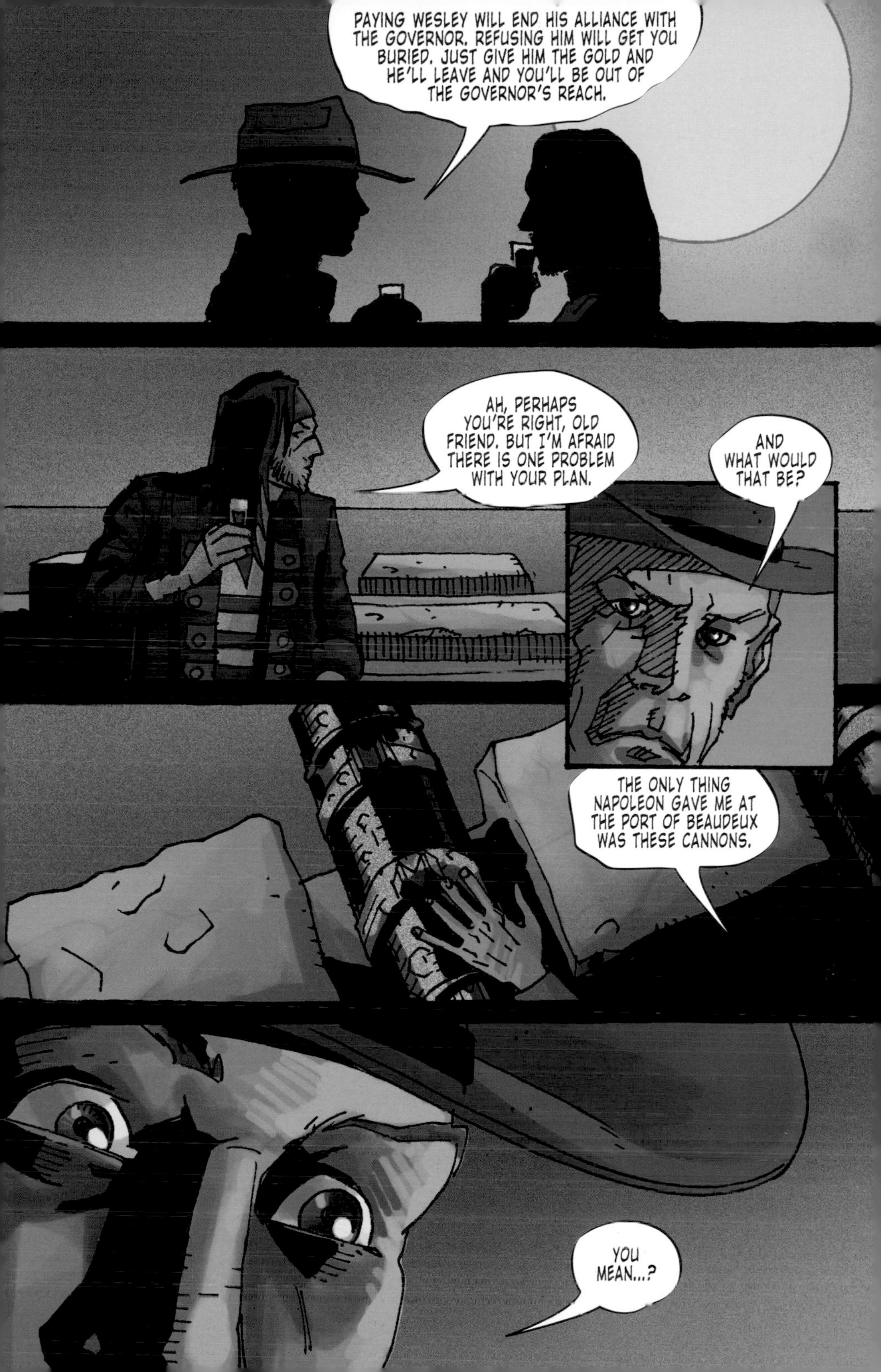
PAYING WESLEY WILL END HIS ALLIANCE WITH THE GOVERNOR. REFUSING HIM WILL GET YOU BURIED. JUST GIVE HIM THE GOLD AND HE'LL LEAVE AND YOU'LL BE OUT OF THE GOVERNOR'S REACH.
AH, PERHAPS YOU'RE RIGHT, OLD FRIEND. BUT I'M AFRAID THERE IS ONE PROBLEM WITH YOUR PLAN.
AND WHAT WOULD THAT BE?
THE ONLY THING NAPOLEON GAVE ME AT THE PORT OF BEAUDEUX WAS THESE CANNONS.
YOU MEAN...?

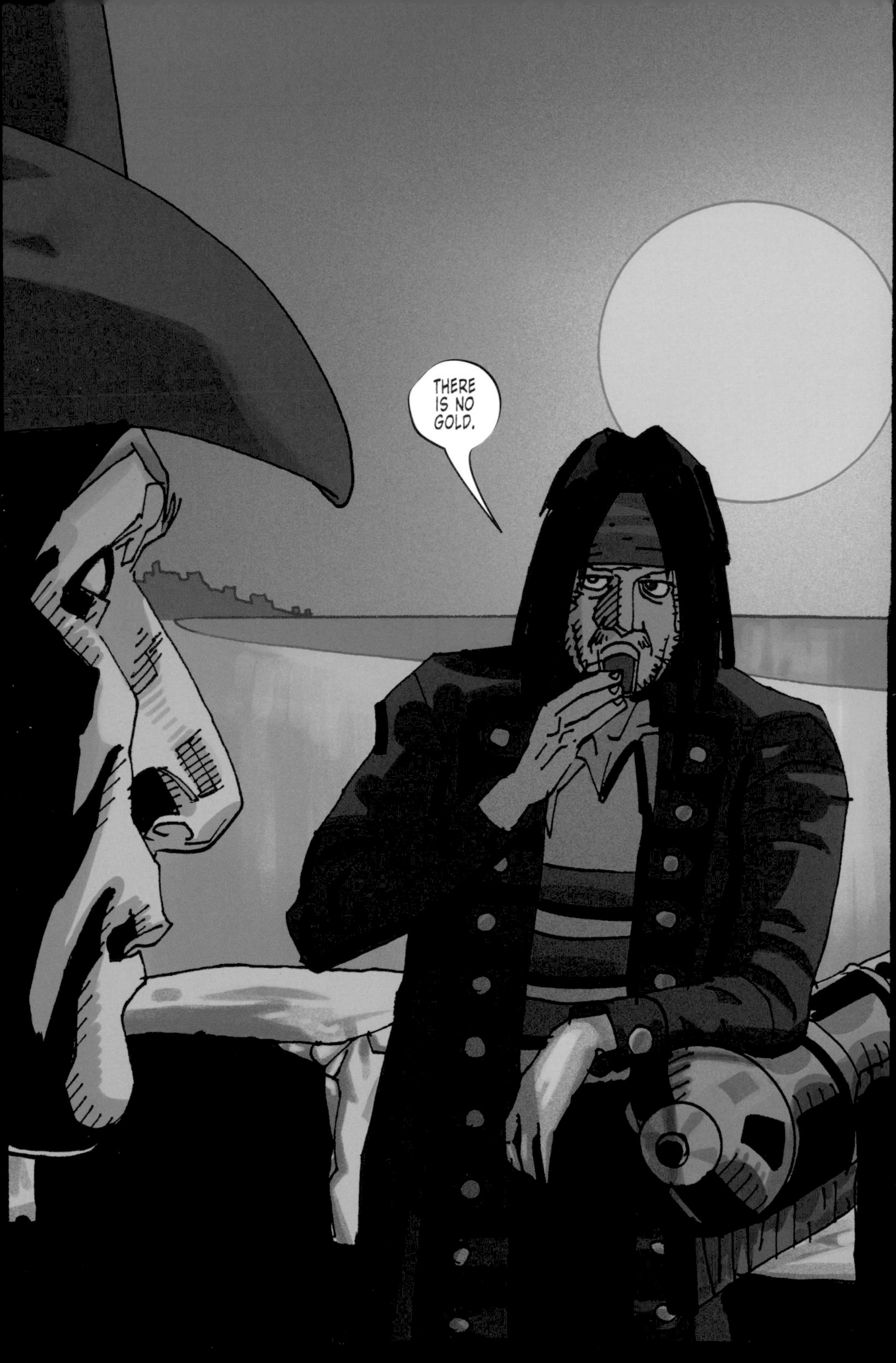
THERE IS NO GOLD.

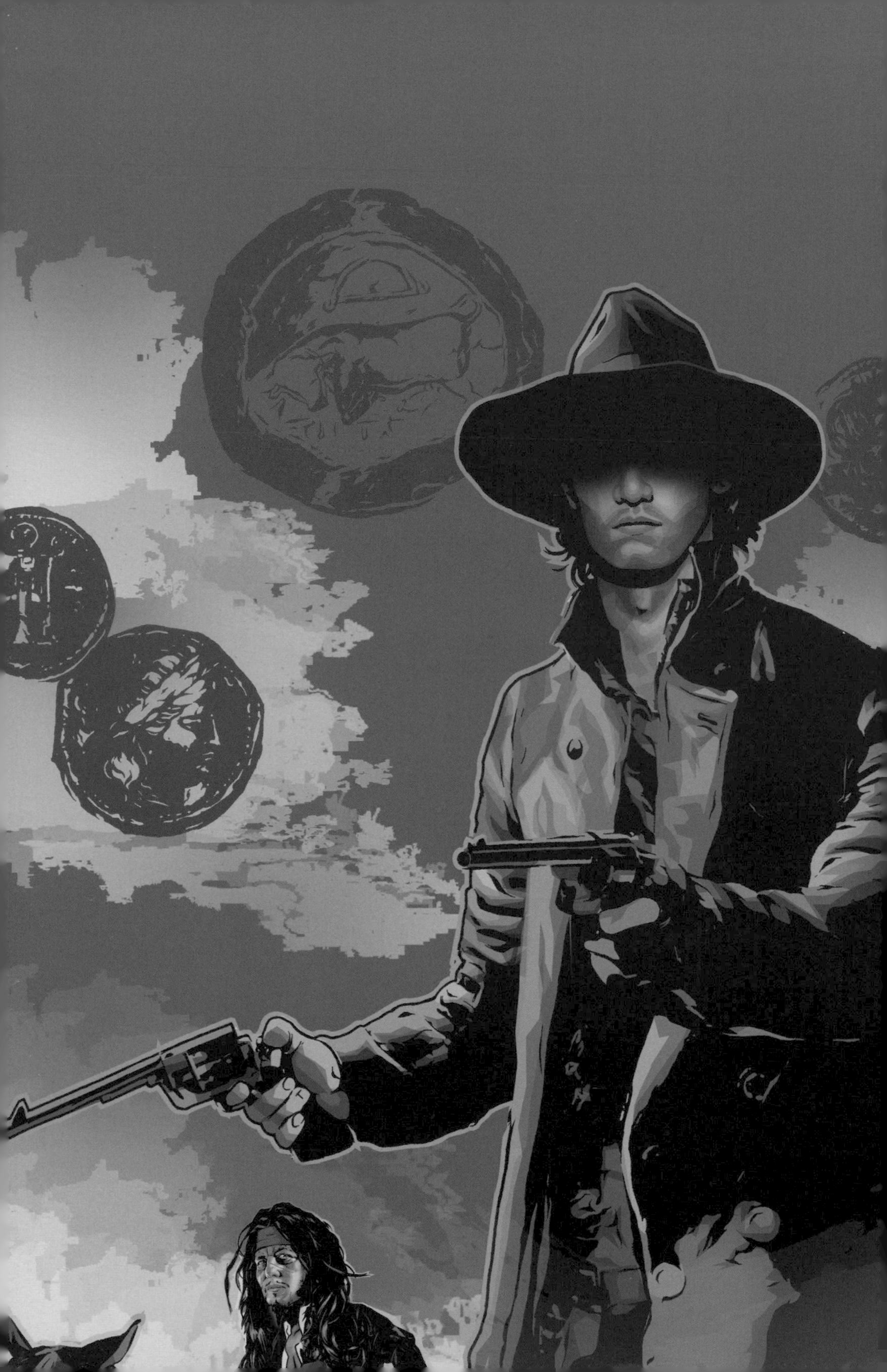

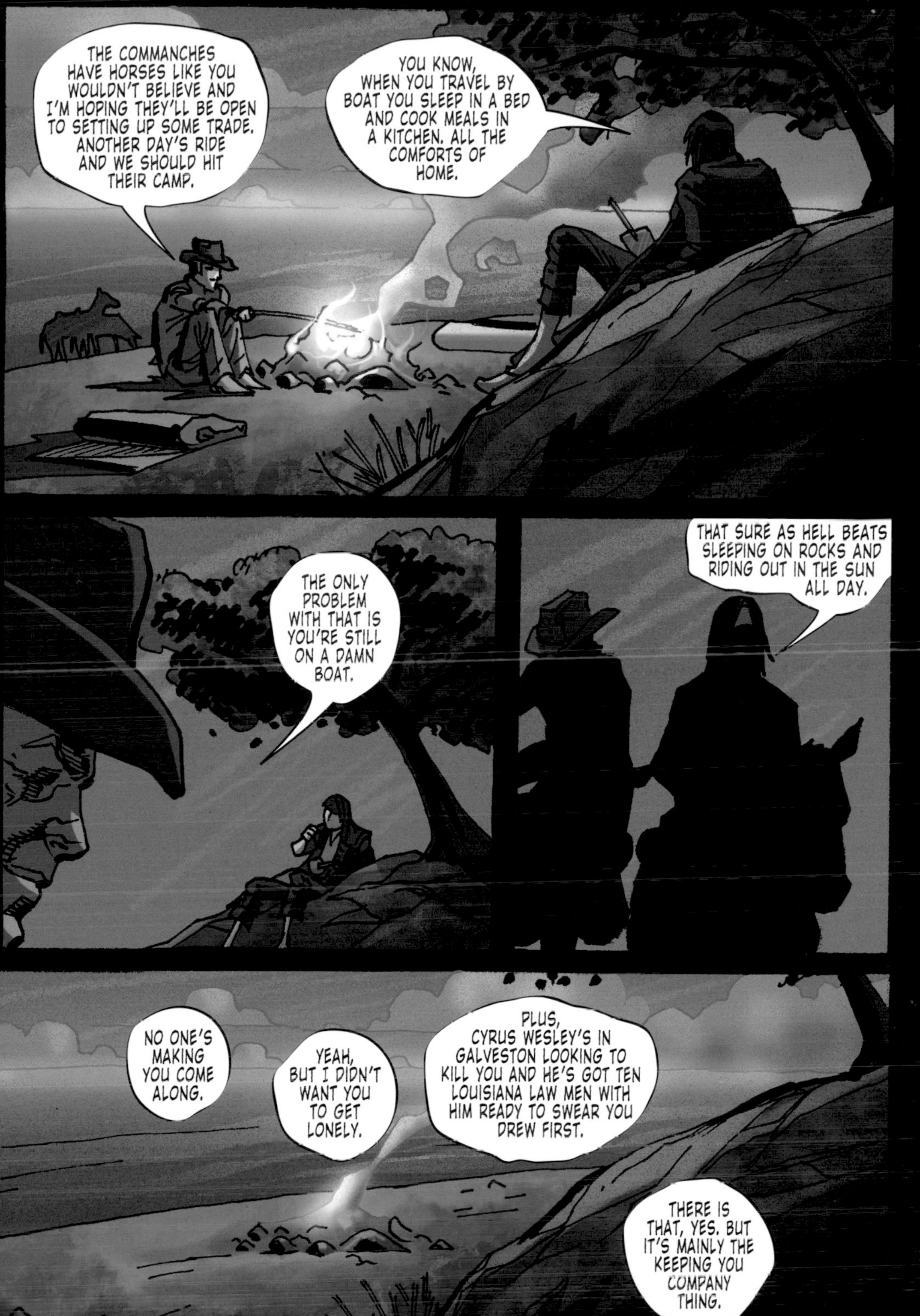
THE COMMANCHES HAVE HORSES LIKE YOU WOULDN'T BELIEVE AND I'M HOPING THEY'LL BE OPEN TO SETTING UP SOME TRADE. ANOTHER DAY'S RIDE AND WE SHOULD HIT THEIR CAMP.
YOU KNOW, WHEN YOU TRAVEL BY BOAT YOU SLEEP IN A BED AND COOK MEALS IN A KITCHEN. ALL THE COMFORTS OF HOME.
THE ONLY PROBLEM WITH THAT IS YOU'RE STILL ON A DAMN BOAT.
THAT SURE AS HELL BEATS SLEEPING ON ROCKS AND RIDING OUT IN THE SUN ALL DAY.
NO ONE'S MAKING YOU COME ALONG.
YEAH, BUT I DIDN'T WANT YOU TO GET LONELY.
PLUS, CYRUS WESLEY'S IN GALVESTON LOOKING TO KILL YOU AND HE'S GOT TEN LOUISIANA LAW MEN WITH HIM READY TO SWEAR YOU DREW FIRST.
THERE IS THAT, YES. BUT IT'S MAINLY THE KEEPING YOU COMPANY THING.

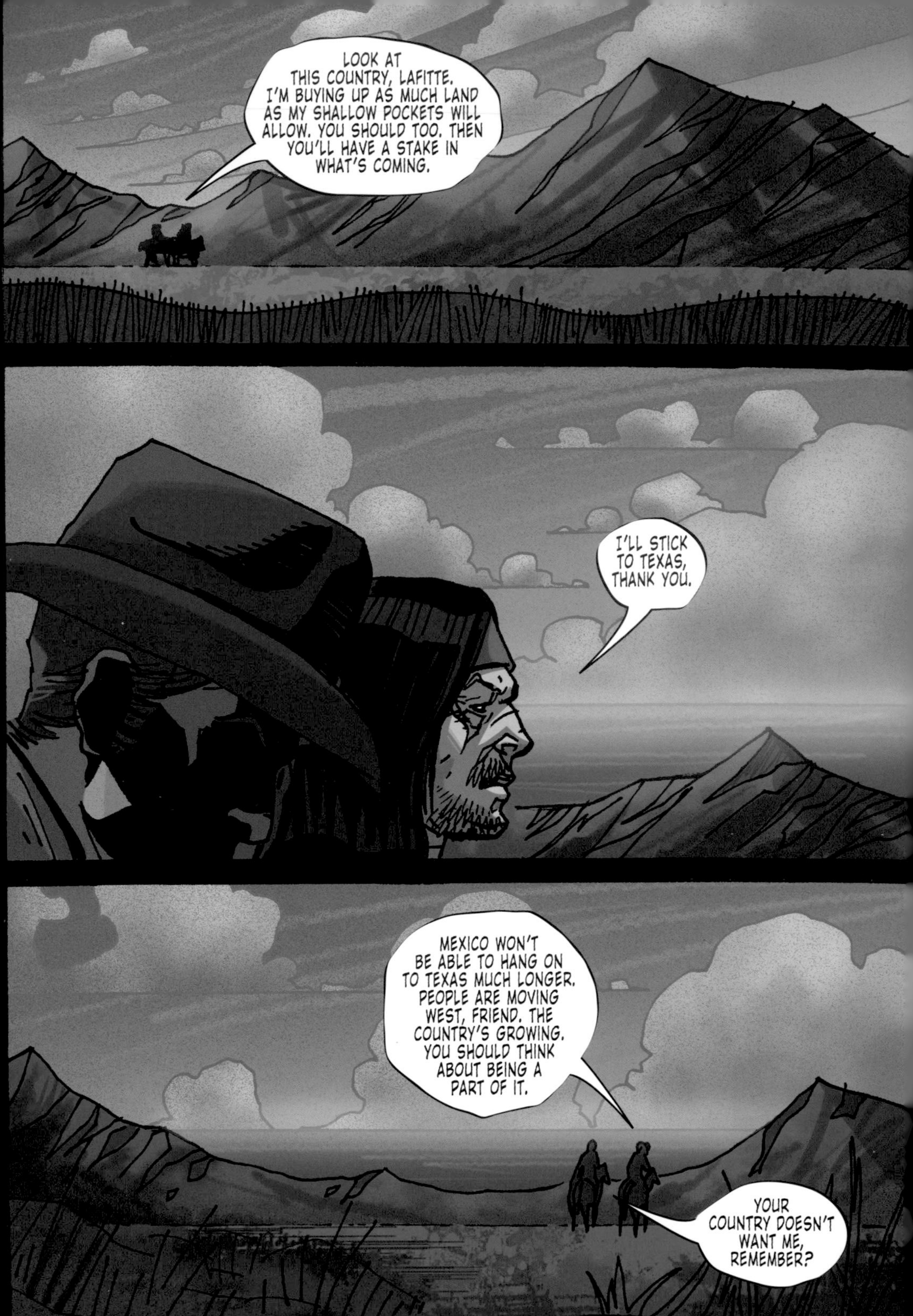
LOOK AT THIS COUNTRY, LAFITTE. I'M BUYING UP AS MUCH LAND AS MY SHALLOW POCKETS WILL ALLOW. YOU SHOULD TOO. THEN YOU'LL HAVE A STAKE IN WHAT'S COMING.
I'LL STICK TO TEXAS, THANK YOU.
MEXICO WON'T BE ABLE TO HANG ON TO TEXAS MUCH LONGER. PEOPLE ARE MOVING WEST, FRIEND. THE COUNTRY'S GROWING. YOU SHOULD THINK ABOUT BEING A PART OF IT.
YOUR COUNTRY DOESN'T WANT ME, REMEMBER?

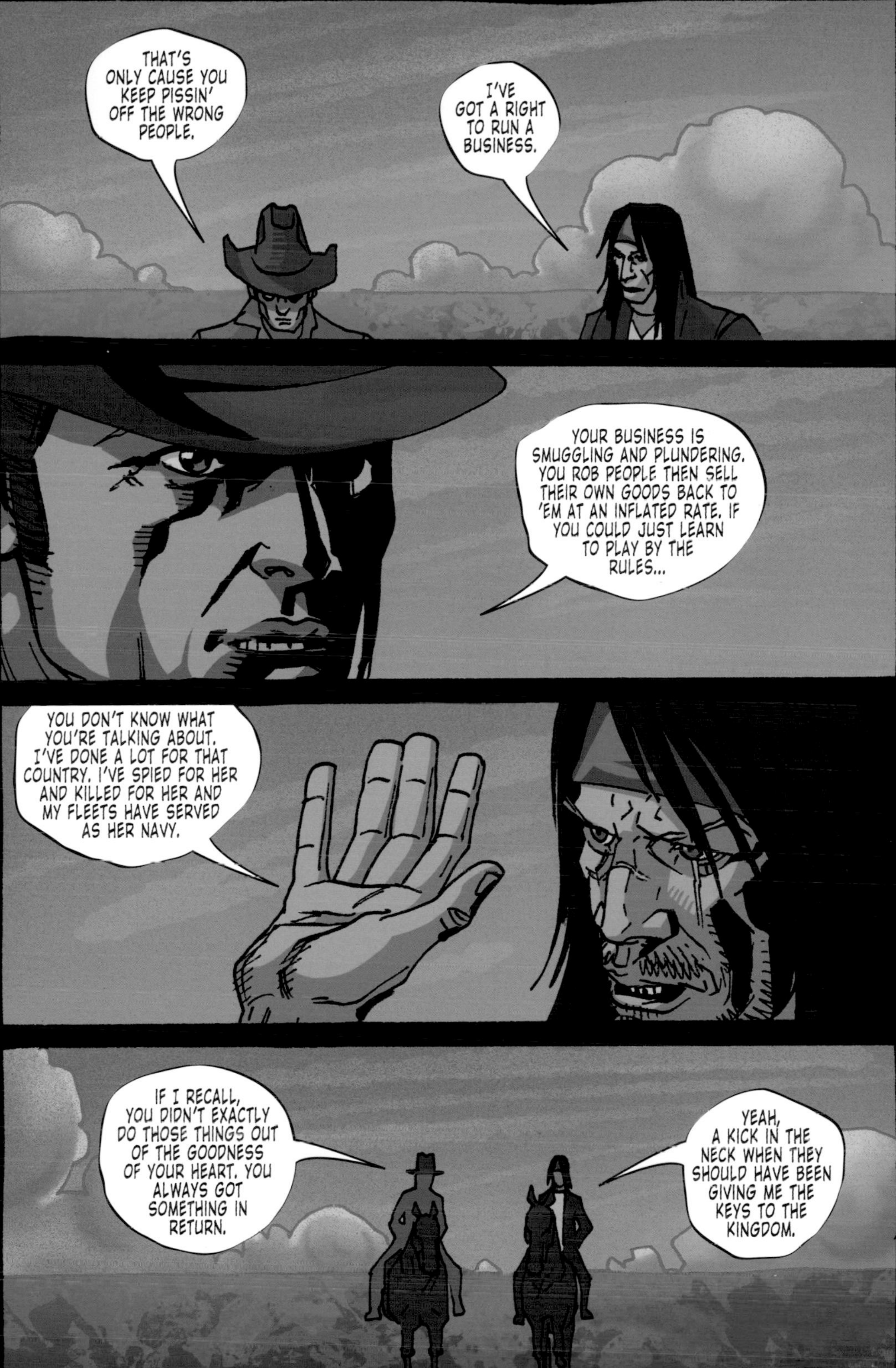
THAT'S ONLY CAUSE YOU KEEP PISSIN' OFF THE WRONG PEOPLE.
I'VE GOT A RIGHT TO RUN A BUSINESS.
YOUR BUSINESS IS SMUGGLING AND PLUNDERING. YOU ROB PEOPLE THEN SELL THEIR OWN GOODS BACK TO 'EM AT AN INFLATED RATE. IF YOU COULD JUST LEARN TO PLAY BY THE RULES...
YOU DON'T KNOW WHAT YOU'RE TALKING ABOUT. I'VE DONE A LOT FOR THAT COUNTRY. I'VE SPIED FOR HER AND KILLED FOR HER AND MY FLEETS HAVE SERVED AS HER NAVY.
IF I RECALL, YOU DIDN'T EXACTLY DO THOSE THINGS OUT OF THE GOODNESS OF YOUR HEART. YOU ALWAYS GOT SOMETHING IN RETURN.
YEAH, A KICK IN THE NECK WHEN THEY SHOULD HAVE BEEN GIVING ME THE KEYS TO THE KINGDOM.

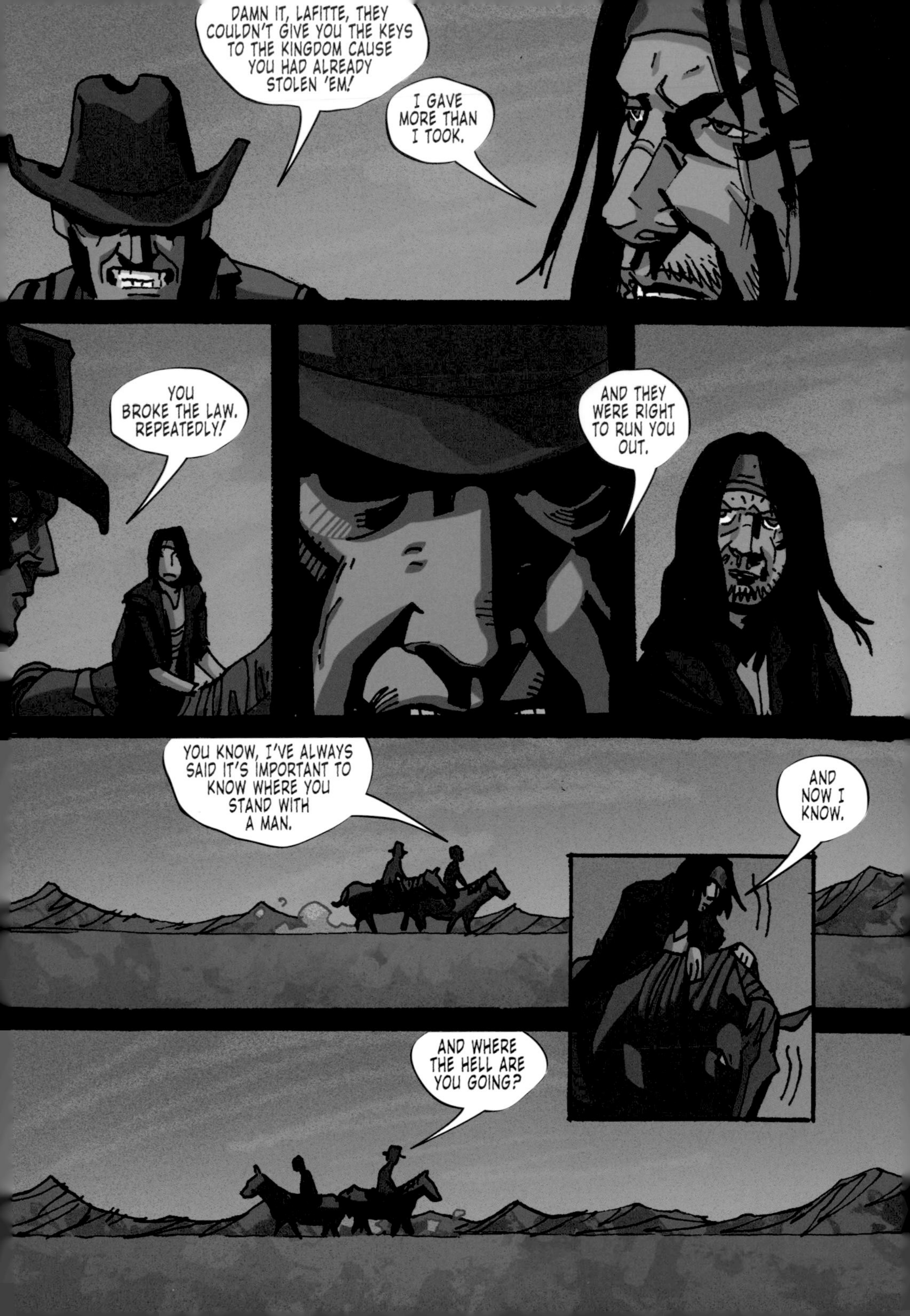
DAMN IT, LAFITTE, THEY COULDN'T GIVE YOU THE KEYS TO THE KINGDOM CAUSE YOU HAD ALREADY STOLEN 'EM!
I GAVE MORE THAN I TOOK.
YOU BROKE THE LAW. REPEATEDLY!
AND THEY WERE RIGHT TO RUN YOU OUT.
YOU KNOW, I'VE ALWAYS SAID IT'S IMPORTANT TO KNOW WHERE YOU STAND WITH A MAN.
AND NOW I KNOW.
AND WHERE THE HELL ARE YOU GOING?

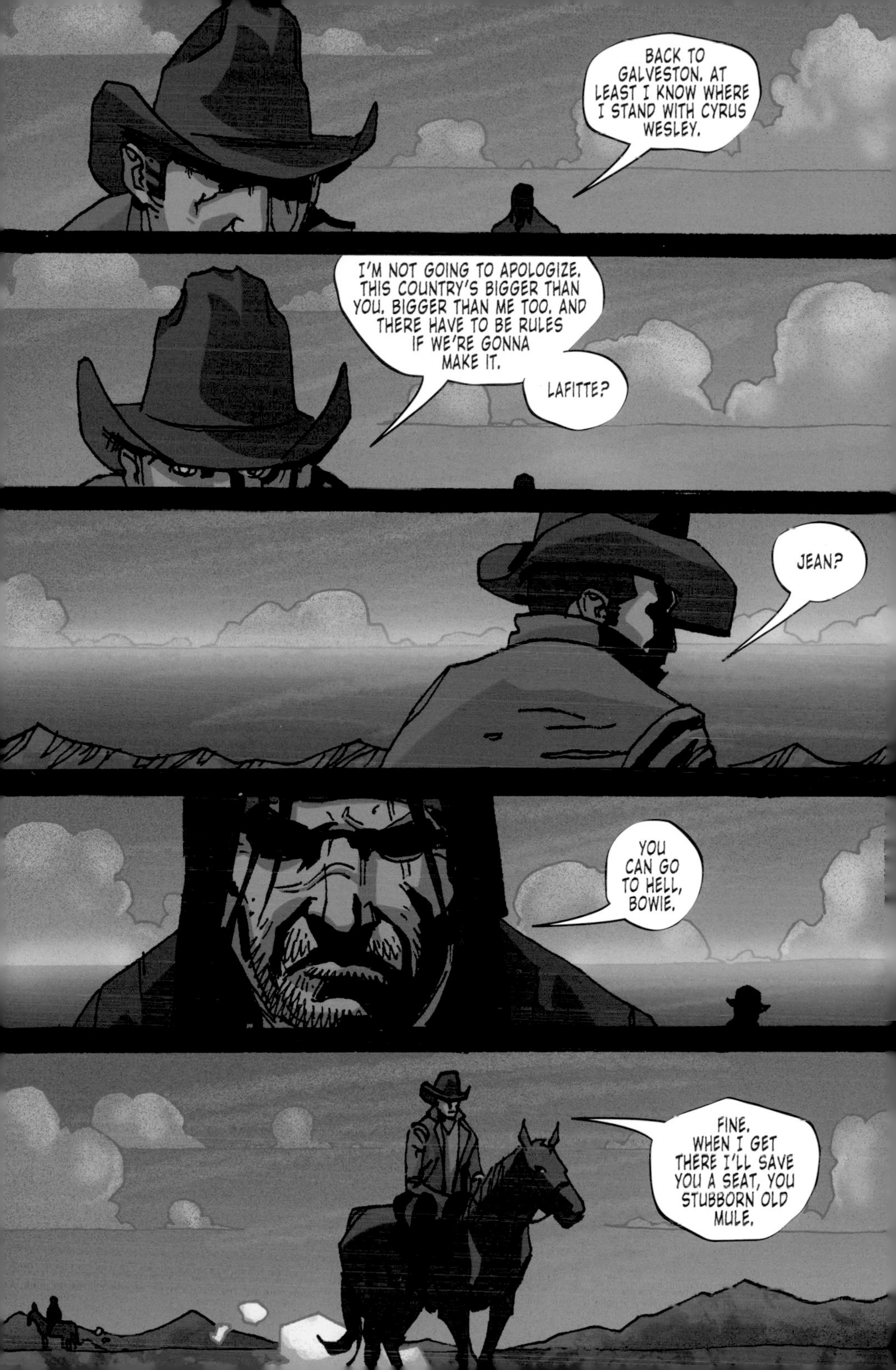
BACK TO GALVESTON. AT LEAST I KNOW WHERE I STAND WITH CYRUS WESLEY.
I'M NOT GOING TO APOLOGIZE. THIS COUNTRY'S BIGGER THAN YOU. BIGGER THAN ME TOO. AND THERE HAVE TO BE RULES IF WE'RE GONNA MAKE IT.
LAFITTE?
JEAN?
YOU CAN GO TO HELL, BOWIE.
FINE. WHEN I GET THERE I'LL SAVE YOU A SEAT, YOU STUBBORN OLD MULE.

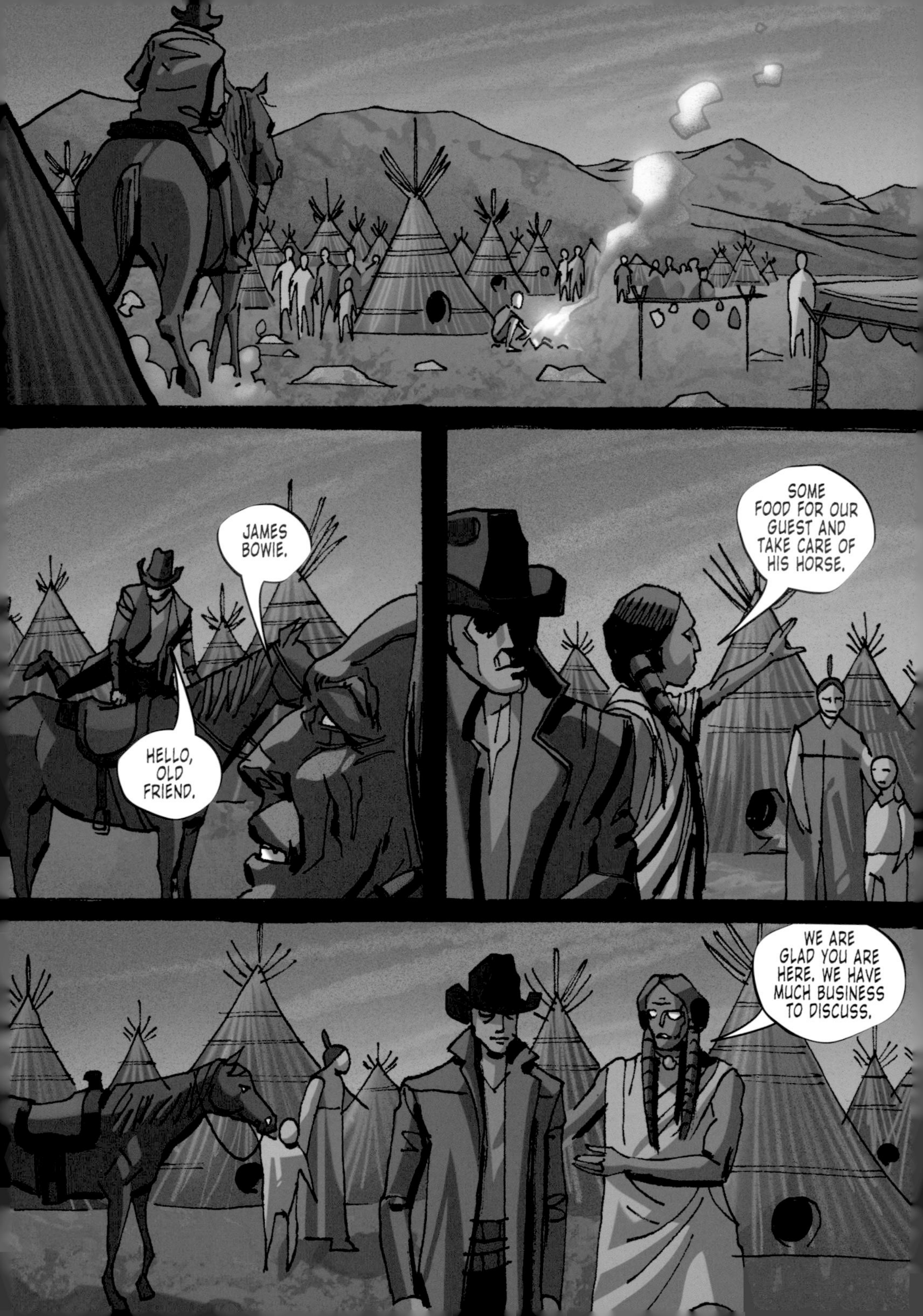
JAMES BOWIE.
HELLO, OLD FRIEND.
SOME FOOD FOR OUR GUEST AND TAKE CARE OF HIS HORSE.
WE ARE GLAD YOU ARE HERE. WE HAVE MUCH BUSINESS TO DISCUSS.

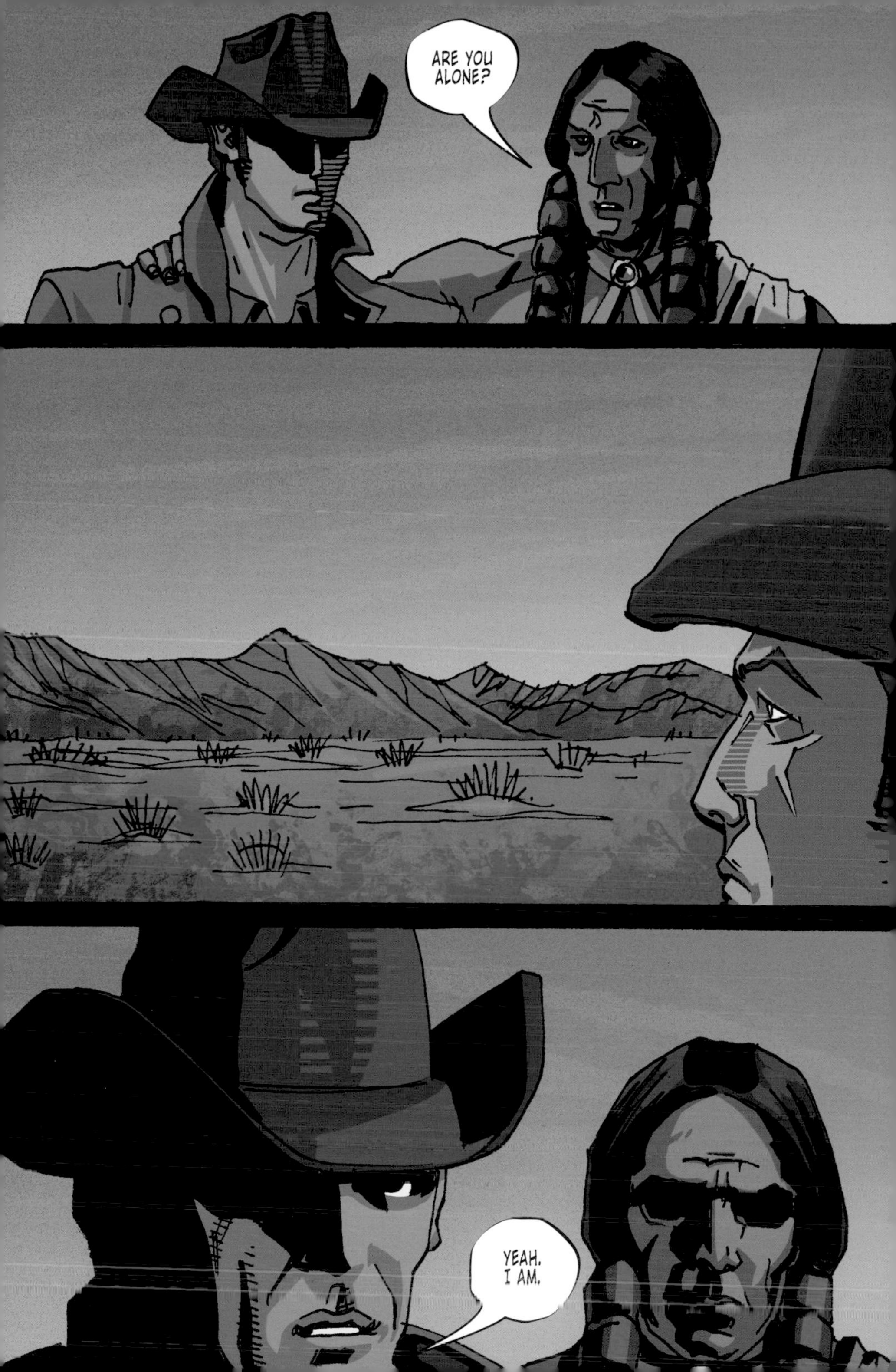
ARE YOU ALONE?
YEAH. I AM.

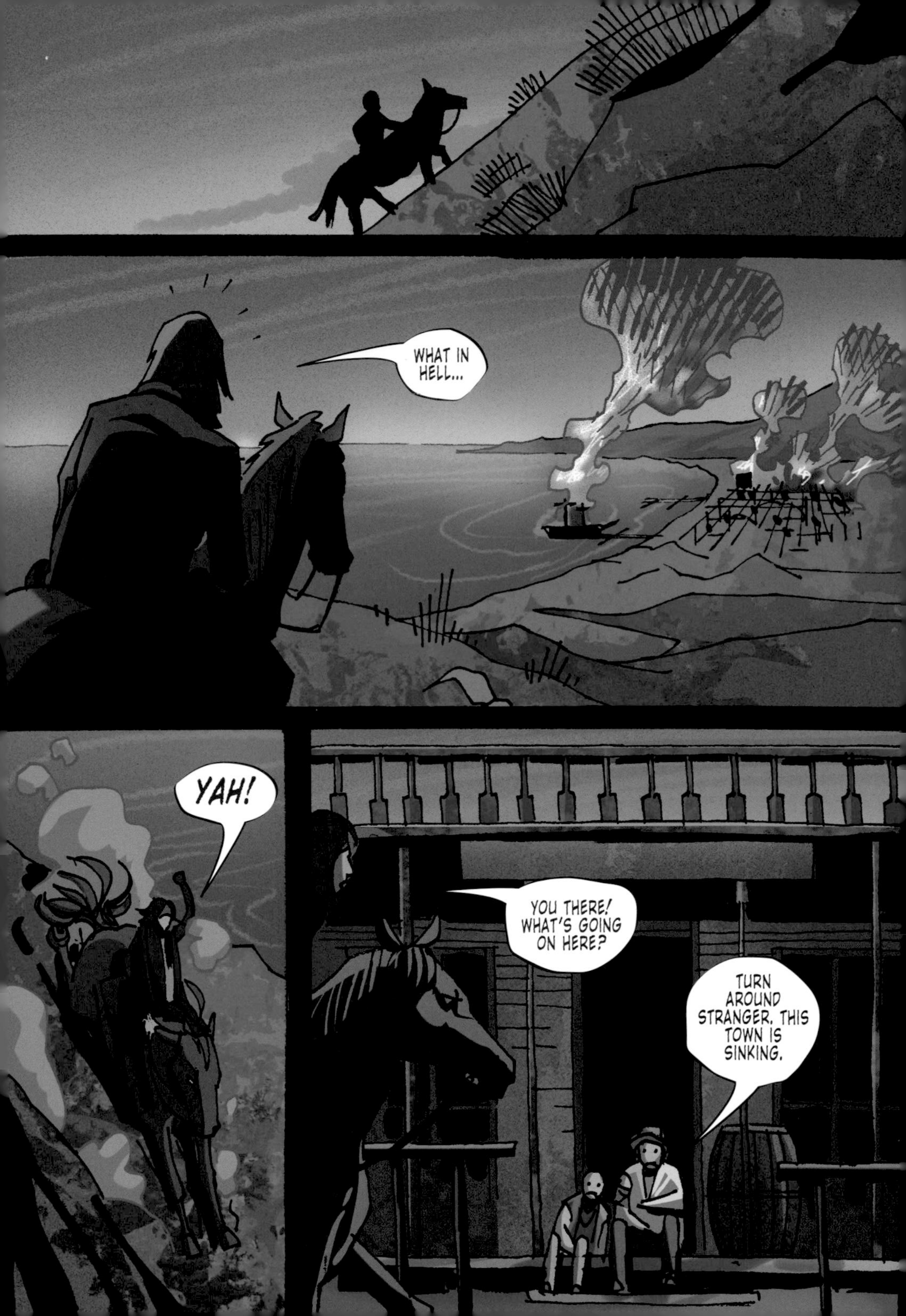
WHAT IN HELL...
YAH!
YOU THERE! WHAT'S GOING ON HERE?
TURN AROUND STRANGER. THIS TOWN IS SINKING.

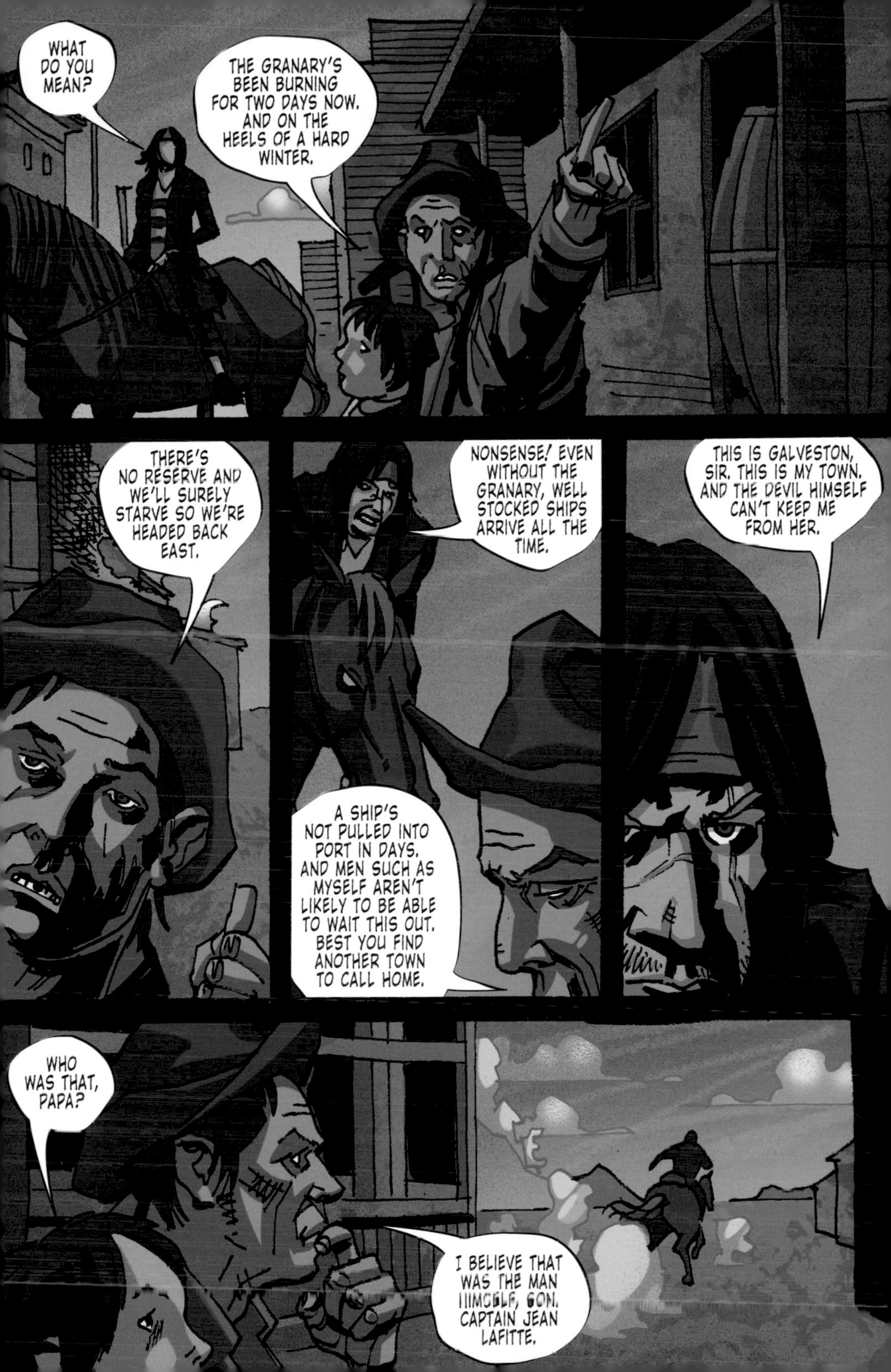
WHAT DO YOU MEAN?
THE GRANARY'S BEEN BURNING FOR TWO DAYS NOW. AND ON THE HEELS OF A HARD WINTER.
THERE'S NO RESERVE AND WE'LL SURELY STARVE SO WE'RE HEADED BACK EAST.
NONSENSE! EVEN WITHOUT THE GRANARY, WELL STOCKED SHIPS ARRIVE ALL THE TIME.
A SHIP'S NOT PULLED INTO PORT IN DAYS. AND MEN SUCH AS MYSELF AREN'T LIKELY TO BE ABLE TO WAIT THIS OUT. BEST YOU FIND ANOTHER TOWN TO CALL HOME.
THIS IS GALVESTON, SIR. THIS IS MY TOWN. AND THE DEVIL HIMSELF CAN'T KEEP ME FROM HER.
WHO WAS THAT, PAPA?
I BELIEVE THAT WAS THE MAN HIMSELF, SON. CAPTAIN JEAN LAFITTE.

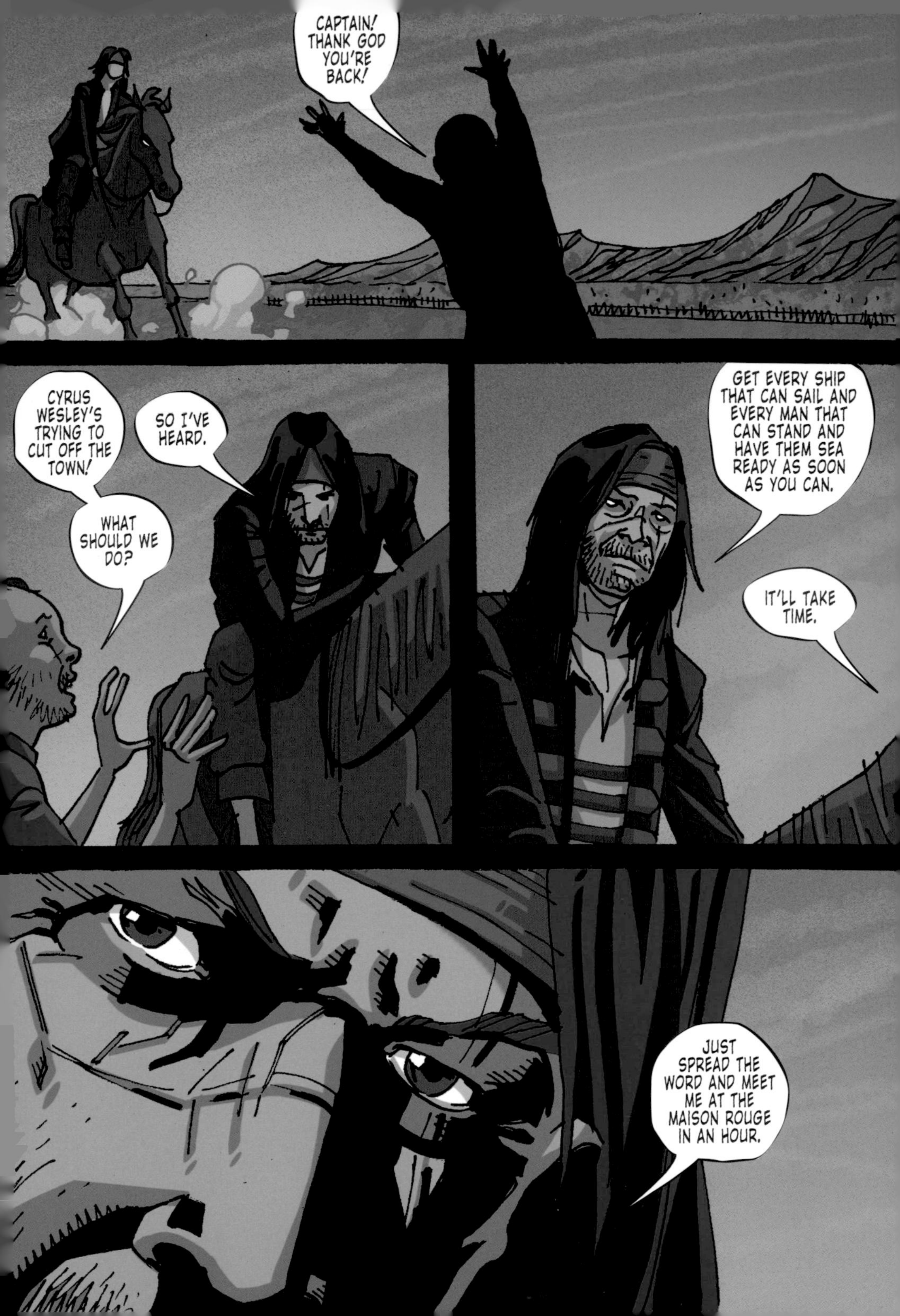
CAPTAIN! THANK GOD YOU'RE BACK!
CYRUS WESLEY'S TRYING TO CUT OFF THE TOWN!
SO I'VE HEARD.
WHAT SHOULD WE DO?
GET EVERY SHIP THAT CAN SAIL AND EVERY MAN THAT CAN STAND AND HAVE THEM SEA READY AS SOON AS YOU CAN.
IT'LL TAKE TIME.
JUST SPREAD THE WORD AND MEET ME AT THE MAISON ROUGE IN AN HOUR.

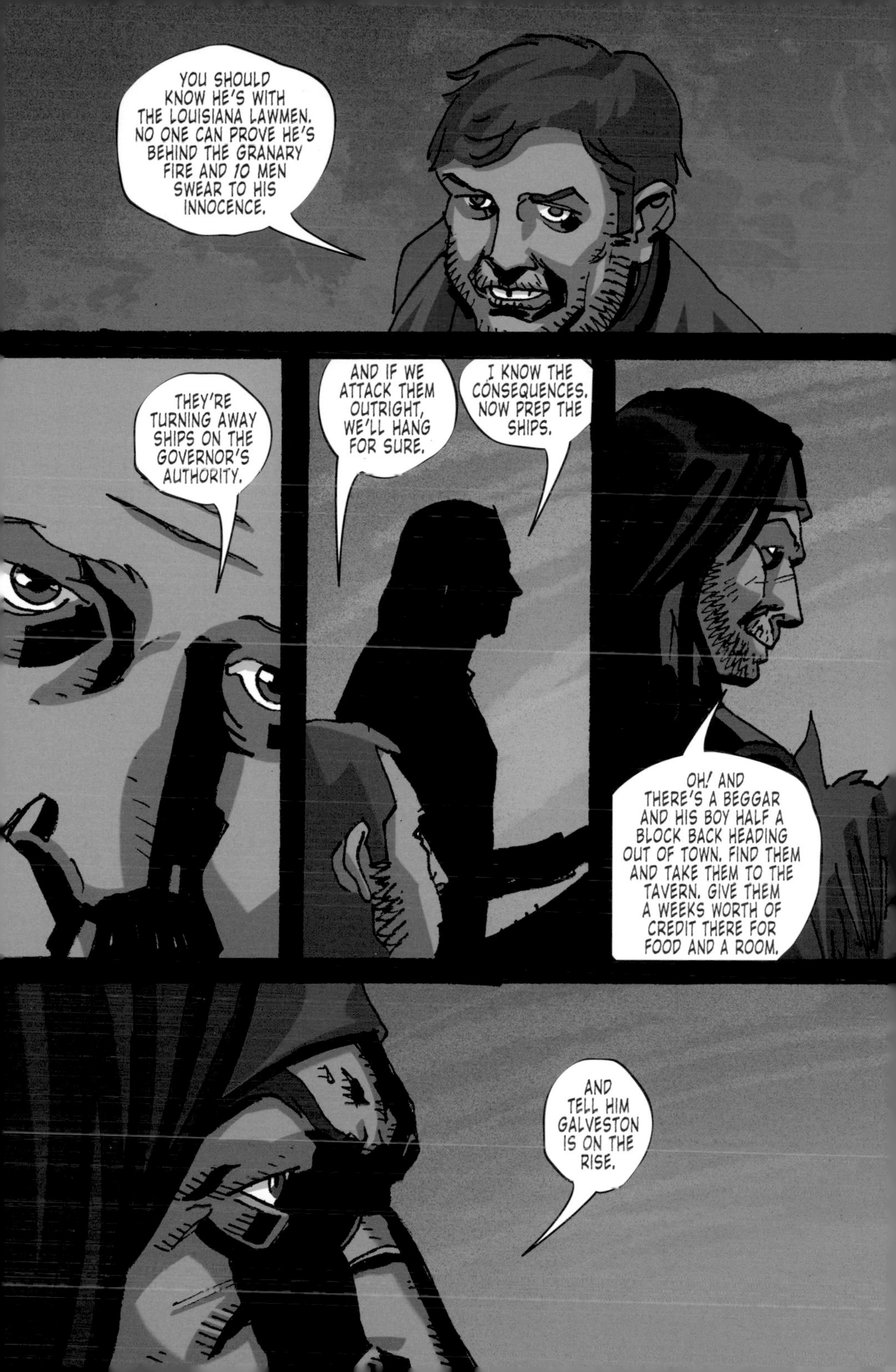
YOU SHOULD KNOW HE'S WITH THE LOUISIANA LAWMEN. NO ONE CAN PROVE HE'S BEHIND THE GRANARY FIRE AND 10 MEN SWEAR TO HIS INNOCENCE.
THEY'RE TURNING AWAY SHIPS ON THE GOVERNOR'S AUTHORITY.
AND IF WE ATTACK THEM OUTRIGHT, WE'LL HANG FOR SURE.
I KNOW THE CONSEQUENCES. NOW PREP THE SHIPS.
OH! AND THERE'S A BEGGAR AND HIS BOY HALF A BLOCK BACK HEADING OUT OF TOWN. FIND THEM AND TAKE THEM TO THE TAVERN. GIVE THEM A WEEKS WORTH OF CREDIT THERE FOR FOOD AND A ROOM.
AND TELL HIM GALVESTON IS ON THE RISE.

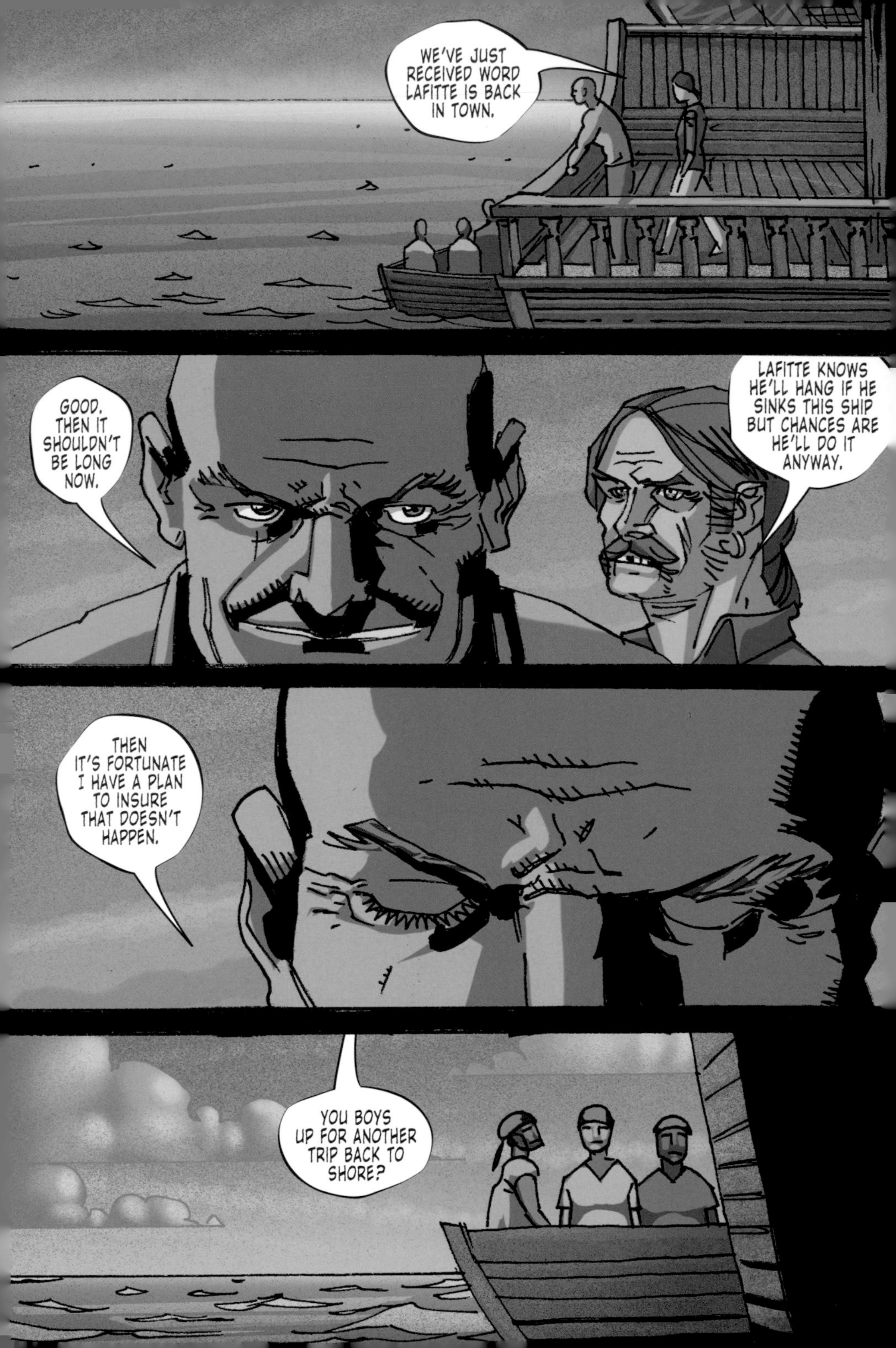
WE'VE JUST RECEIVED WORD LAFITTE IS BACK IN TOWN.
GOOD. THEN IT SHOULDN'T BE LONG NOW.
LAFITTE KNOWS HE'LL HANG IF HE SINKS THIS SHIP BUT CHANCES ARE HE'LL DO IT ANYWAY.
THEN IT'S FORTUNATE I HAVE A PLAN TO INSURE THAT DOESN'T HAPPEN.
YOU BOYS UP FOR ANOTHER TRIP BACK TO SHORE?

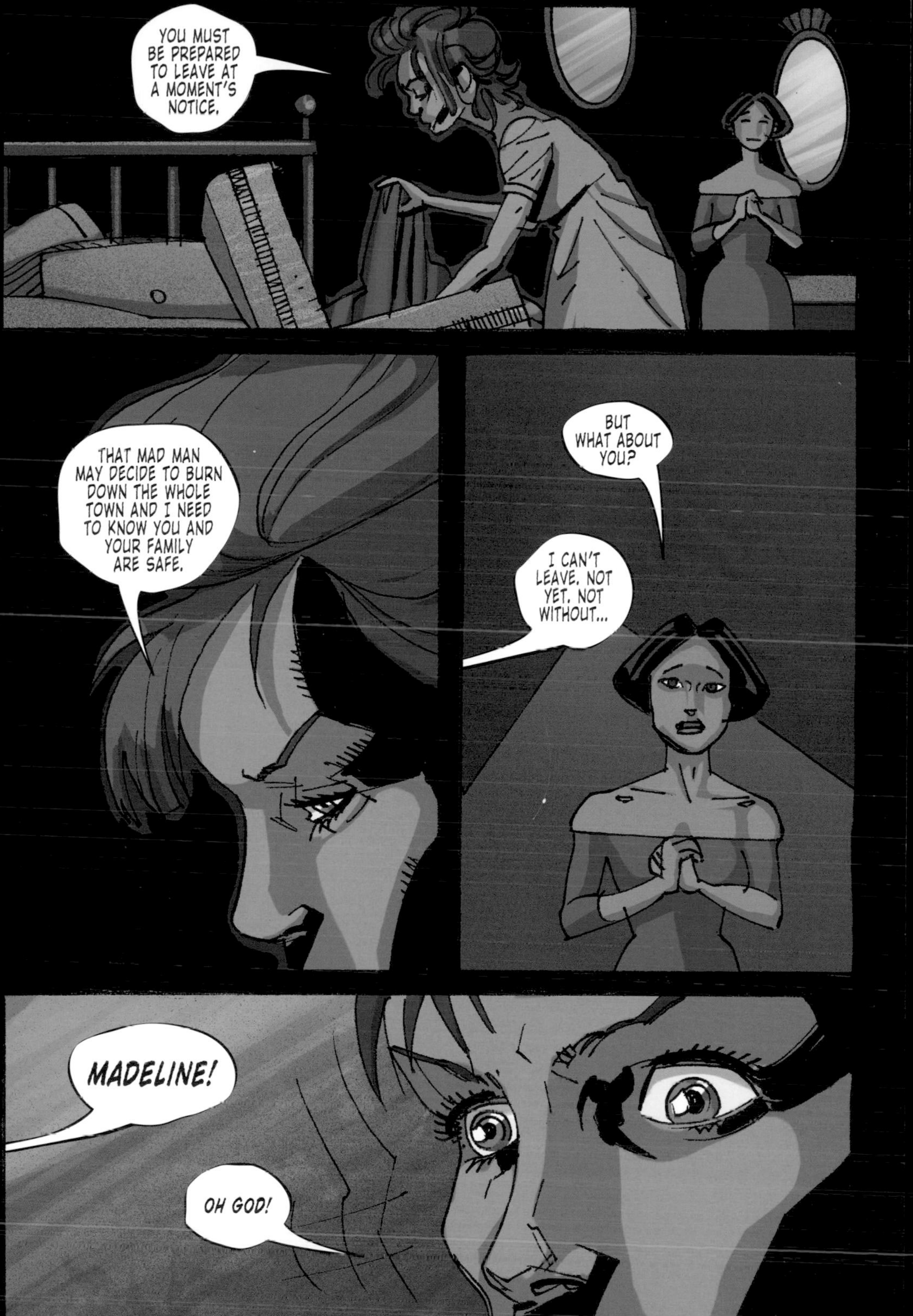
YOU MUST BE PREPARED TO LEAVE AT A MOMENT'S NOTICE.
THAT MAD MAN MAY DECIDE TO BURN DOWN THE WHOLE TOWN AND I NEED TO KNOW YOU AND YOUR FAMILY ARE SAFE.
BUT WHAT ABOUT YOU?
I CAN'T LEAVE. NOT YET. NOT WITHOUT...
MADELINE!
OH GOD!

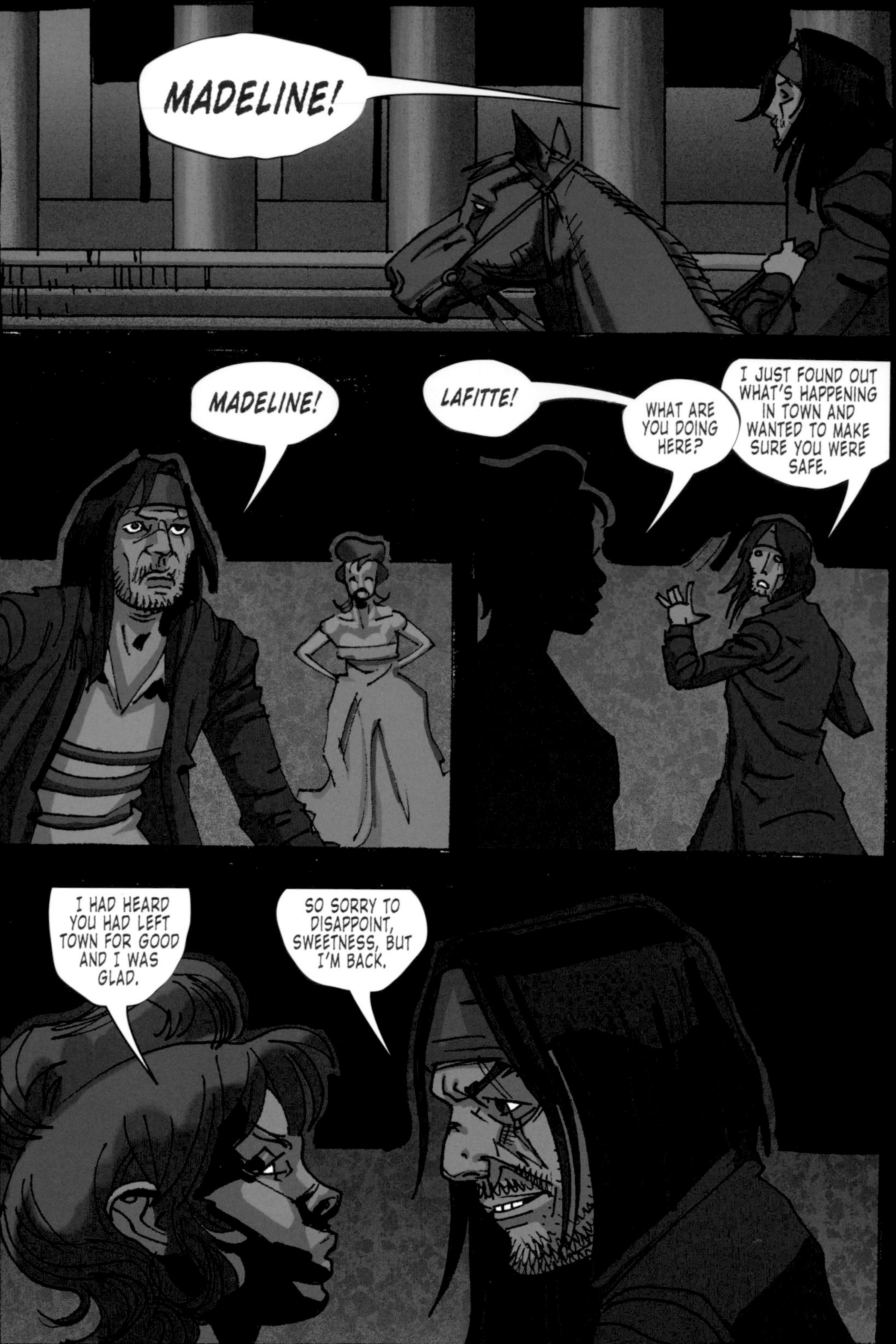
MADELINE!
MADELINE!
LAFITTE!
WHAT ARE YOU DOING HERE?
I JUST FOUND OUT WHAT'S HAPPENING IN TOWN AND WANTED TO MAKE SURE YOU WERE SAFE.
I HAD HEARD YOU HAD LEFT TOWN FOR GOOD AND I WAS GLAD.
SO SORRY TO DISAPPOINT, SWEETNESS, BUT I'M BACK.

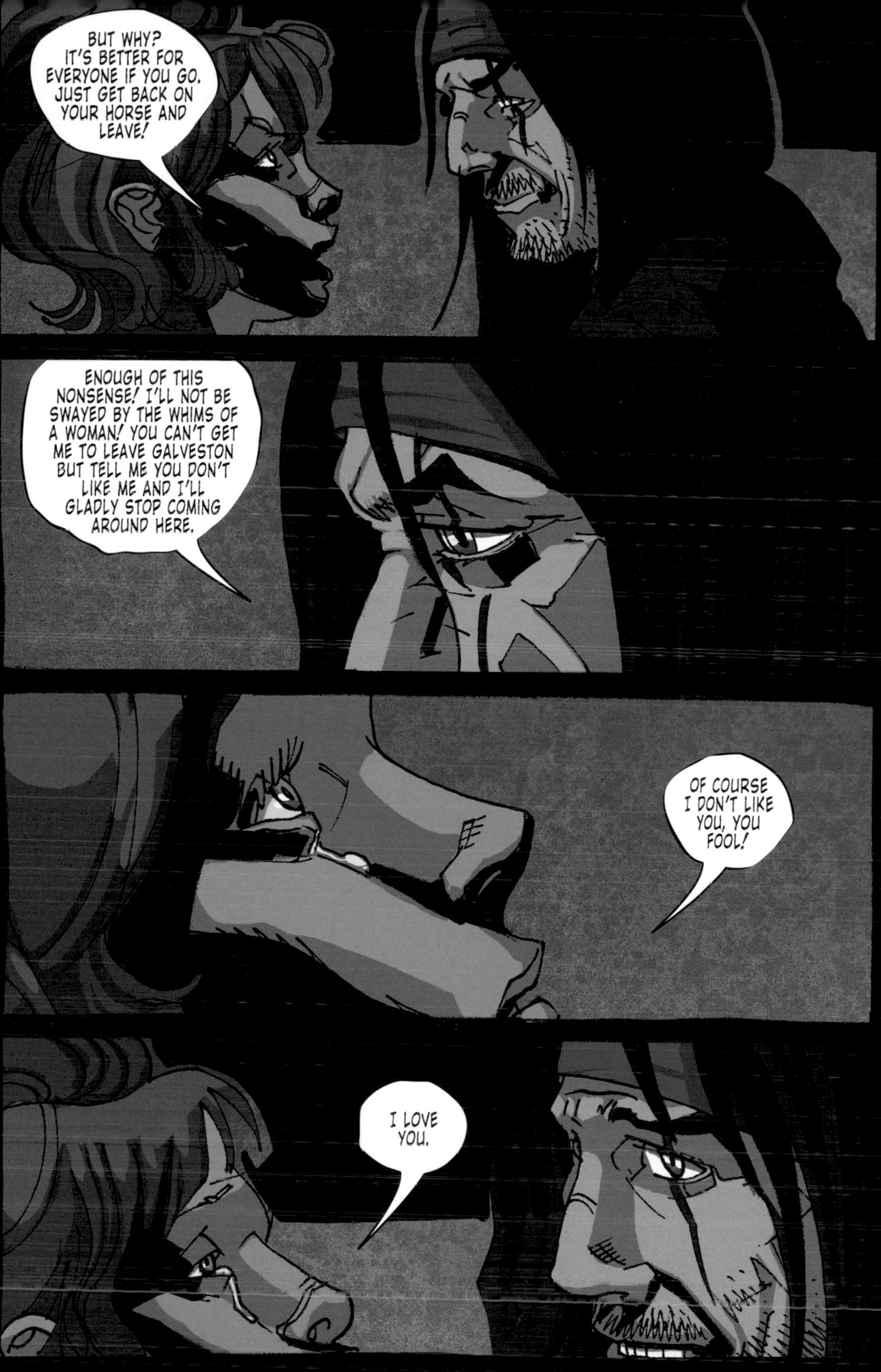
BUT WHY? IT'S BETTER FOR EVERYONE IF YOU GO. JUST GET BACK ON YOUR HORSE AND LEAVE!
ENOUGH OF THIS NONSENSE! I'LL NOT BE SWAYED BY THE WHIMS OF A WOMAN! YOU CAN'T GET ME TO LEAVE GALVESTON BUT TELL ME YOU DON'T LIKE ME AND I'LL GLADLY STOP COMING AROUND HERE.
OF COURSE I DON'T LIKE YOU, YOU FOOL!
I LOVE YOU.

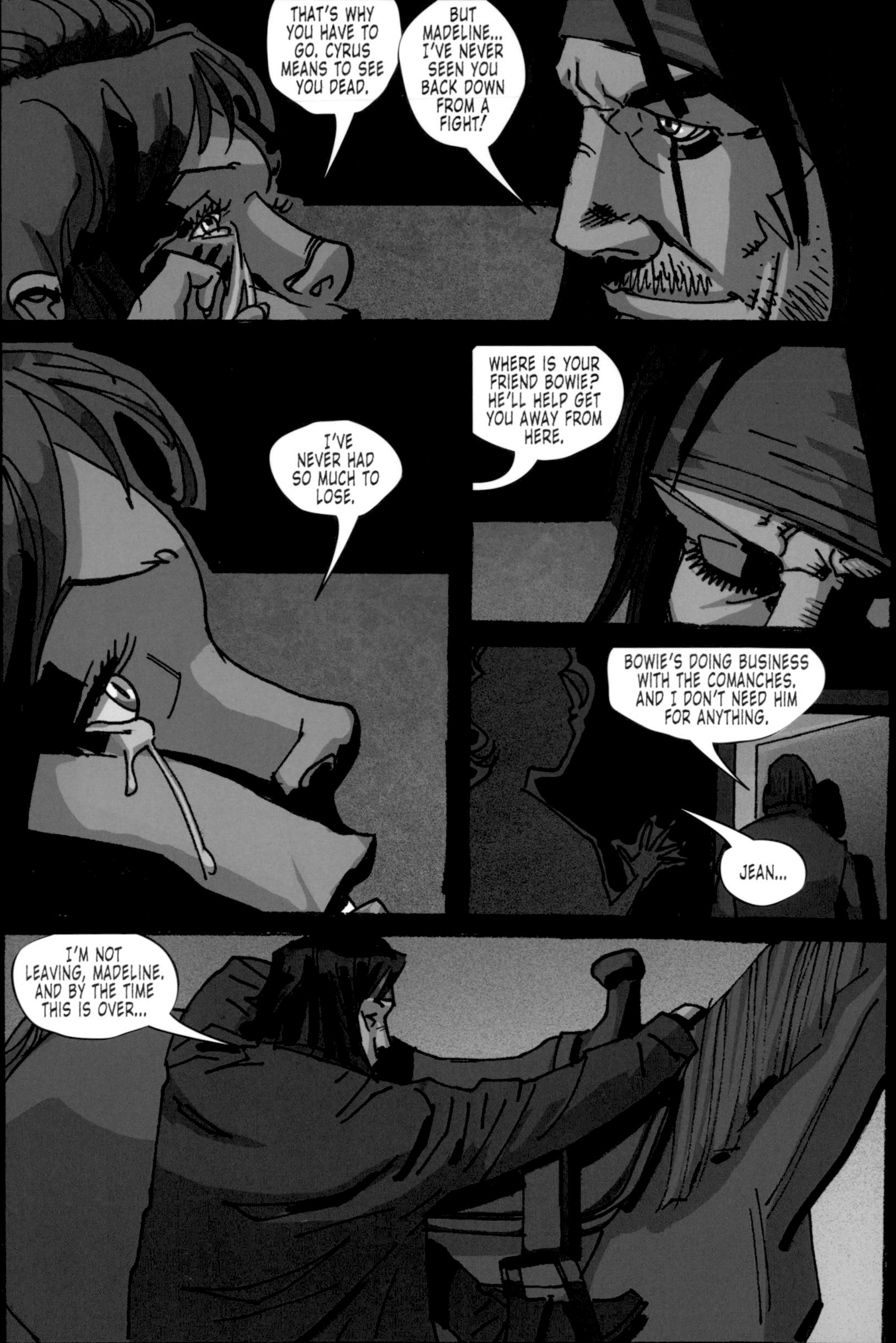
THAT'S WHY YOU HAVE TO GO. CYRUS MEANS TO SEE YOU DEAD.
BUT MADELINE... I'VE NEVER SEEN YOU BACK DOWN FROM A FIGHT!
I'VE NEVER HAD SO MUCH TO LOSE.
WHERE IS YOUR FRIEND BOWIE? HE'LL HELP GET YOU AWAY FROM HERE.
BOWIE'S DOING BUSINESS WITH THE COMANCHES. AND I DON'T NEED HIM FOR ANYTHING.
JEAN...
I'M NOT LEAVING, MADELINE. AND BY THE TIME THIS IS OVER...

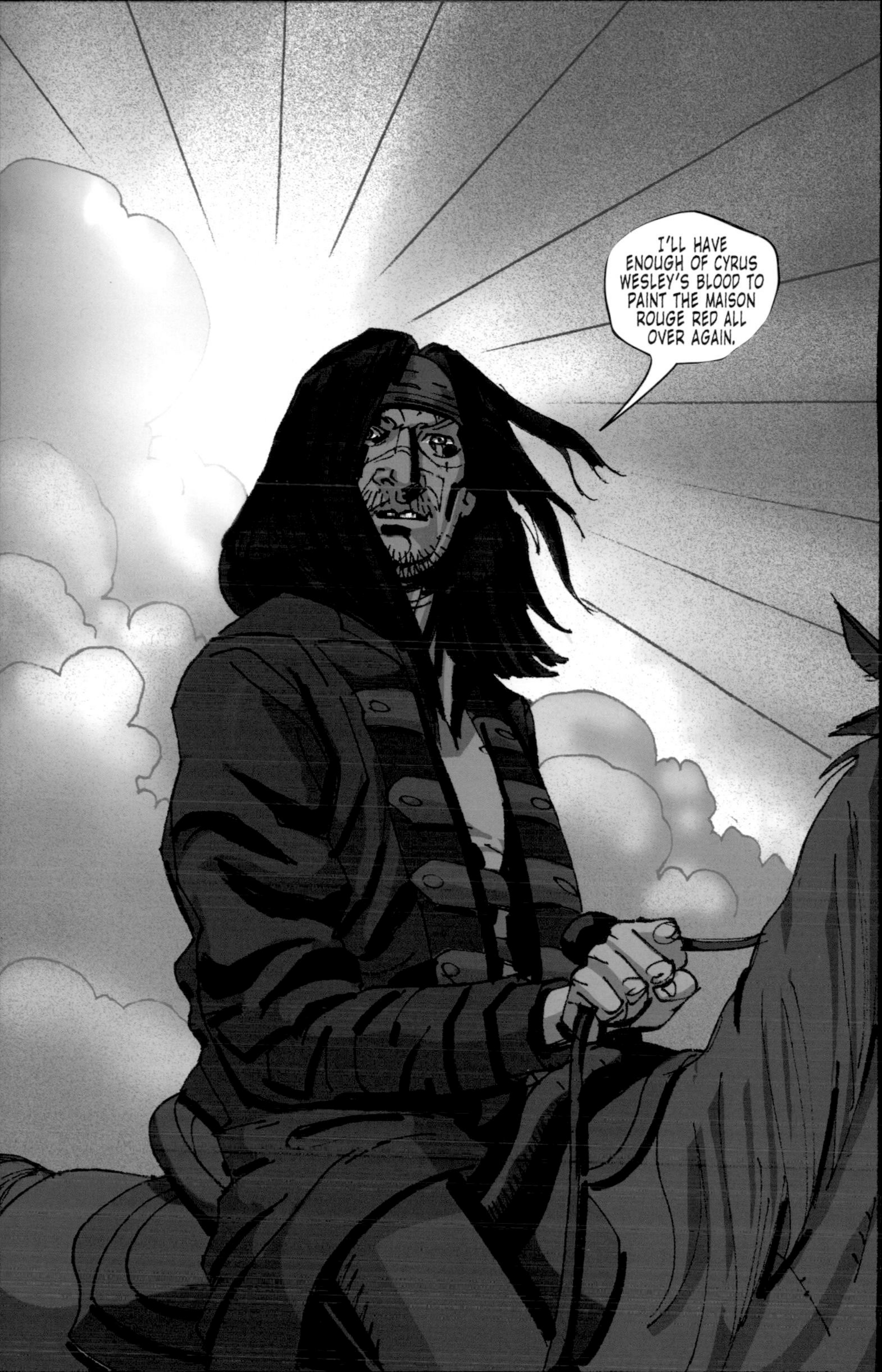
I'LL HAVE ENOUGH OF CYRUS WESLEY'S BLOOD TO PAINT THE MAISON ROUGE RED ALL OVER AGAIN.

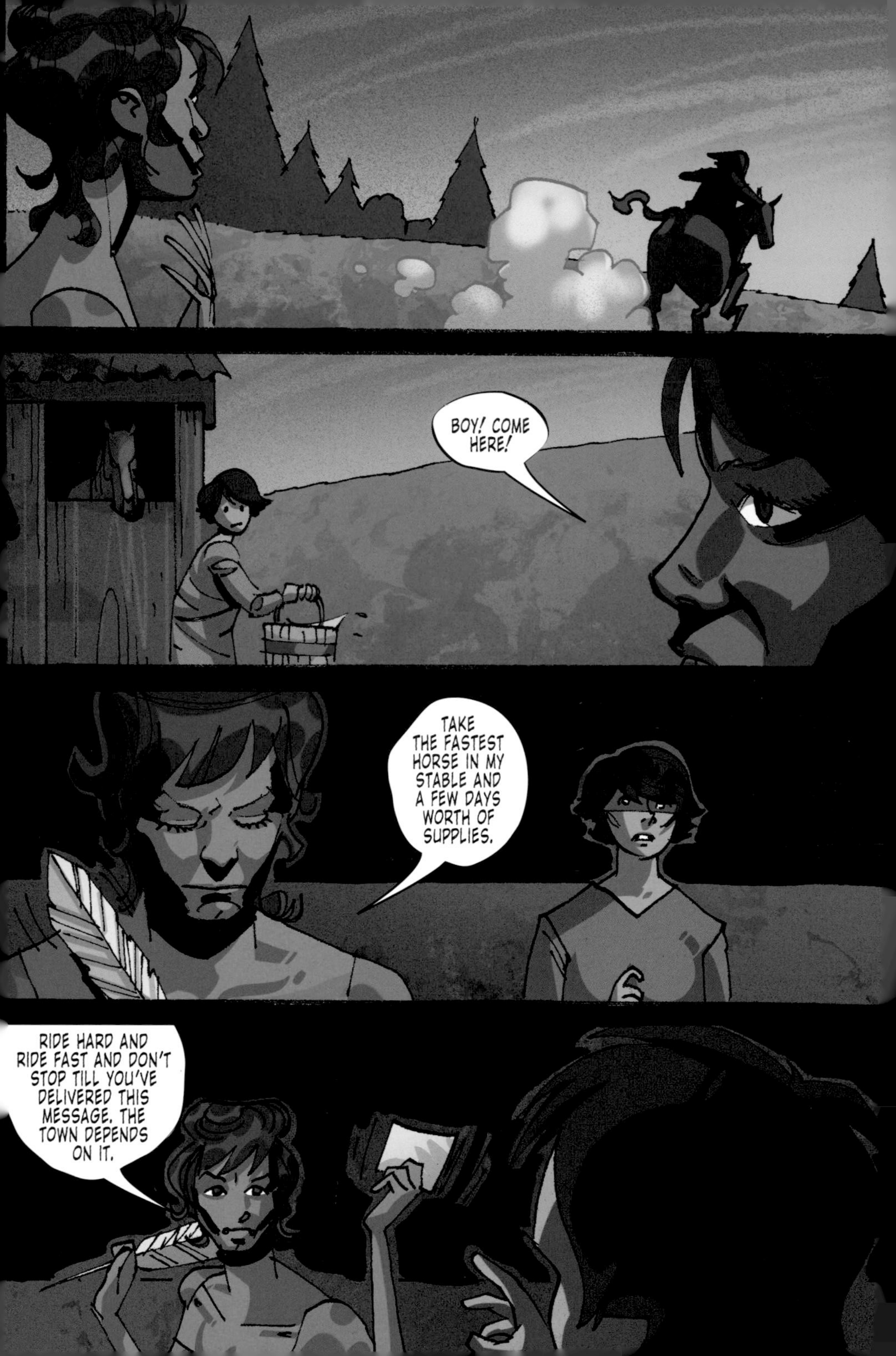
BOY! COME HERE!
TAKE THE FASTEST HORSE IN MY STABLE AND A FEW DAYS WORTH OF SUPPLIES.
RIDE HARD AND RIDE FAST AND DON'T STOP TILL YOU'VE DELIVERED THIS MESSAGE. THE TOWN DEPENDS ON IT.

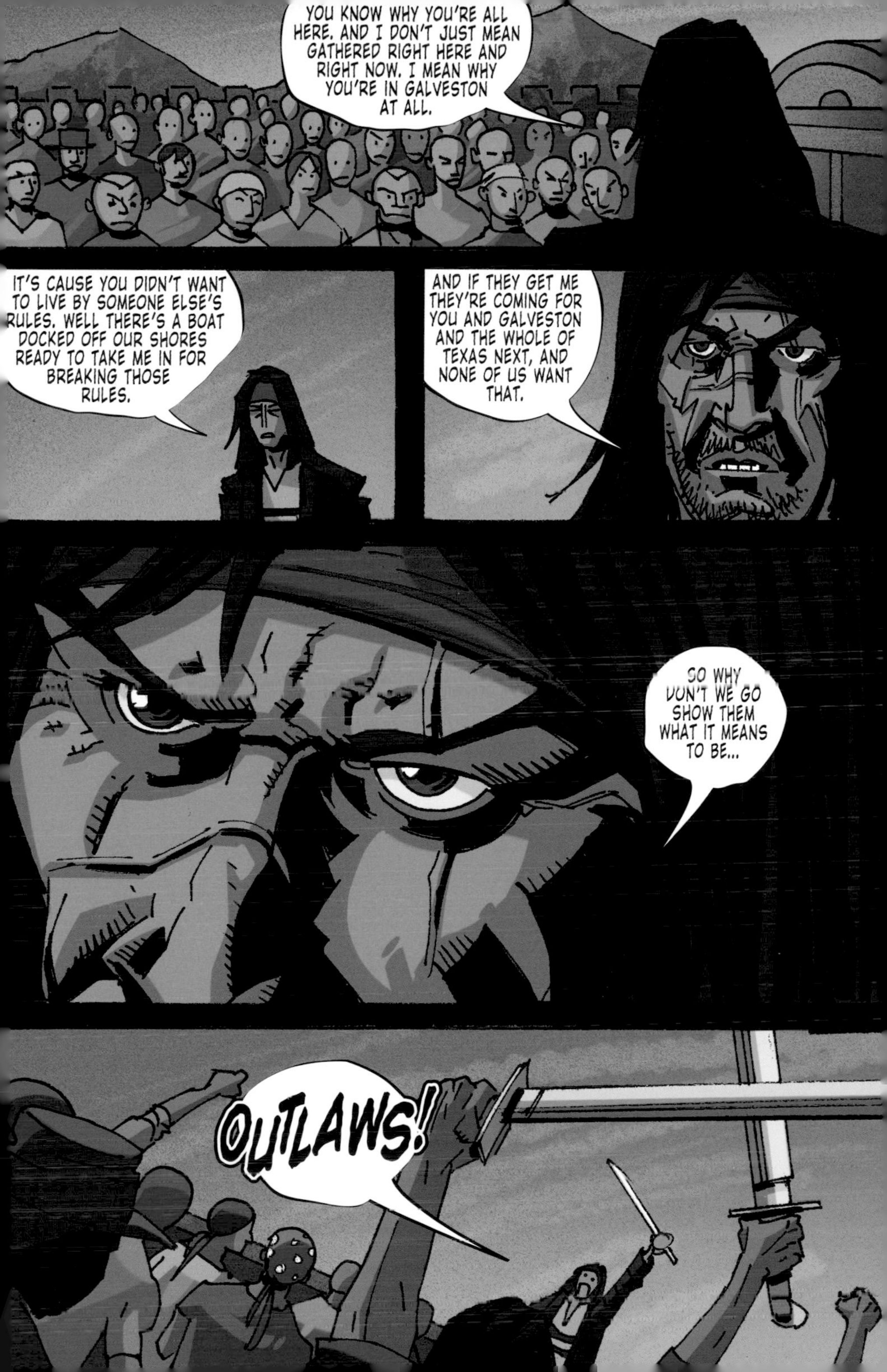

YOU KNOW WHY YOU'RE ALL HERE. AND I DON'T JUST MEAN GATHERED RIGHT HERE AND RIGHT NOW. I MEAN WHY YOU'RE IN GALVESTON AT ALL.
IT'S CAUSE YOU DIDN'T WANT TO LIVE BY SOMEONE ELSE'S RULES. WELL THERE'S A BOAT DOCKED OFF OUR SHORES READY TO TAKE ME IN FOR BREAKING THOSE RULES.
AND IF THEY GET ME THEY'RE COMING FOR YOU AND GALVESTON AND THE WHOLE OF TEXAS NEXT, AND NONE OF US WANT THAT.
SO WHY DON'T WE GO SHOW THEM WHAT IT MEANS TO BE...
OUTLAWS!

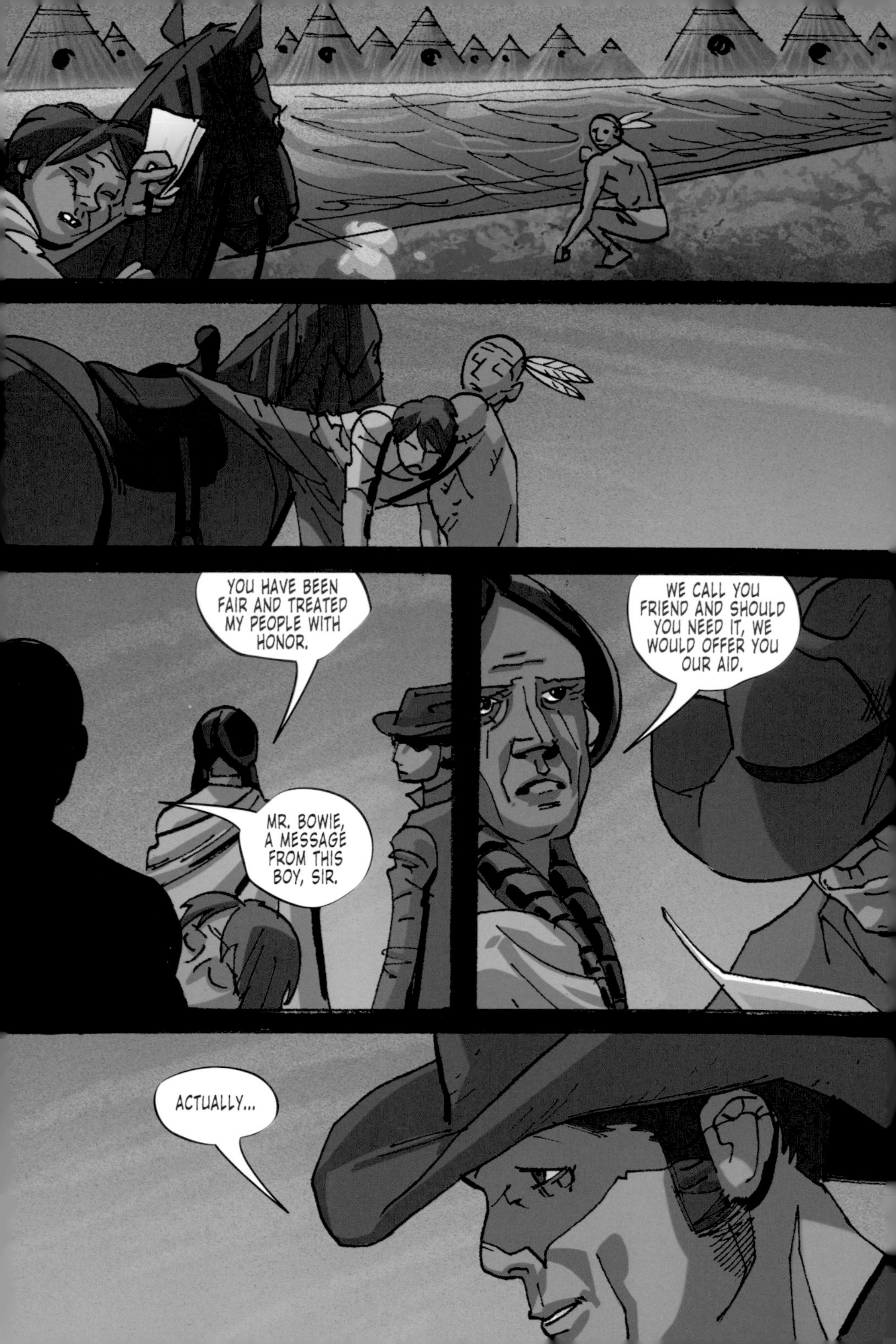
YOU HAVE BEEN FAIR AND TREATED MY PEOPLE WITH HONOR.
MR. BOWIE, A MESSAGE FROM THIS BOY, SIR.
WE CALL YOU FRIEND AND SHOULD YOU NEED IT, WE WOULD OFFER YOU OUR AID.
ACTUALLY...

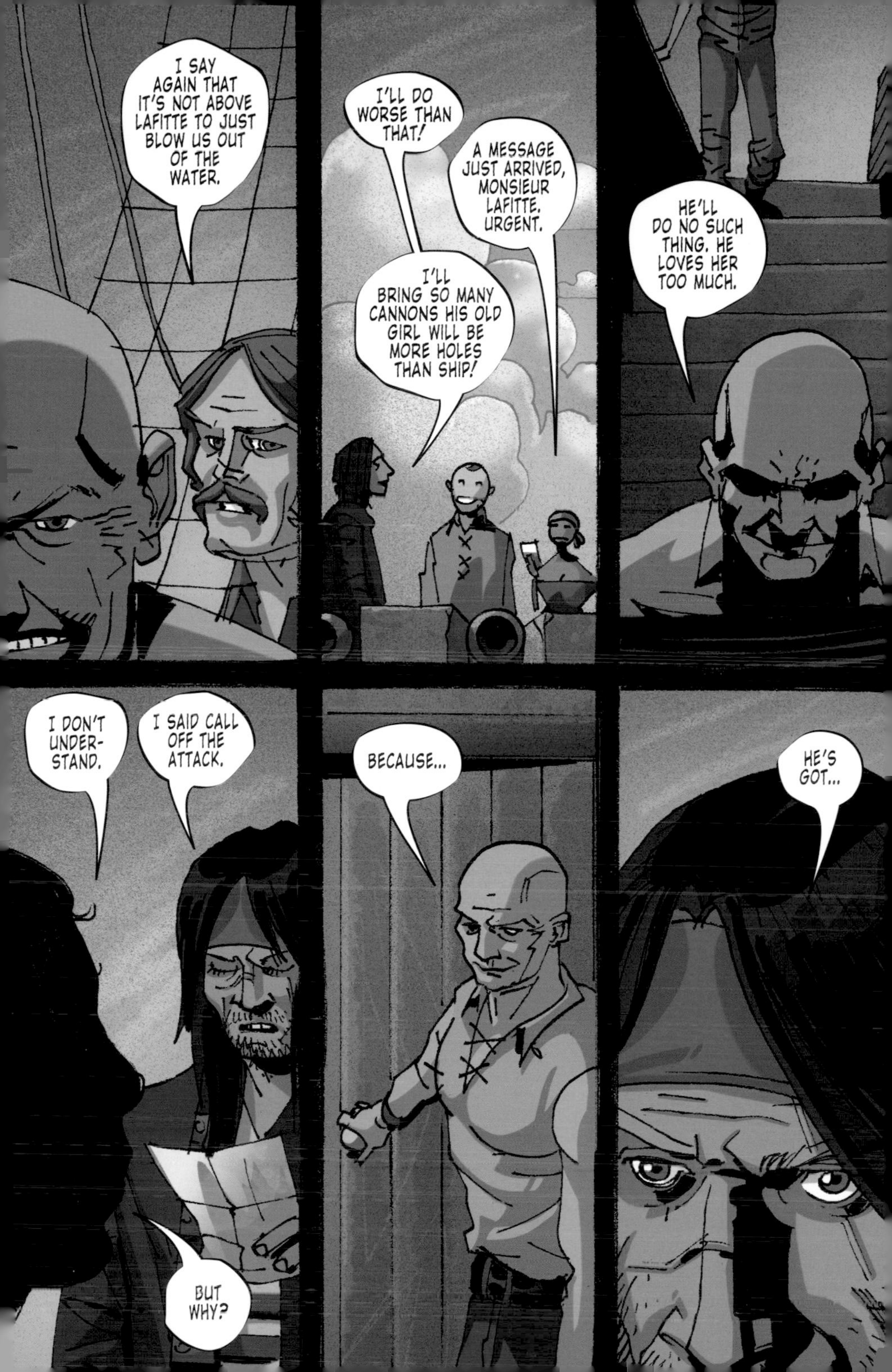
I SAY AGAIN THAT IT'S NOT ABOVE LAFITTE TO JUST BLOW US OUT OF THE WATER.
I'LL DO WORSE THAN THAT!
I'LL BRING SO MANY CANNONS HIS OLD GIRL WILL BE MORE HOLES THAN SHIP!
A MESSAGE JUST ARRIVED, MONSIEUR LAFITTE. URGENT.
HE'LL DO NO SUCH THING. HE LOVES HER TOO MUCH.
I DON'T UNDER-STAND.
I SAID CALL OFF THE ATTACK.
BUT WHY?
BECAUSE...
HE'S GOT...

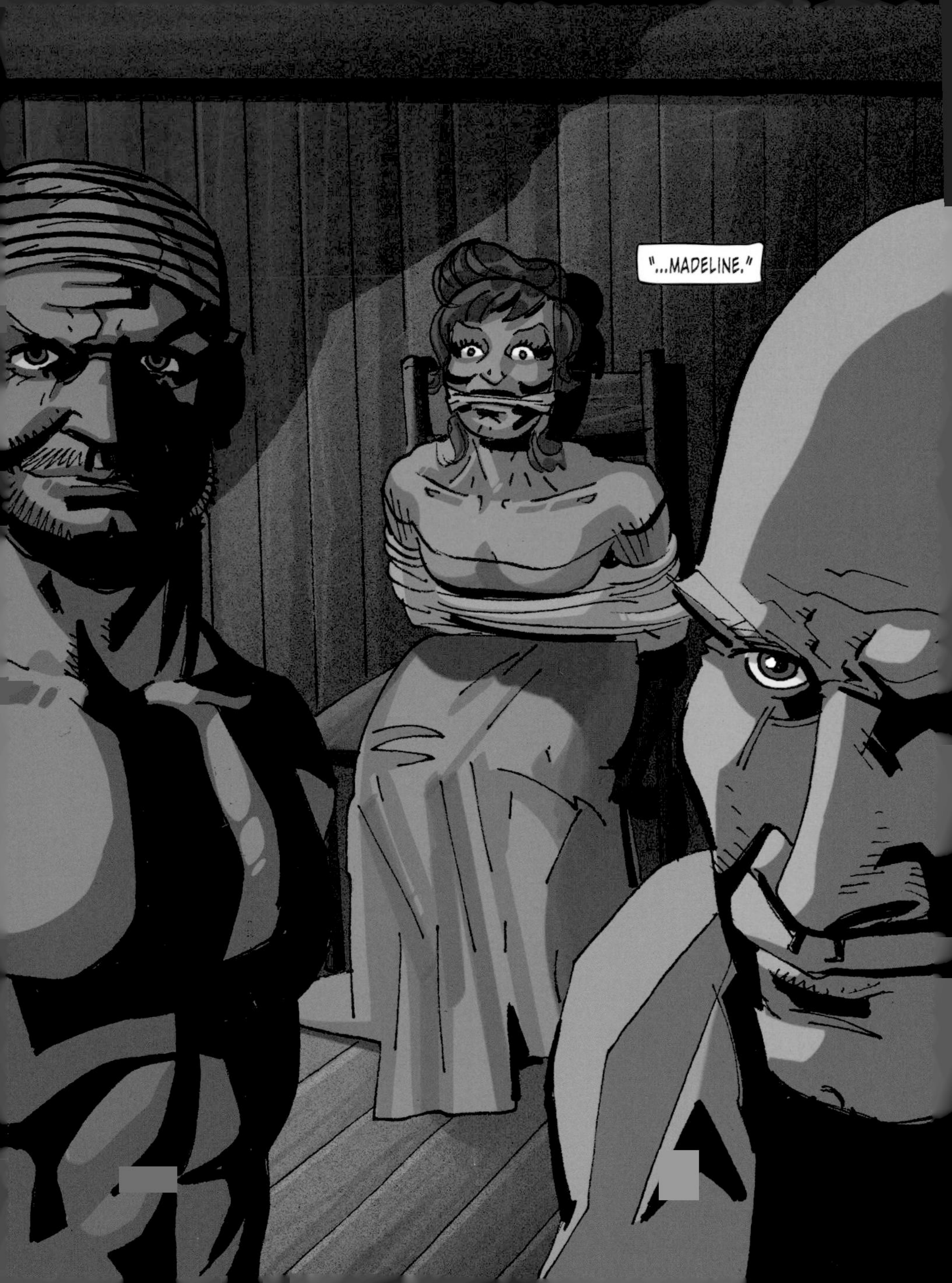
"...MADELINE."

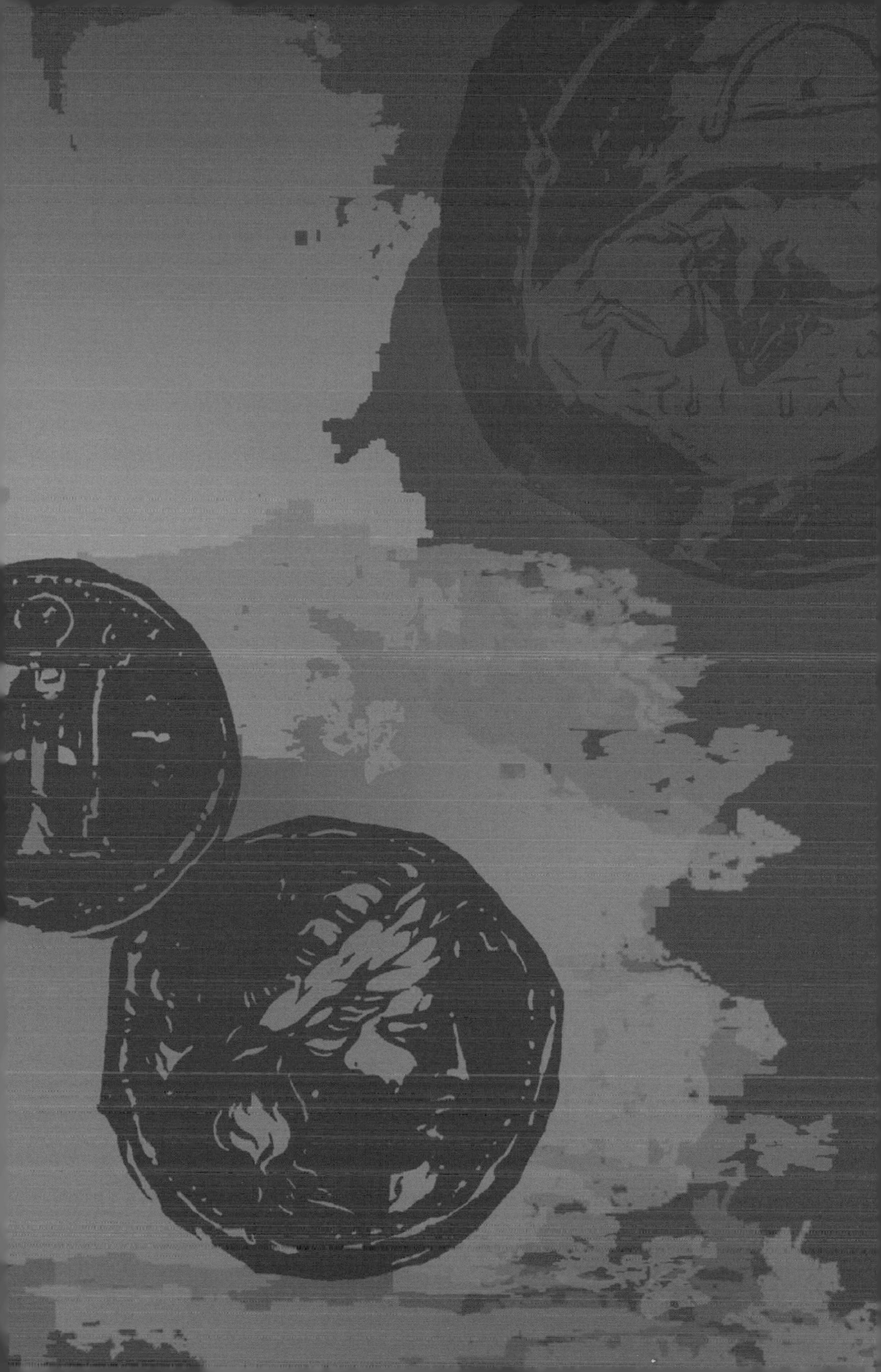

CHAPTER IV

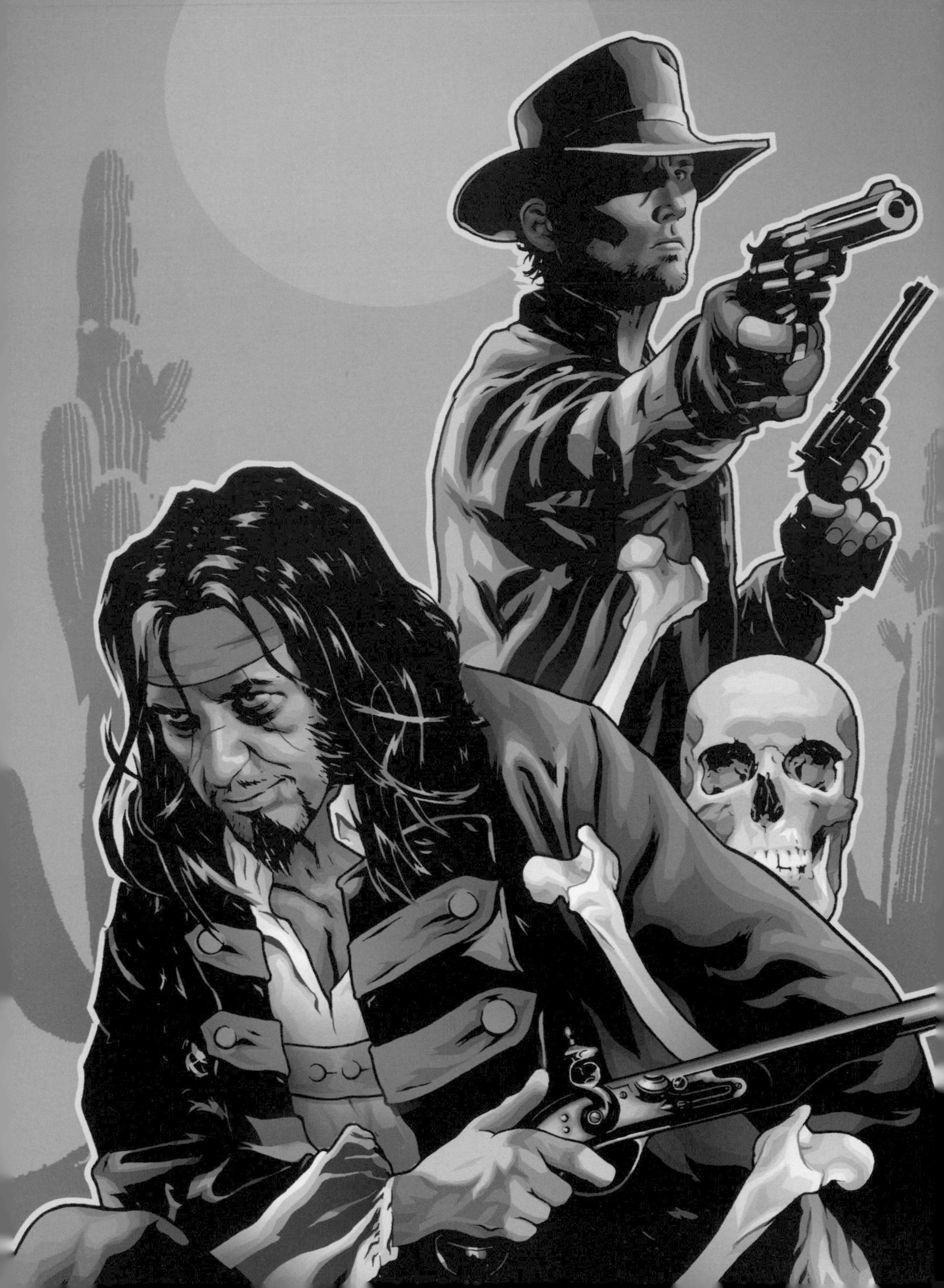

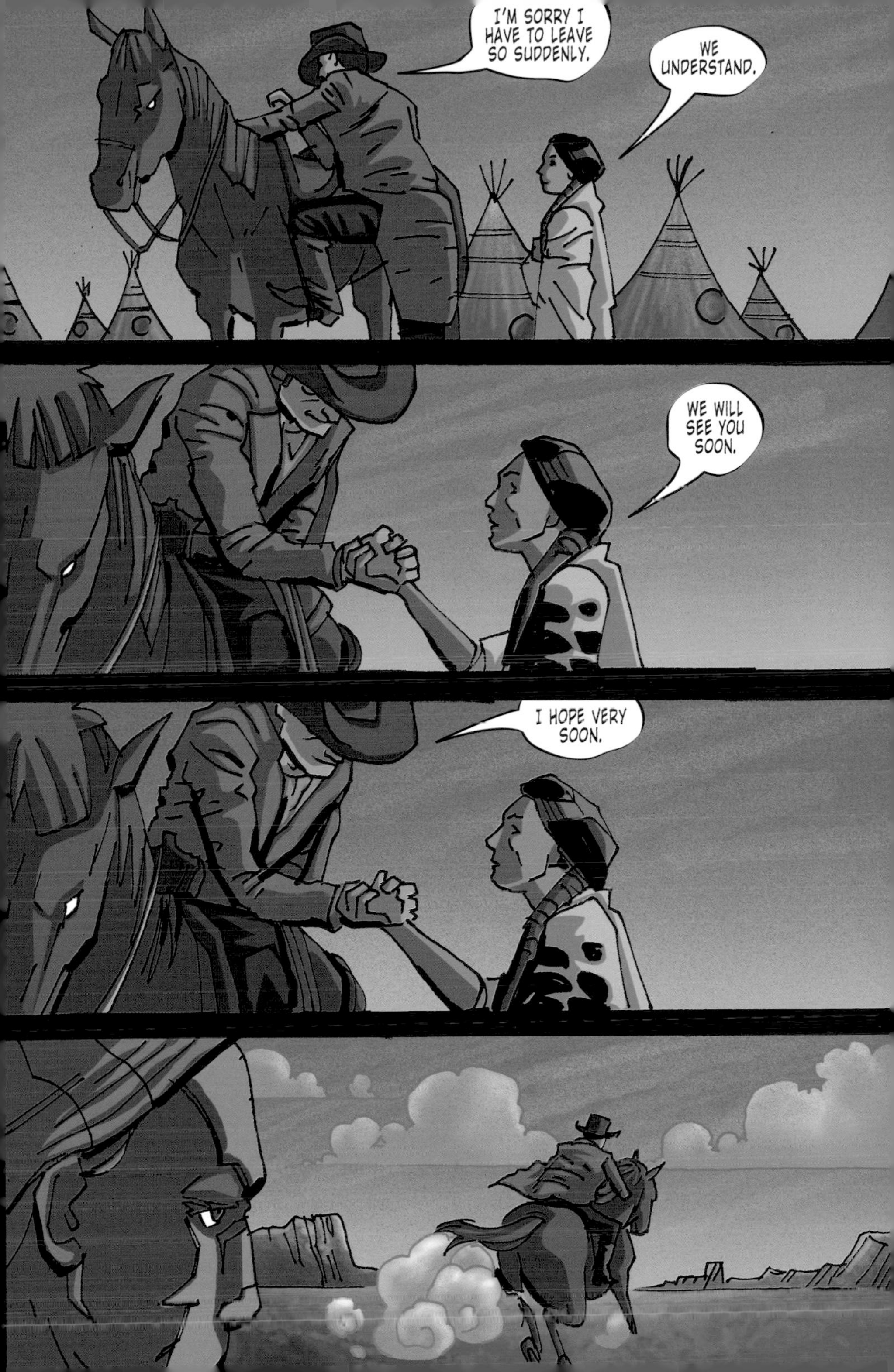
I'M SORRY I HAVE TO LEAVE SO SUDDENLY.
WE UNDERSTAND.
WE WILL SEE YOU SOON.
I HOPE VERY SOON.

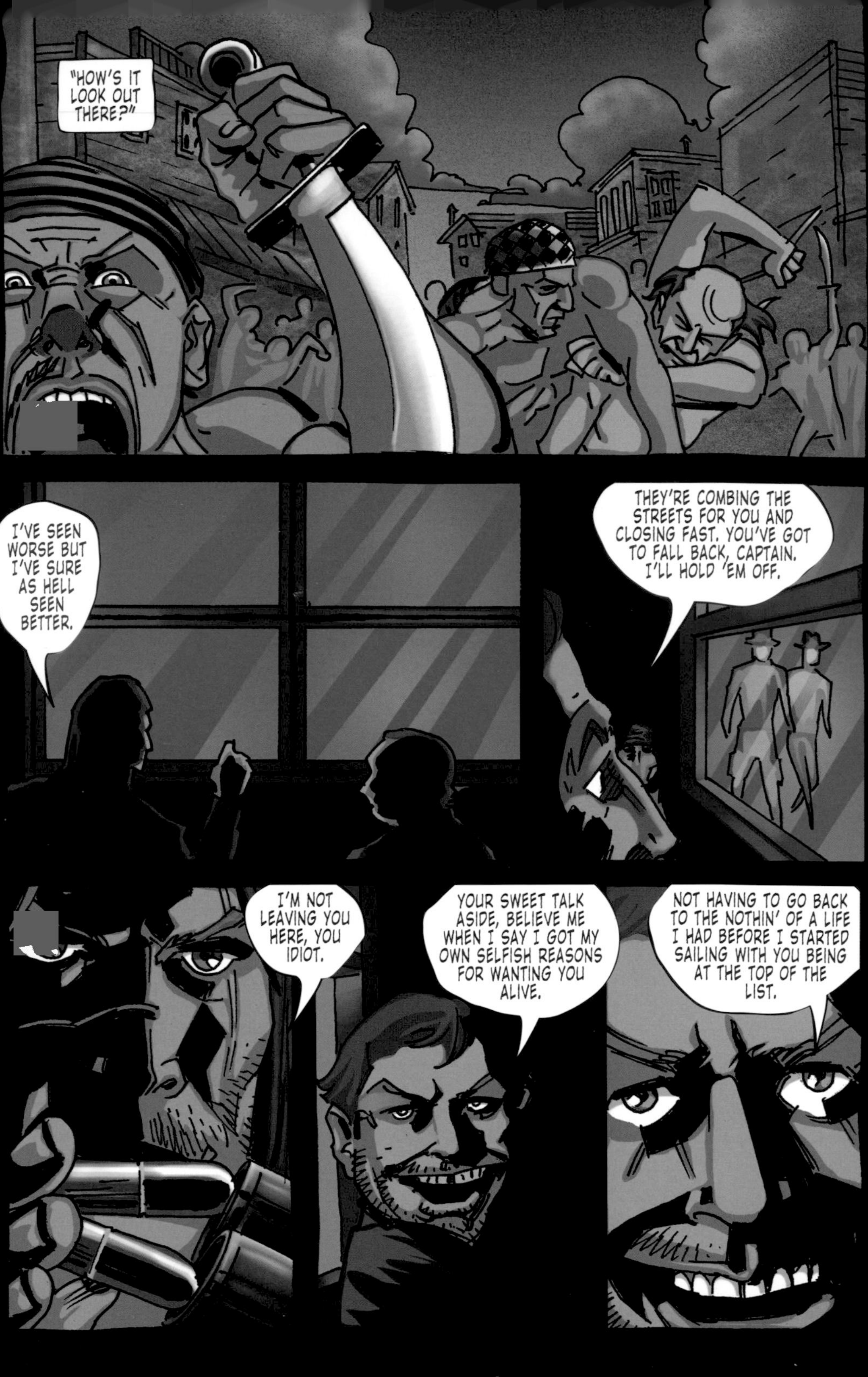
"HOW'S IT LOOK OUT THERE?"
I'VE SEEN WORSE BUT I'VE SURE AS HELL SEEN BETTER.
THEY'RE COMBING THE STREETS FOR YOU AND CLOSING FAST. YOU'VE GOT TO FALL BACK, CAPTAIN. I'LL HOLD 'EM OFF.
I'M NOT LEAVING YOU HERE, YOU IDIOT.
YOUR SWEET TALK ASIDE, BELIEVE ME WHEN I SAY I GOT MY OWN SELFISH REASONS FOR WANTING YOU ALIVE.
NOT HAVING TO GO BACK TO THE NOTHIN' OF A LIFE I HAD BEFORE I STARTED SAILING WITH YOU BEING AT THE TOP OF THE LIST.

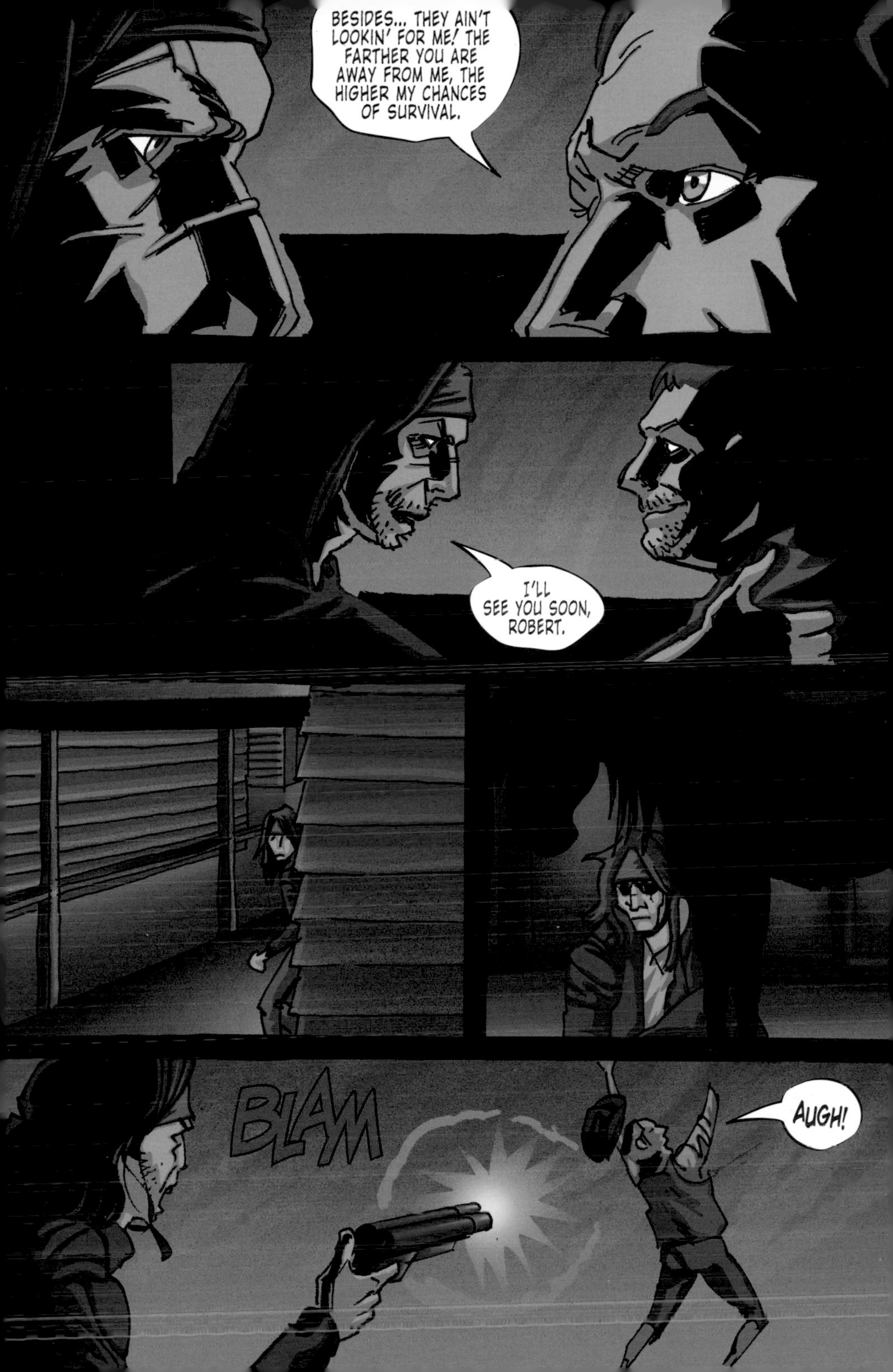
BESIDES... THEY AIN'T LOOKIN' FOR ME! THE FARTHER YOU ARE AWAY FROM ME, THE HIGHER MY CHANCES OF SURVIVAL.
I'LL SEE YOU SOON, ROBERT.
BLAM
AUGH!

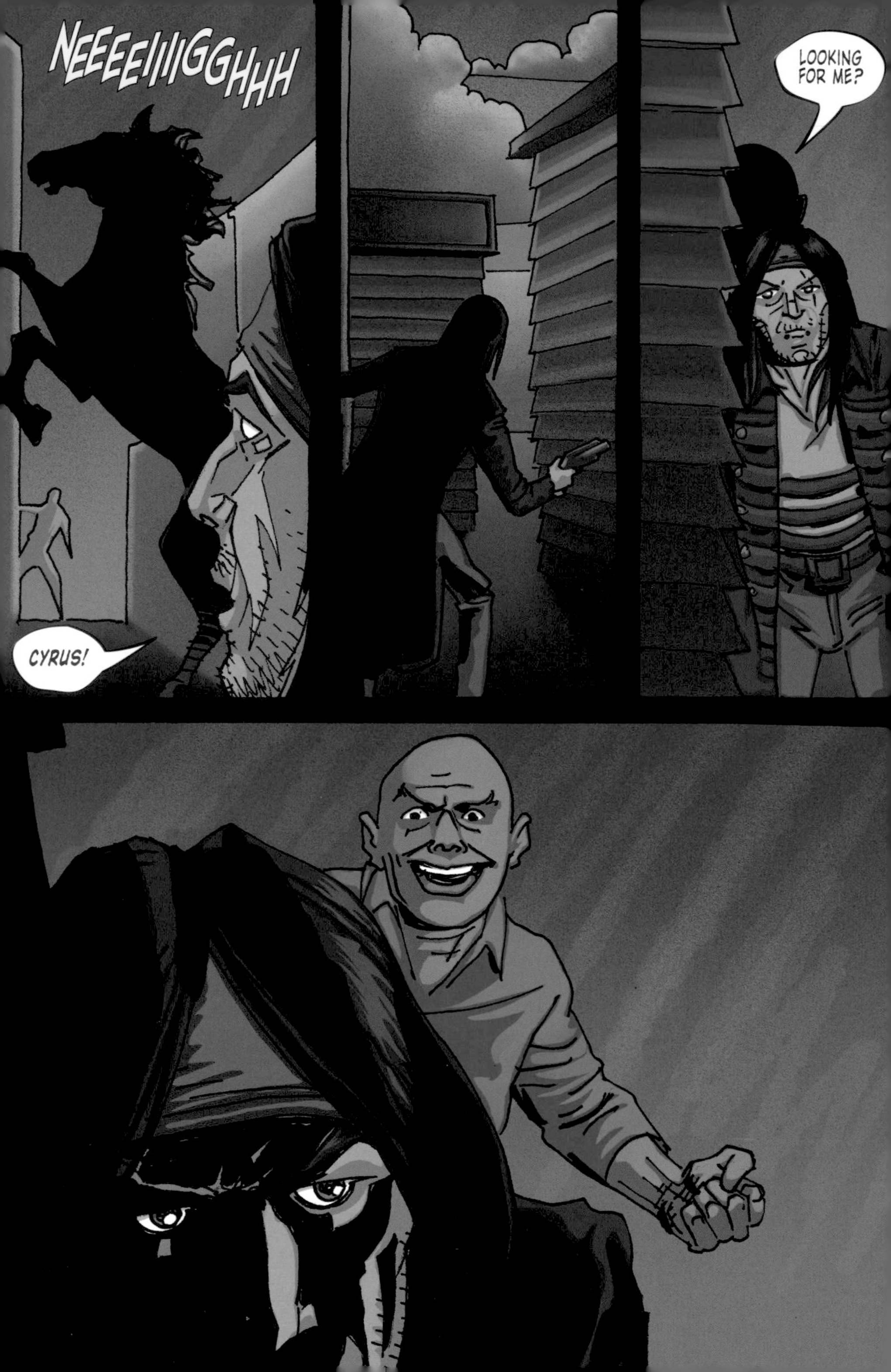
NEEEEIIIIGGHHH
CYRUS!
LOOKING FOR ME?

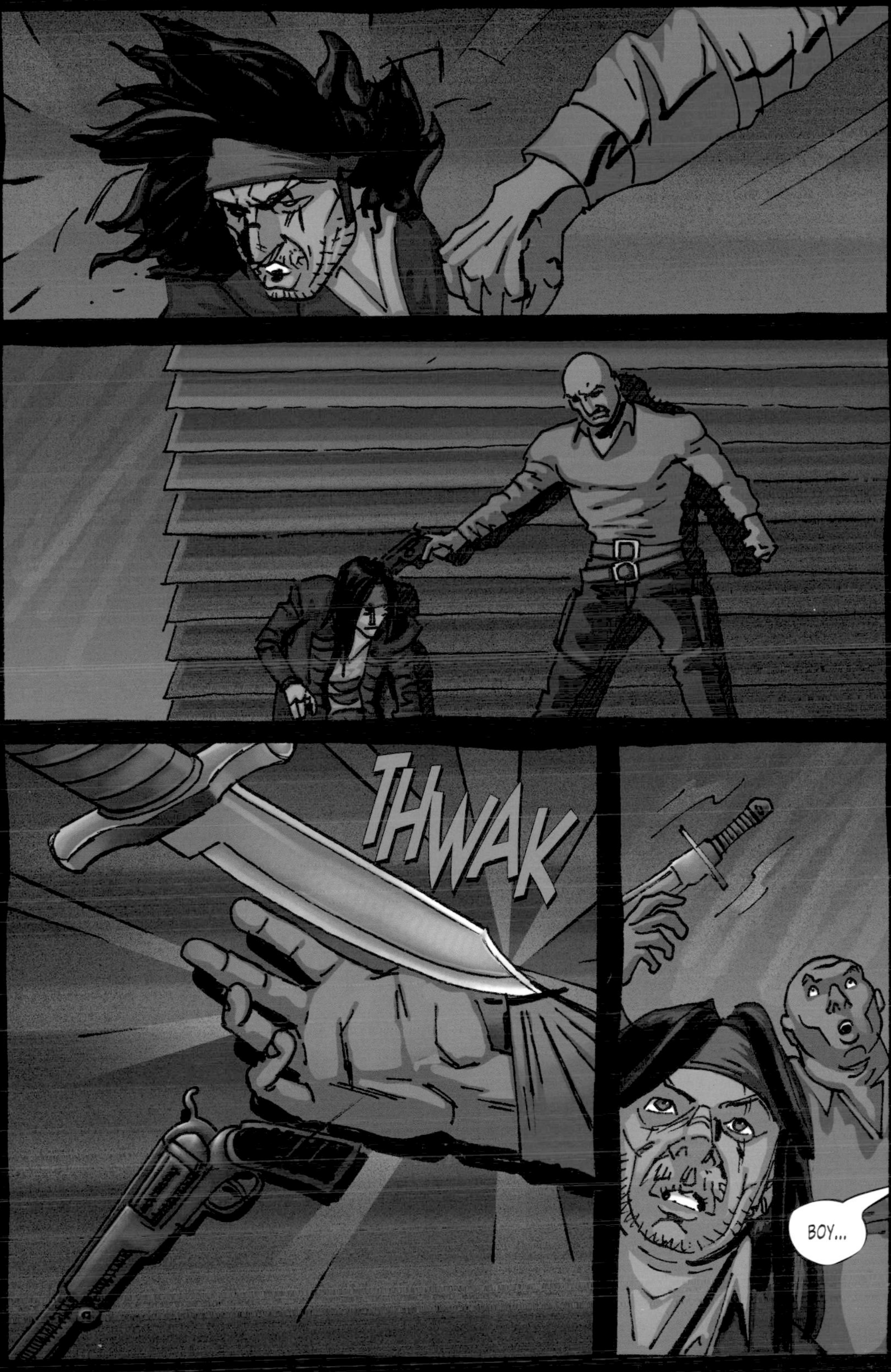
THWAK
BOY...

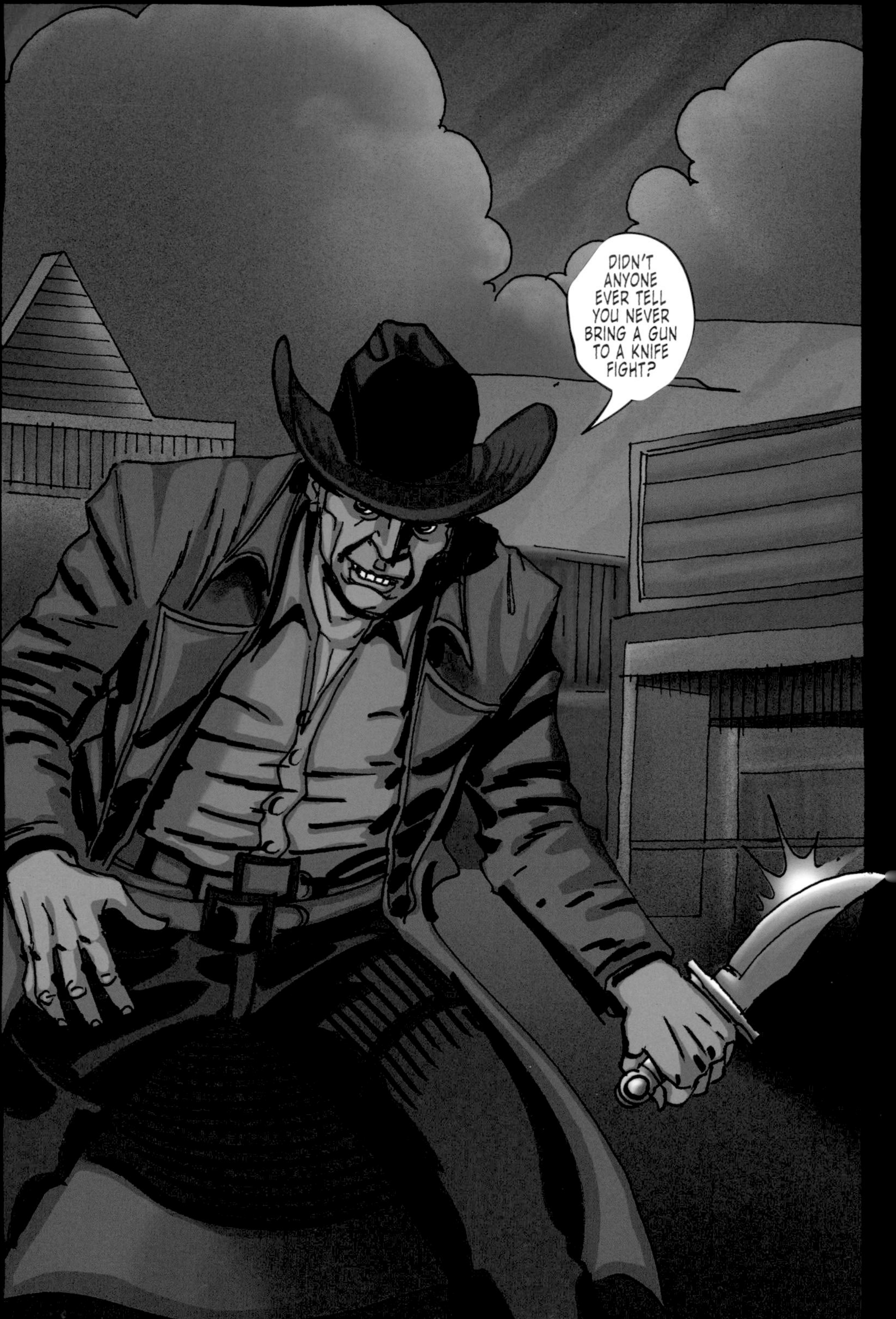
DIDN'T ANYONE EVER TELL YOU NEVER BRING A GUN TO A KNIFE FIGHT?

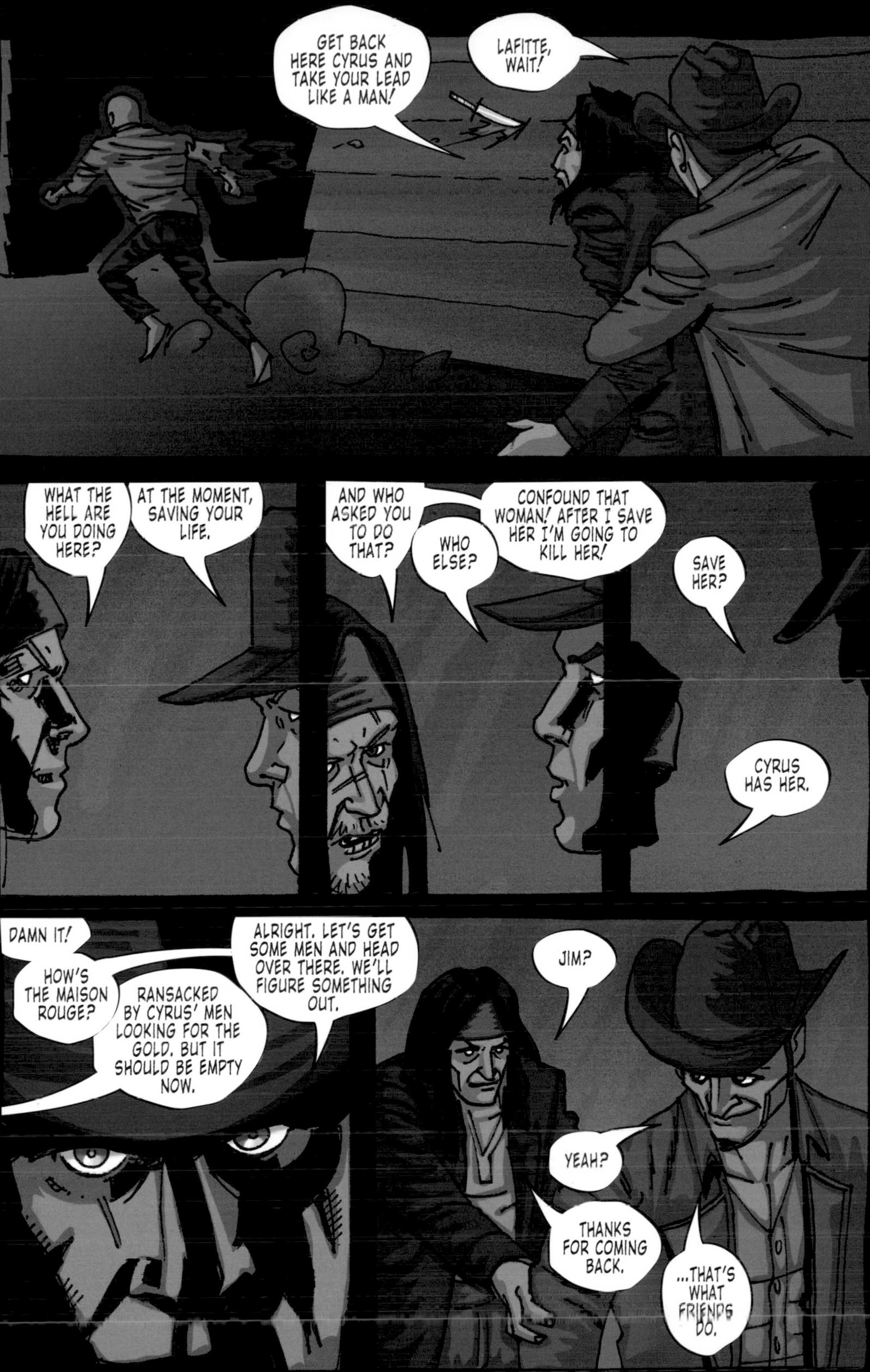
GET BACK HERE CYRUS AND TAKE YOUR LEAD LIKE A MAN!
LAFITTE, WAIT!
WHAT THE HELL ARE YOU DOING HERE?
AT THE MOMENT, SAVING YOUR LIFE.
AND WHO ASKED YOU TO DO THAT?
WHO ELSE?
CONFOUND THAT WOMAN! AFTER I SAVE HER I'M GOING TO KILL HER!
SAVE HER?
CYRUS HAS HER.
DAMN IT!
HOW'S THE MAISON ROUGE?
RANSACKED BY CYRUS' MEN LOOKING FOR THE GOLD. BUT IT SHOULD BE EMPTY NOW.
ALRIGHT. LET'S GET SOME MEN AND HEAD OVER THERE. WE'LL FIGURE SOMETHING OUT.
JIM?
YEAH?
THANKS FOR COMING BACK.
...THAT'S WHAT FRIENDS DO.

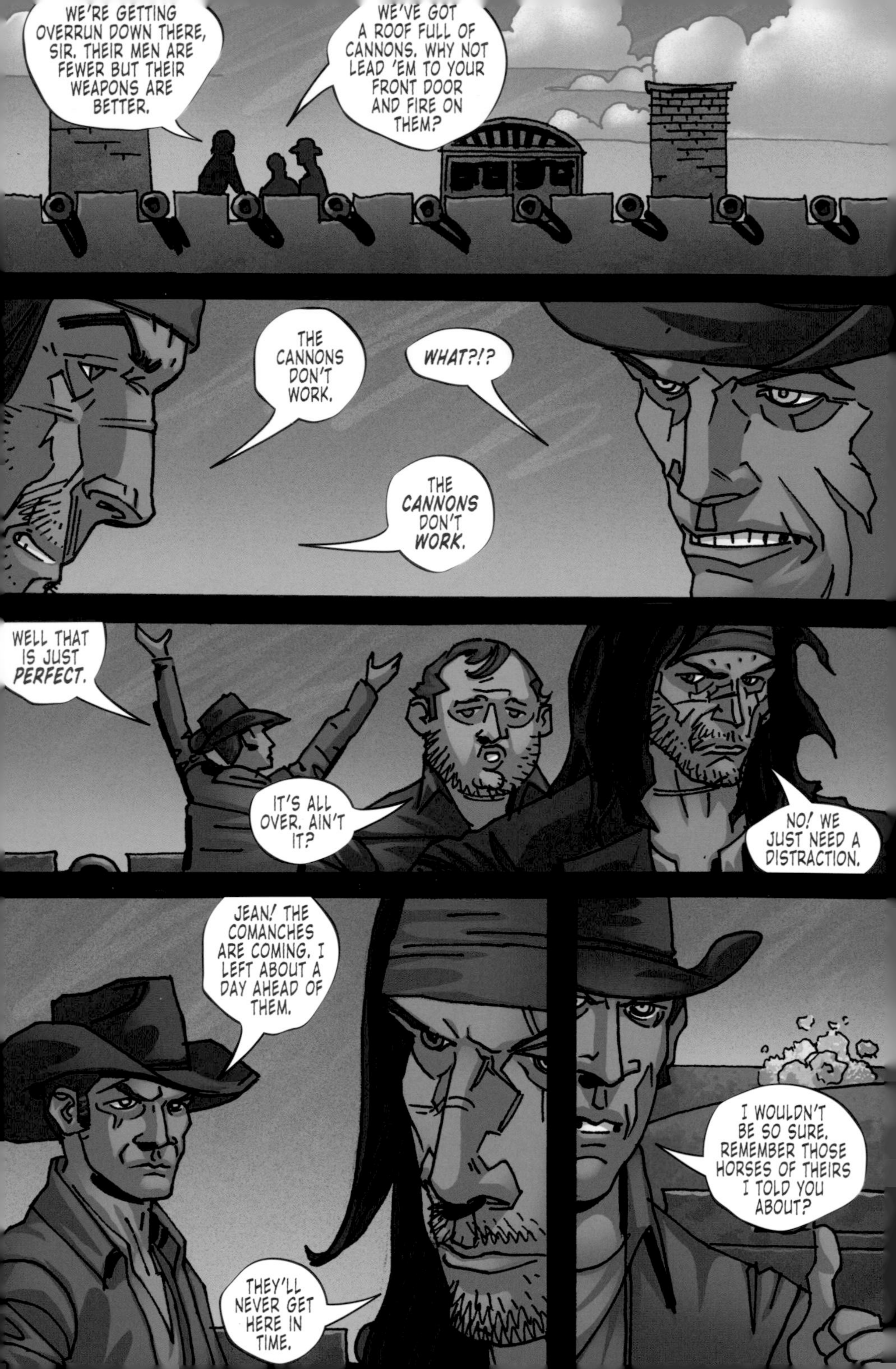
WE'RE GETTING OVERRUN DOWN THERE, SIR. THEIR MEN ARE FEWER BUT THEIR WEAPONS ARE BETTER.
WE'VE GOT A ROOF FULL OF CANNONS. WHY NOT LEAD 'EM TO YOUR FRONT DOOR AND FIRE ON THEM?
THE CANNONS DON'T WORK.
WHAT?!?
THE CANNONS DON'T WORK.
WELL THAT IS JUST PERFECT.
IT'S ALL OVER, AIN'T IT?
NO! WE JUST NEED A DISTRACTION.
JEAN! THE COMANCHES ARE COMING. I LEFT ABOUT A DAY AHEAD OF THEM.
THEY'LL NEVER GET HERE IN TIME.
I WOULDN'T BE SO SURE. REMEMBER THOSE HORSES OF THEIRS I TOLD YOU ABOUT?

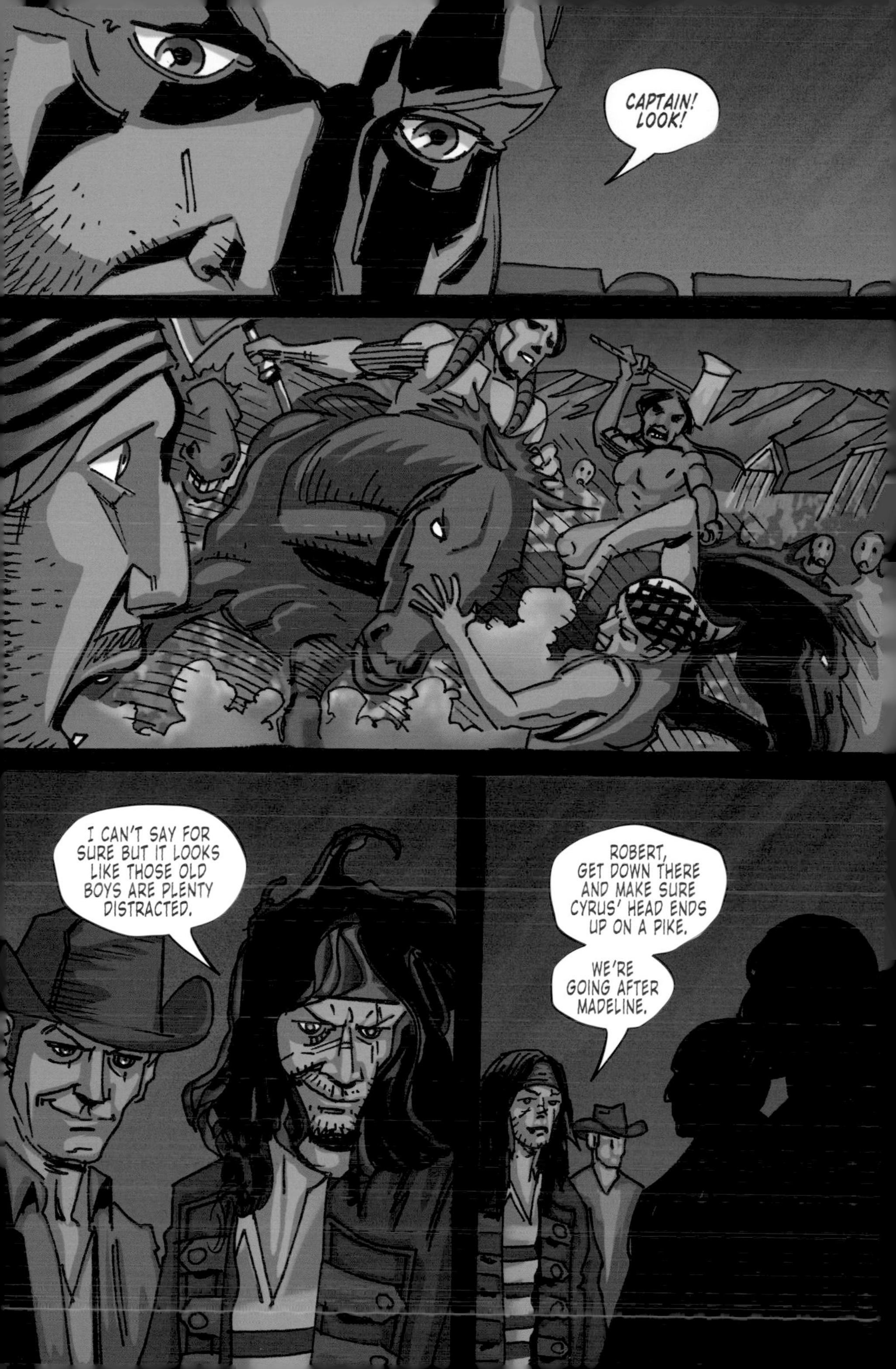
CAPTAIN! LOOK!
I CAN'T SAY FOR SURE BUT IT LOOKS LIKE THOSE OLD BOYS ARE PLENTY DISTRACTED.
ROBERT, GET DOWN THERE AND MAKE SURE CYRUS' HEAD ENDS UP ON A PIKE.
WE'RE GOING AFTER MADELINE.

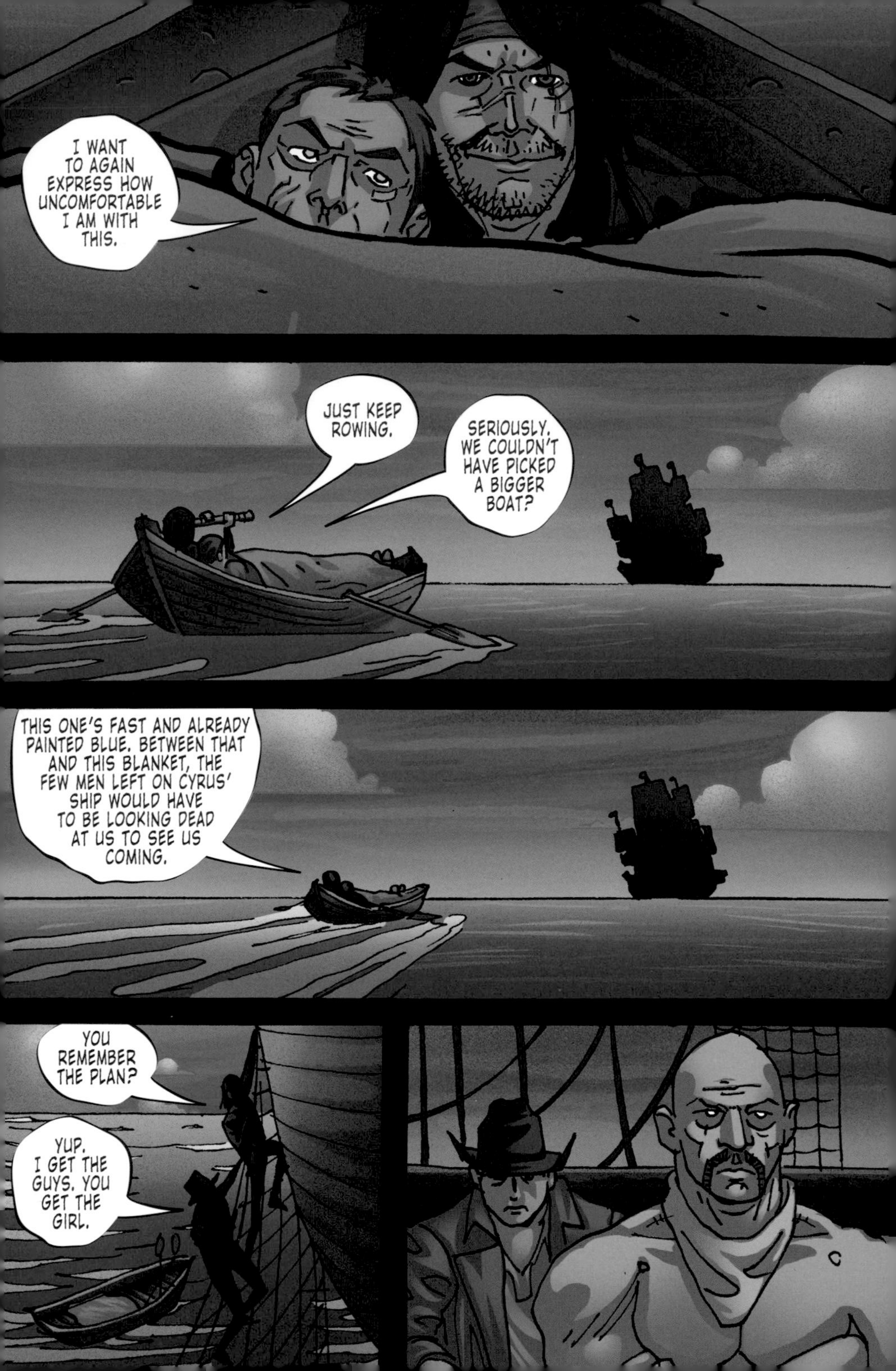
I WANT TO AGAIN EXPRESS HOW UNCOMFORTABLE I AM WITH THIS.
JUST KEEP ROWING.
SERIOUSLY, WE COULDN'T HAVE PICKED A BIGGER BOAT?
THIS ONE'S FAST AND ALREADY PAINTED BLUE. BETWEEN THAT AND THIS BLANKET, THE FEW MEN LEFT ON CYRUS' SHIP WOULD HAVE TO BE LOOKING DEAD AT US TO SEE US COMING.
YOU REMEMBER THE PLAN?
YUP. I GET THE GUYS. YOU GET THE GIRL.

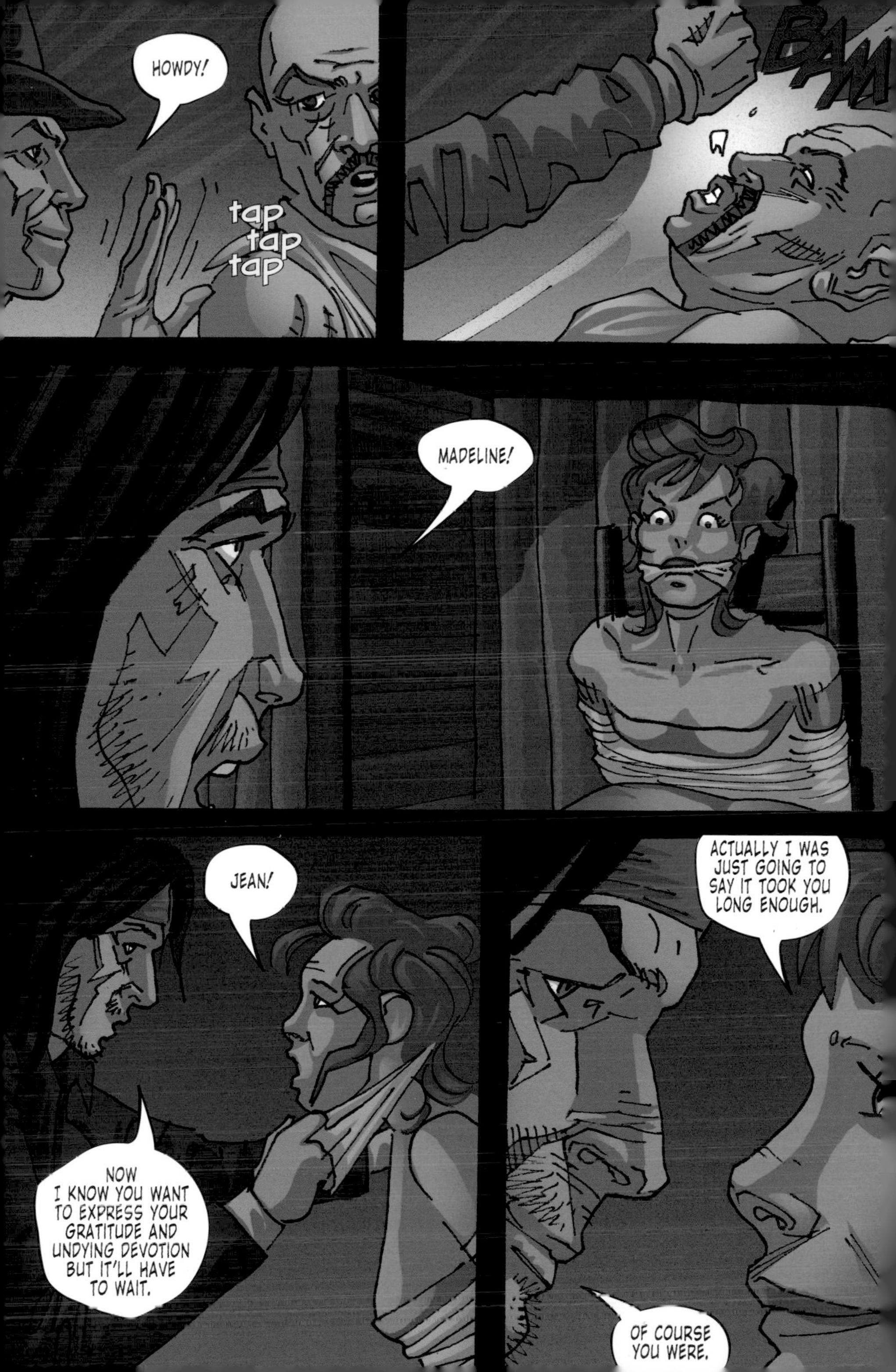
HOWDY!
tap tap tap
BAM
MADELINE!
JEAN!
NOW I KNOW YOU WANT TO EXPRESS YOUR GRATITUDE AND UNDYING DEVOTION BUT IT'LL HAVE TO WAIT.
ACTUALLY I WAS JUST GOING TO SAY IT TOOK YOU LONG ENOUGH.
OF COURSE YOU WERE.

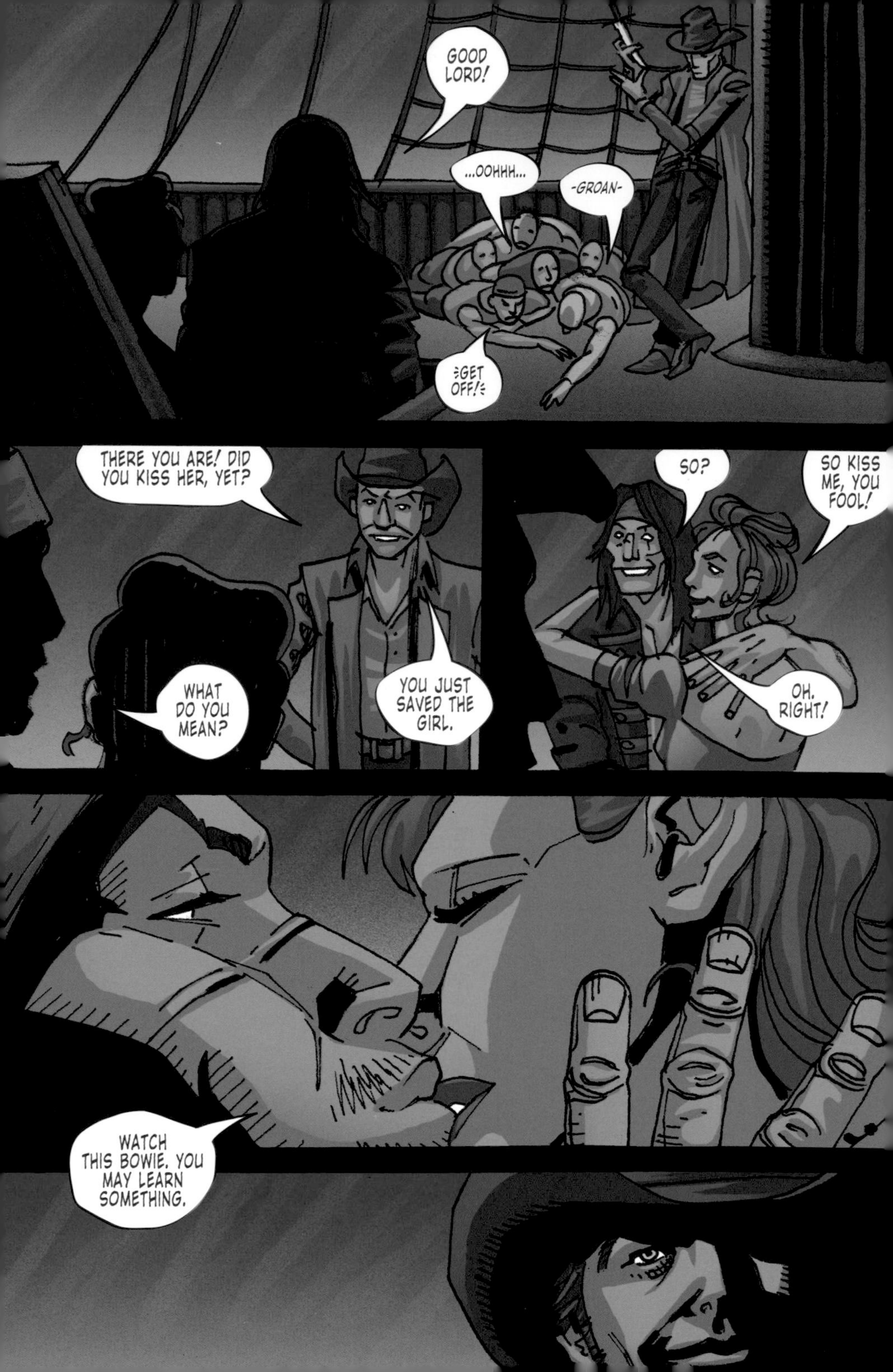
GOOD LORD!
...OOHHH...
-GROAN-
GET OFF!
THERE YOU ARE! DID YOU KISS HER, YET?
WHAT DO YOU MEAN?
YOU JUST SAVED THE GIRL.
SO?
SO KISS ME, YOU FOOL!
OH. RIGHT!
WATCH THIS BOWIE. YOU MAY LEARN SOMETHING.

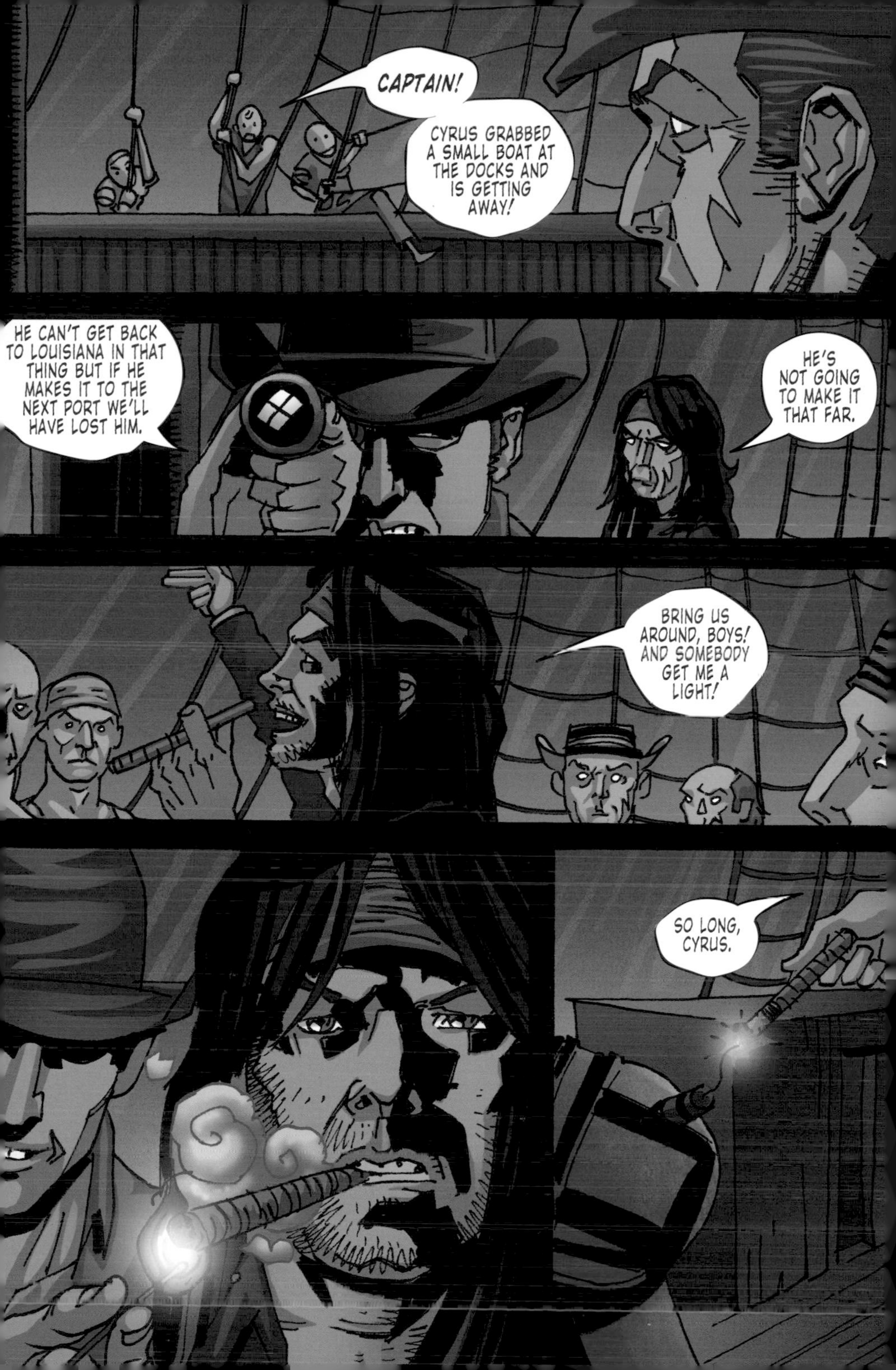
CAPTAIN!
CYRUS GRABBED A SMALL BOAT AT THE DOCKS AND IS GETTING AWAY!
HE CAN'T GET BACK TO LOUISIANA IN THAT THING BUT IF HE MAKES IT TO THE NEXT PORT WE'LL HAVE LOST HIM.
HE'S NOT GOING TO MAKE IT THAT FAR.
BRING US AROUND, BOYS! AND SOMEBODY GET ME A LIGHT!
SO LONG, CYRUS.

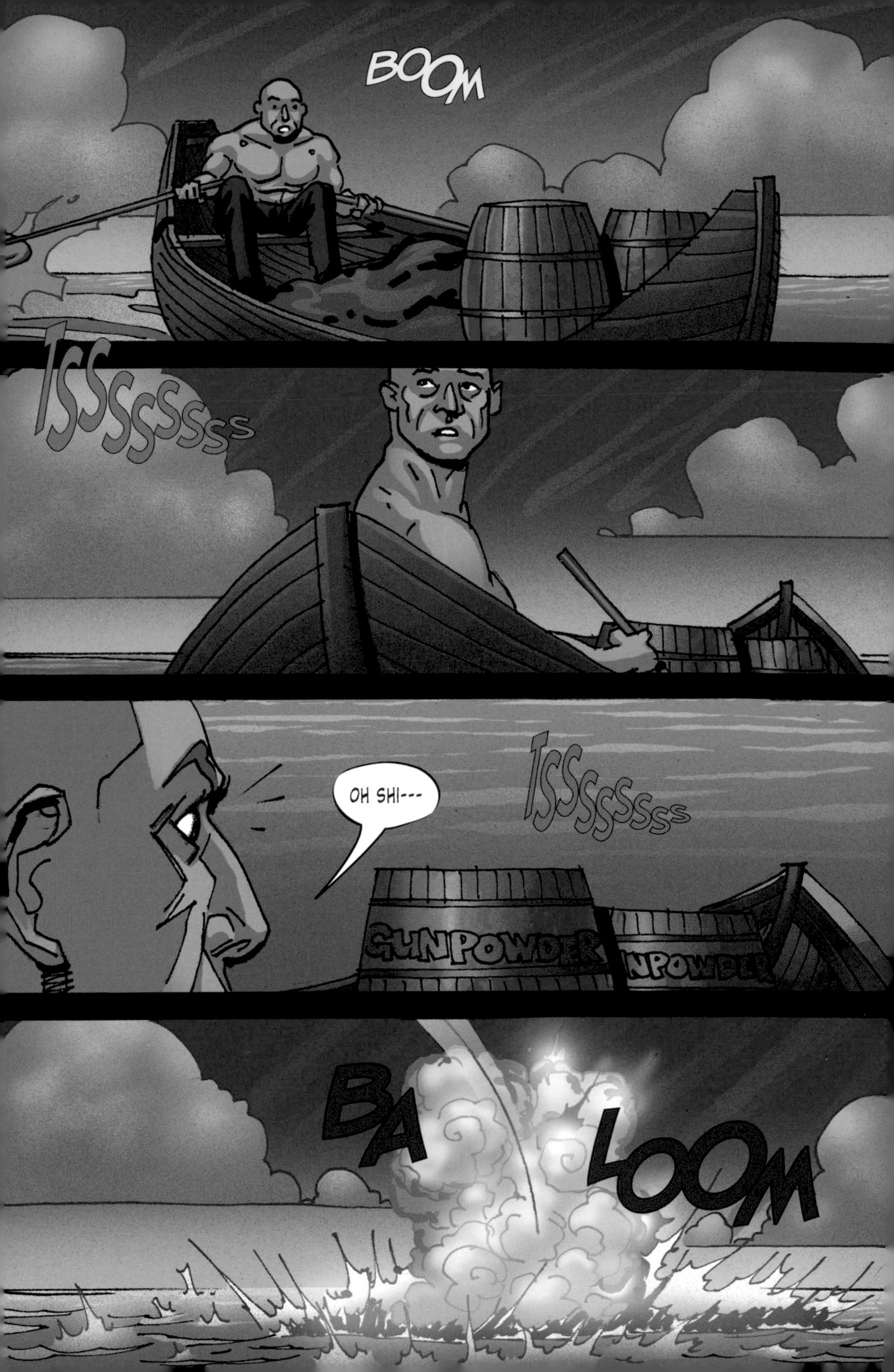
BOOM
TSSSSSSSS
OH SHI---
TSSSSSSSS
GUNPOWDER
NPOWDER
BA
LOOM

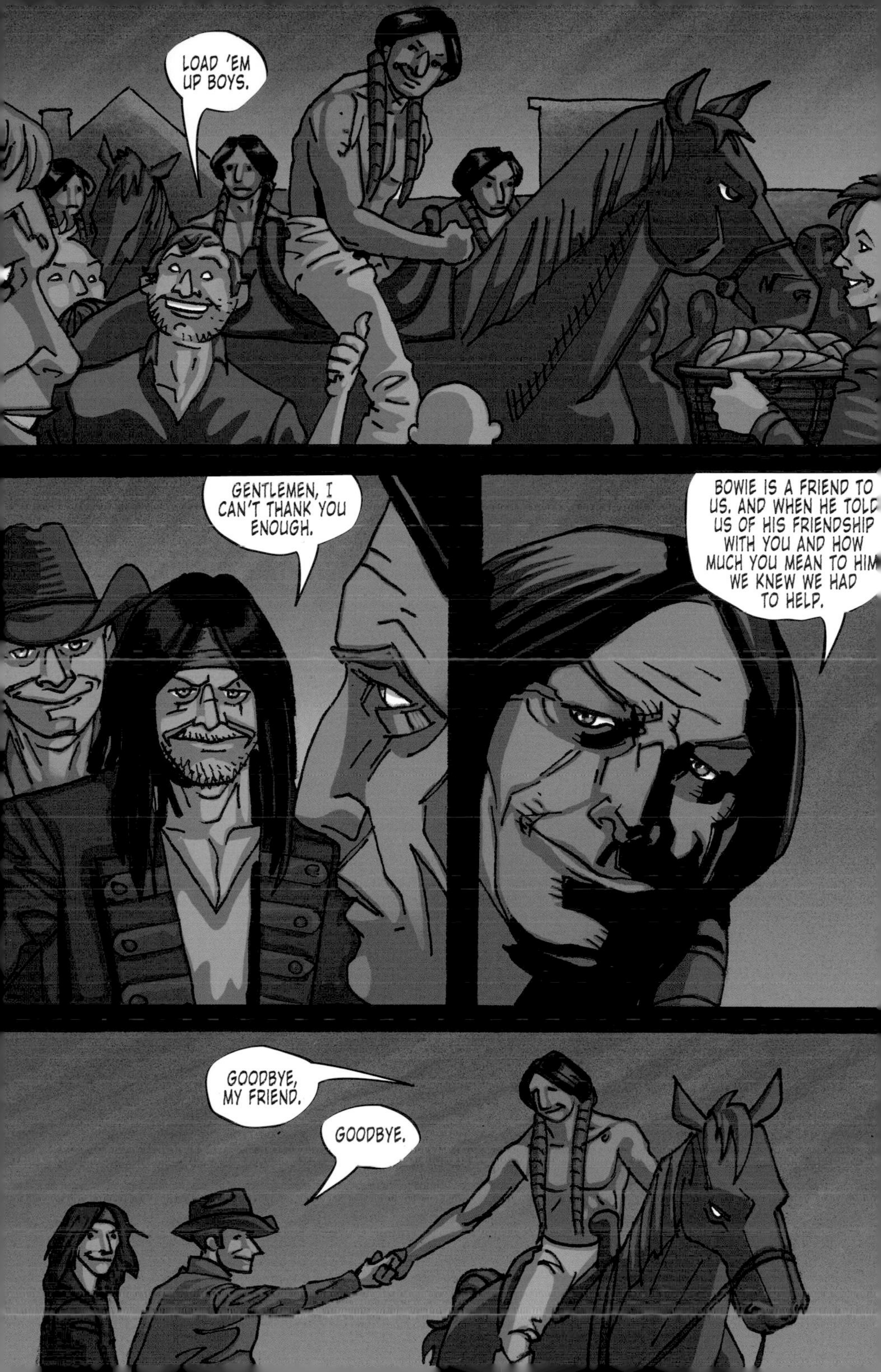
LOAD 'EM UP BOYS.
GENTLEMEN, I CAN'T THANK YOU ENOUGH.
BOWIE IS A FRIEND TO US. AND WHEN HE TOLD US OF HIS FRIENDSHIP WITH YOU AND HOW MUCH YOU MEAN TO HIM WE KNEW WE HAD TO HELP.
GOODBYE, MY FRIEND.
GOODBYE.

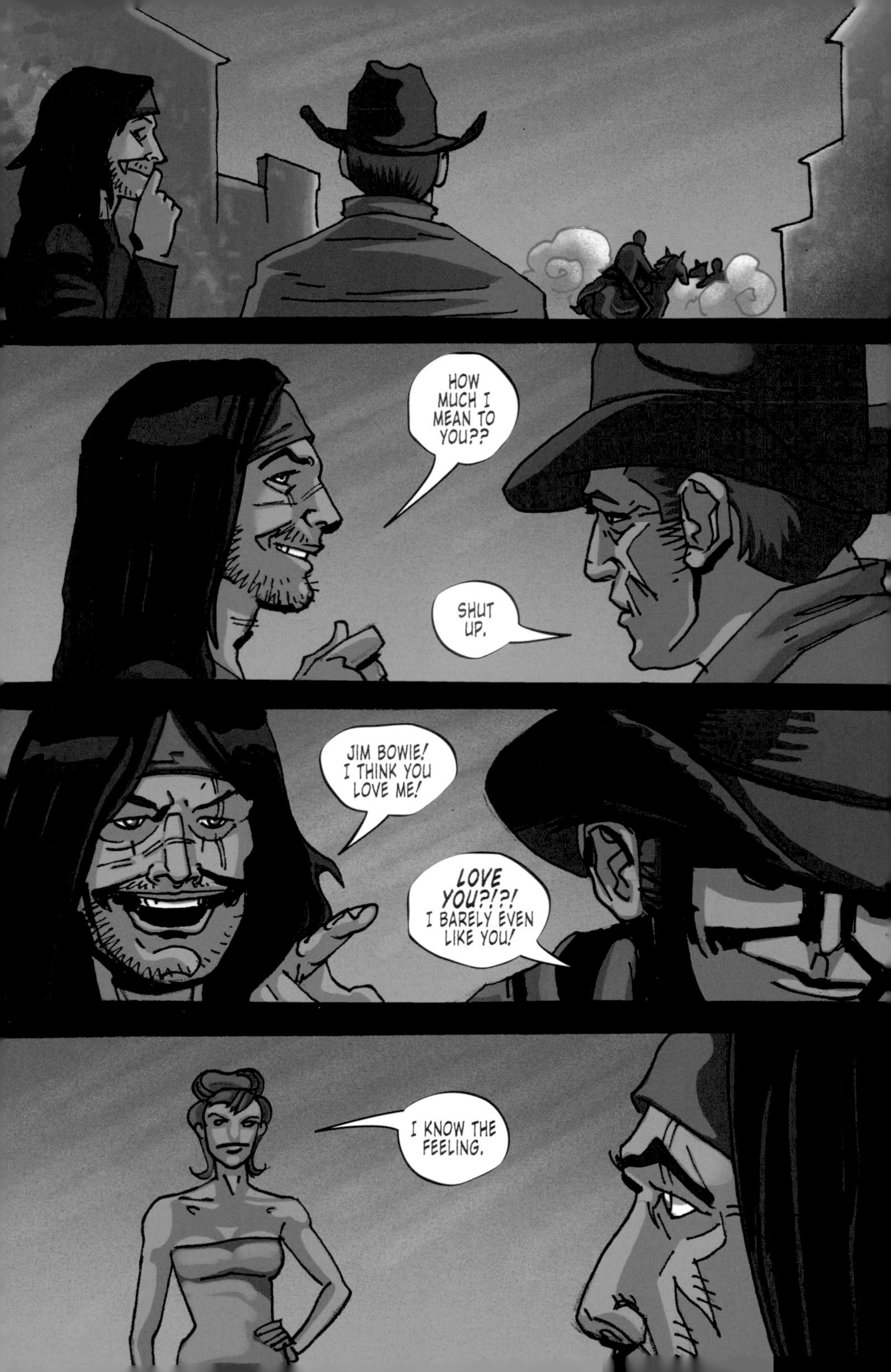
HOW MUCH I MEAN TO YOU??
SHUT UP.
JIM BOWIE! I THINK YOU LOVE ME!
LOVE YOU?!?! I BARELY EVEN LIKE YOU!
I KNOW THE FEELING.

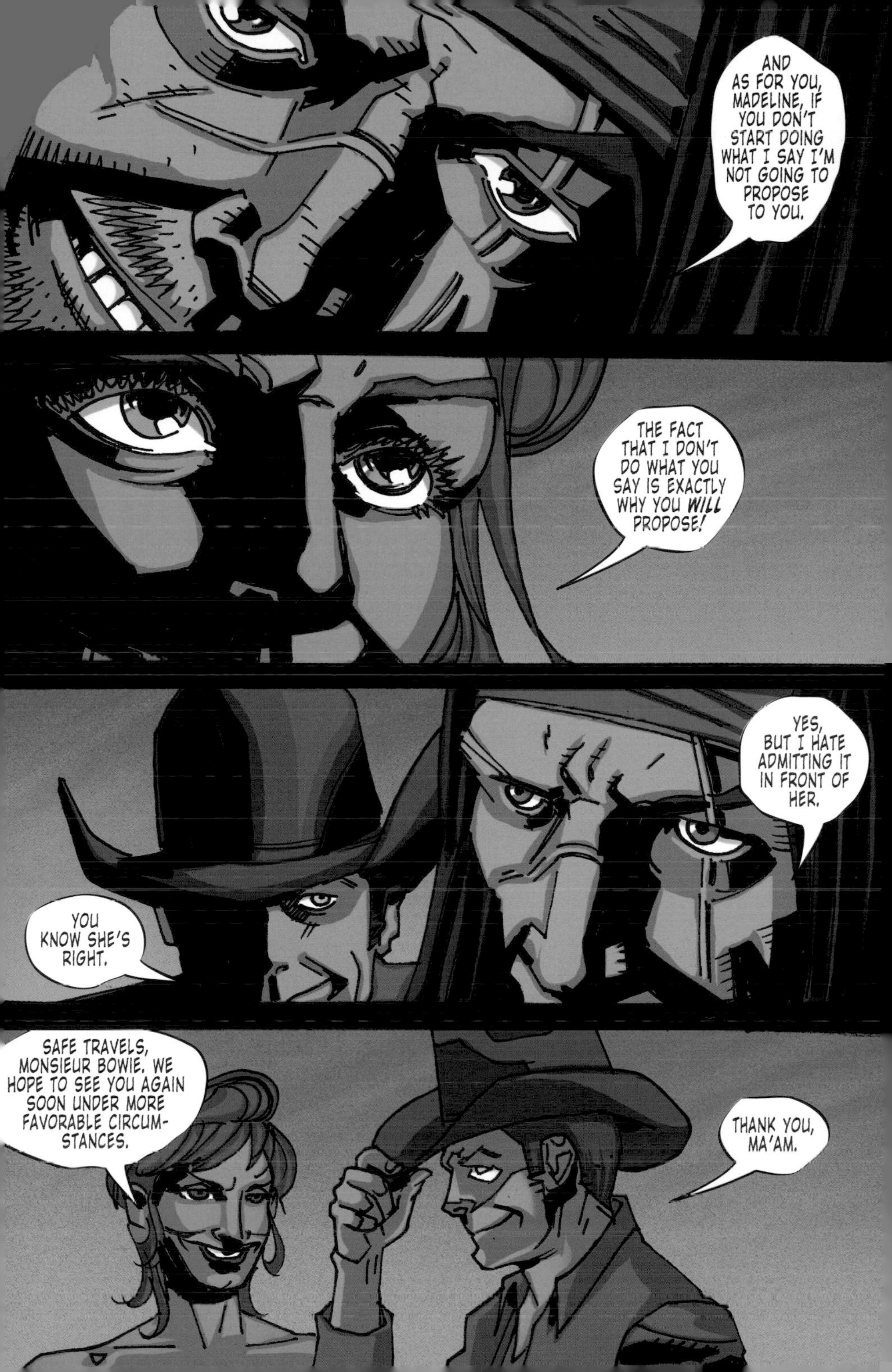
AND AS FOR YOU, MADELINE, IF YOU DON'T START DOING WHAT I SAY I'M NOT GOING TO PROPOSE TO YOU.
THE FACT THAT I DON'T DO WHAT YOU SAY IS EXACTLY WHY YOU *WILL* PROPOSE!
YOU KNOW SHE'S RIGHT.
YES, BUT I HATE ADMITTING IT IN FRONT OF HER.
SAFE TRAVELS, MONSIEUR BOWIE. WE HOPE TO SEE YOU AGAIN SOON UNDER MORE FAVORABLE CIRCUM-STANCES.
THANK YOU, MA'AM.

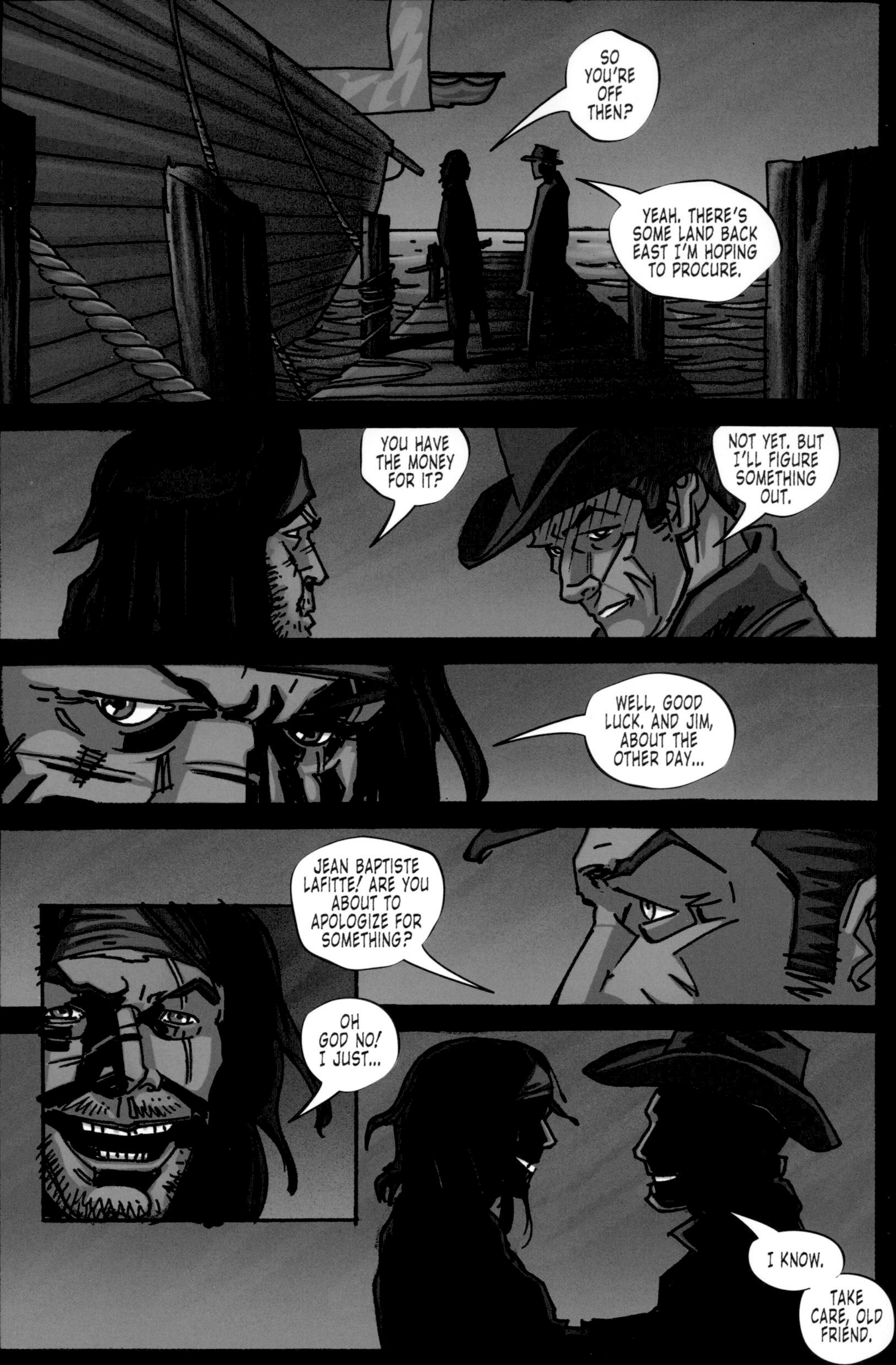
SO YOU'RE OFF THEN?
YEAH. THERE'S SOME LAND BACK EAST I'M HOPING TO PROCURE.
YOU HAVE THE MONEY FOR IT?
NOT YET. BUT I'LL FIGURE SOMETHING OUT.
WELL, GOOD LUCK. AND JIM, ABOUT THE OTHER DAY...
JEAN BAPTISTE LAFITTE! ARE YOU ABOUT TO APOLOGIZE FOR SOMETHING?
OH GOD NO! I JUST...
I KNOW.
TAKE CARE, OLD FRIEND.

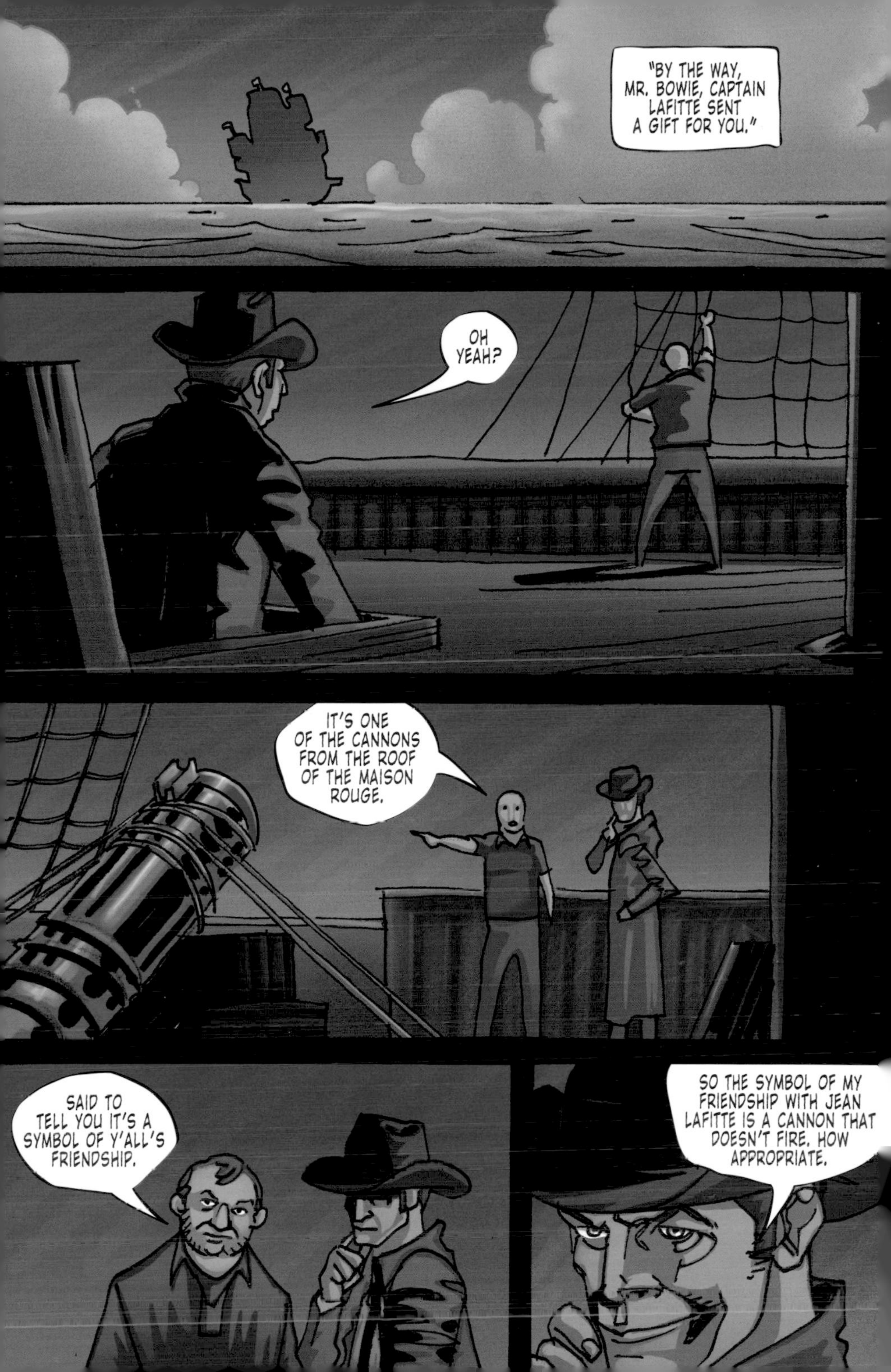
"BY THE WAY, MR. BOWIE, CAPTAIN LAFITTE SENT A GIFT FOR YOU."
OH YEAH?
IT'S ONE OF THE CANNONS FROM THE ROOF OF THE MAISON ROUGE.
SAID TO TELL YOU IT'S A SYMBOL OF Y'ALL'S FRIENDSHIP.
SO THE SYMBOL OF MY FRIENDSHIP WITH JEAN LAFITTE IS A CANNON THAT DOESN'T FIRE. HOW APPROPRIATE.

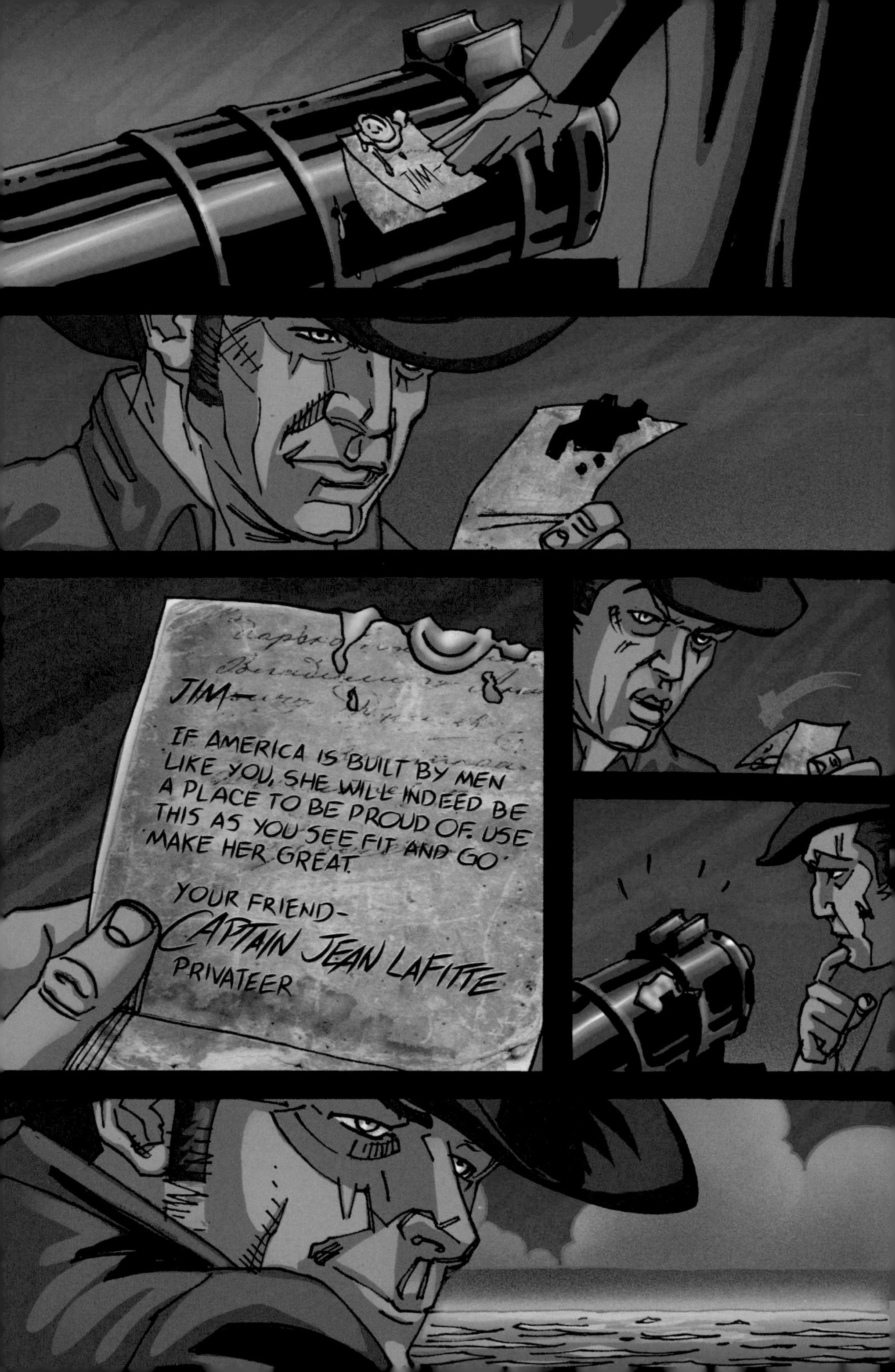
JIM—
JIM—
IF AMERICA IS BUILT BY MEN LIKE YOU, SHE WILL INDEED BE A PLACE TO BE PROUD OF. USE THIS AS YOU SEE FIT AND GO MAKE HER GREAT.
YOUR FRIEND-
CAPTAIN JEAN LAFITTE
PRIVATEER

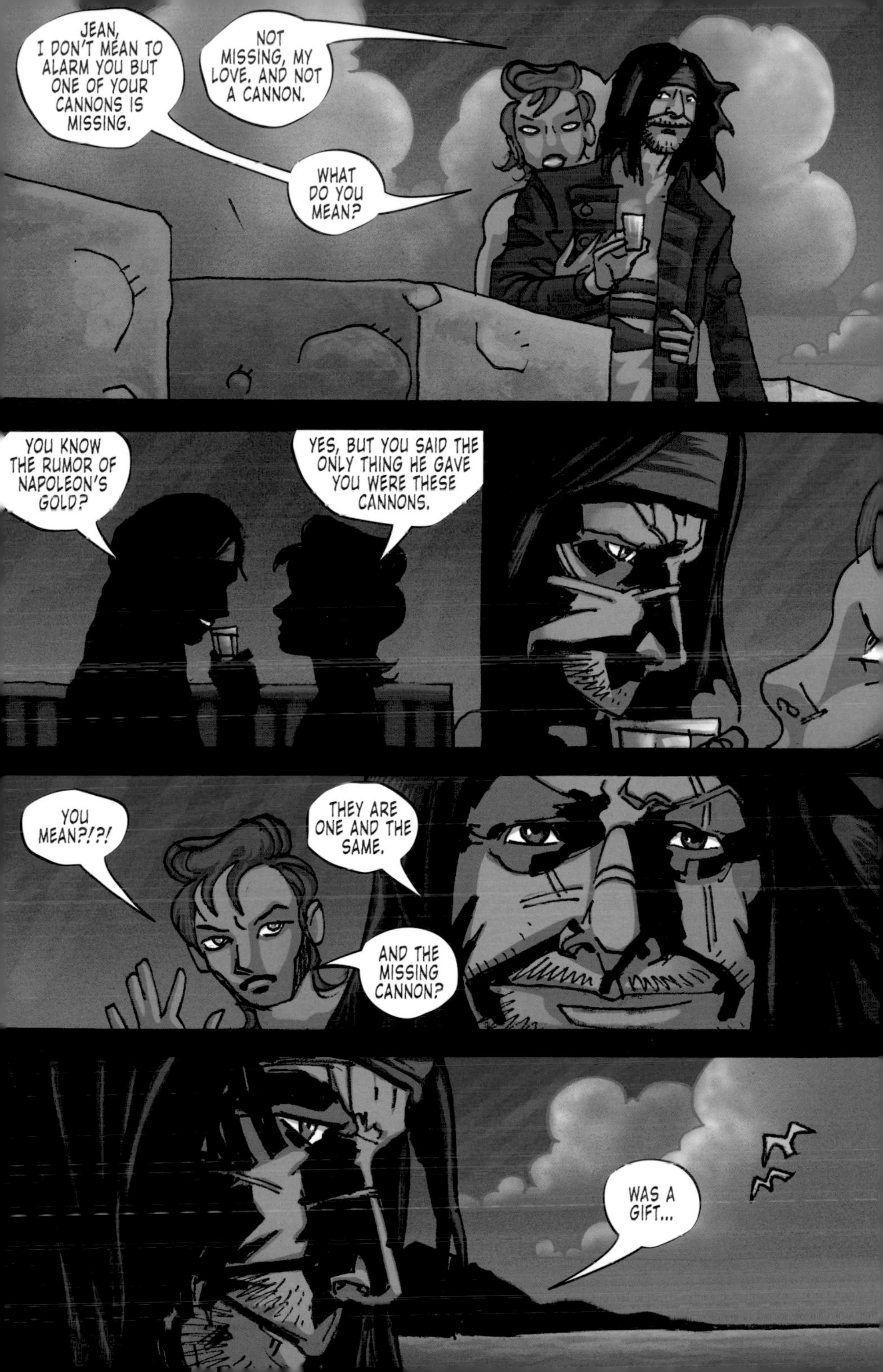
JEAN, I DON'T MEAN TO ALARM YOU BUT ONE OF YOUR CANNONS IS MISSING.
NOT MISSING, MY LOVE. AND NOT A CANNON.
WHAT DO YOU MEAN?
YOU KNOW THE RUMOR OF NAPOLEON'S GOLD?
YES, BUT YOU SAID THE ONLY THING HE GAVE YOU WERE THESE CANNONS.
YOU MEAN?!?!
THEY ARE ONE AND THE SAME.
AND THE MISSING CANNON?
WAS A GIFT...

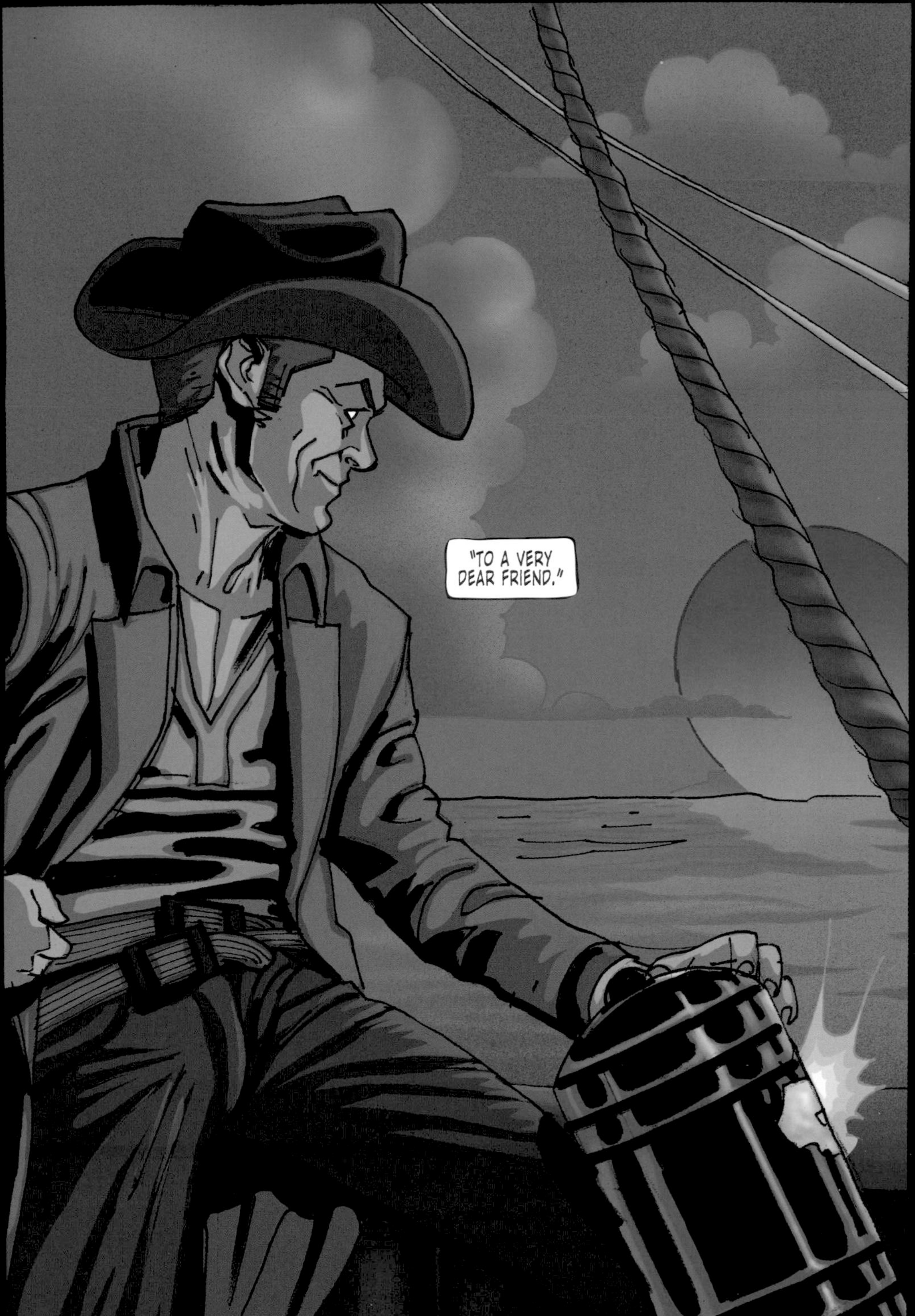
"TO A VERY DEAR FRIEND."

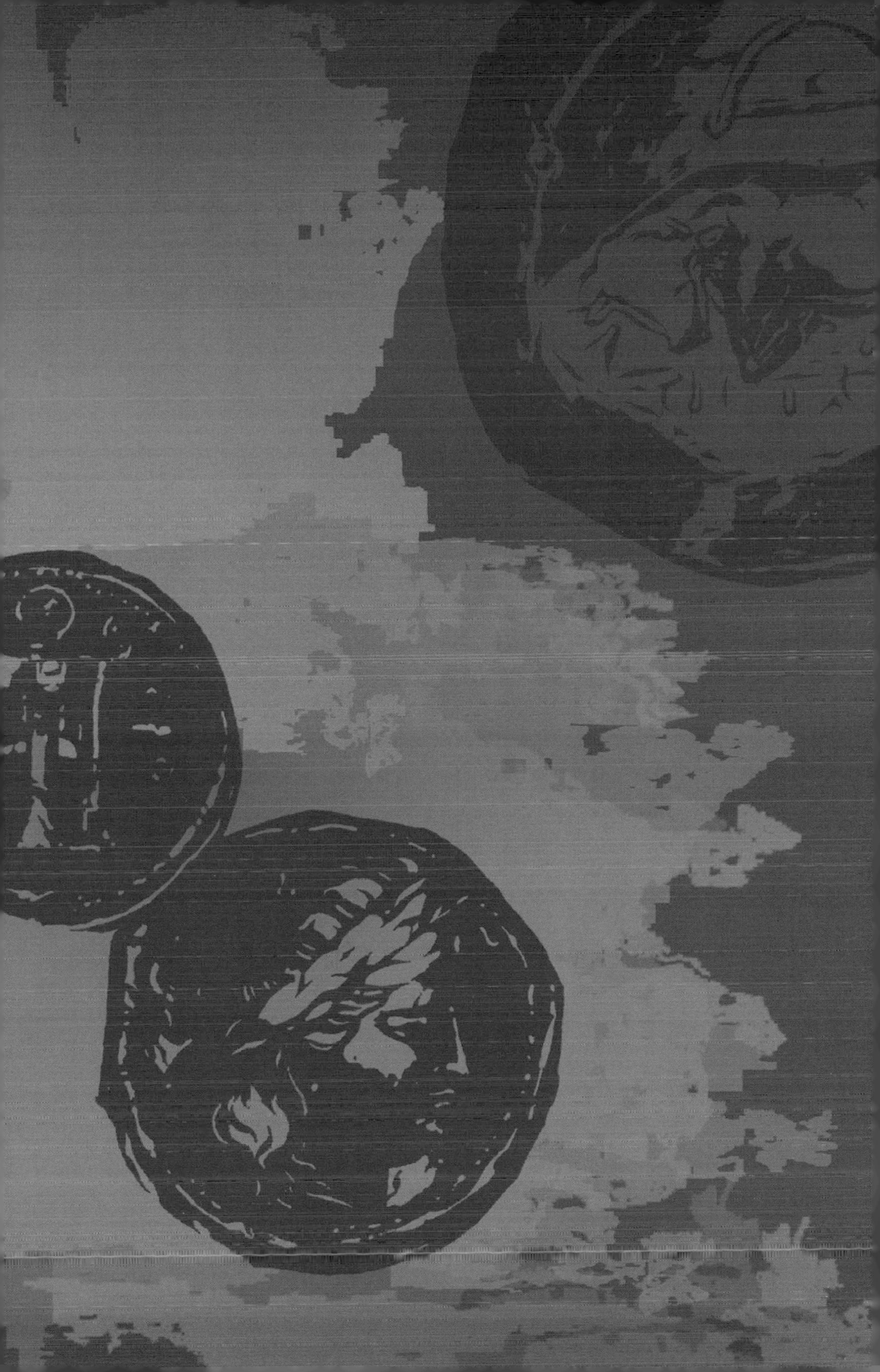

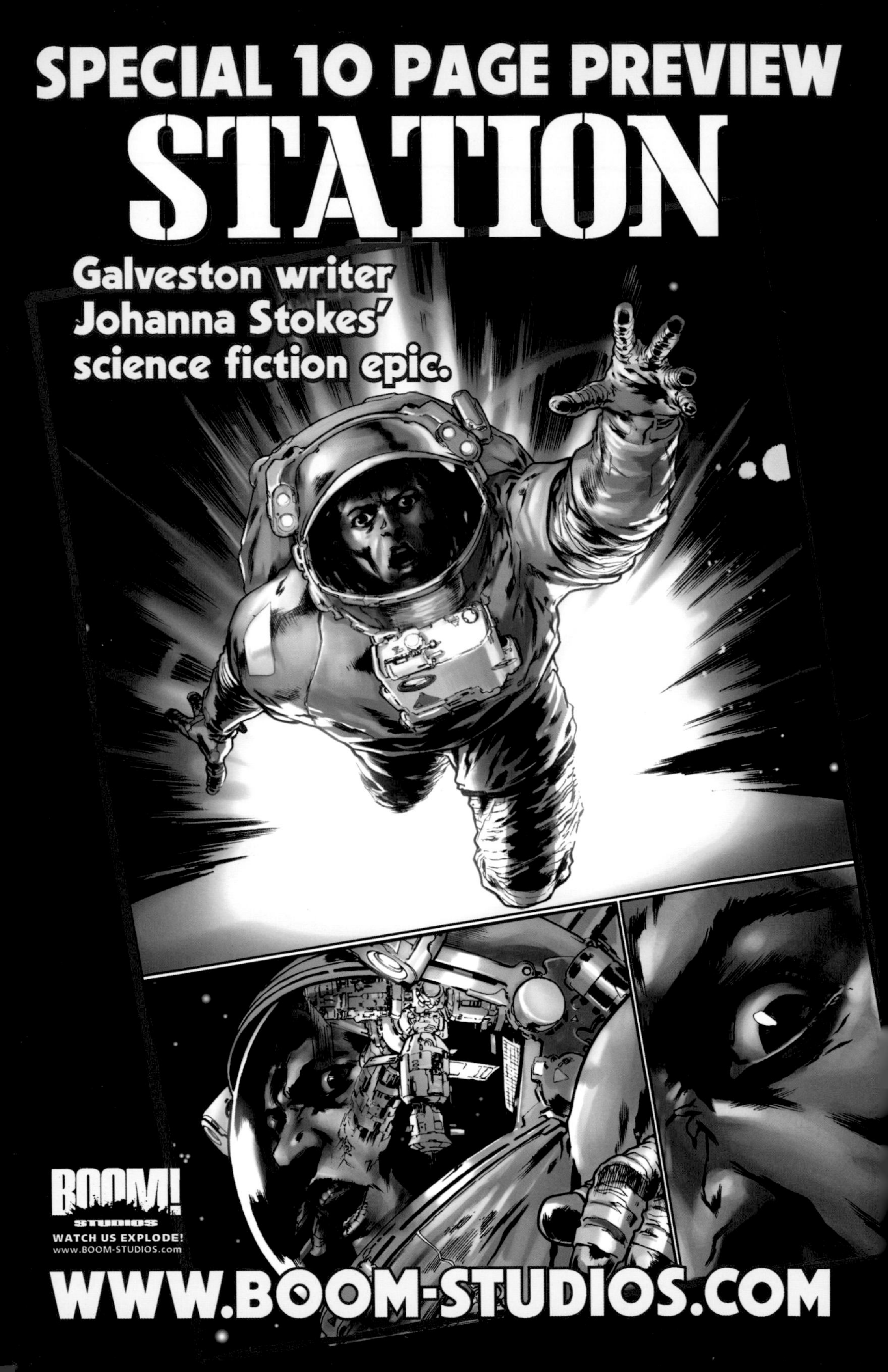
SPECIAL 10 PAGE PREVIEW
STATION
Galveston writer Johanna Stokes' science fiction epic.
BOOM! STUDIOS
WATCH US EXPLODE!
www.BOOM-STUDIOS.com
WWW.BOOM-STUDIOS.COM

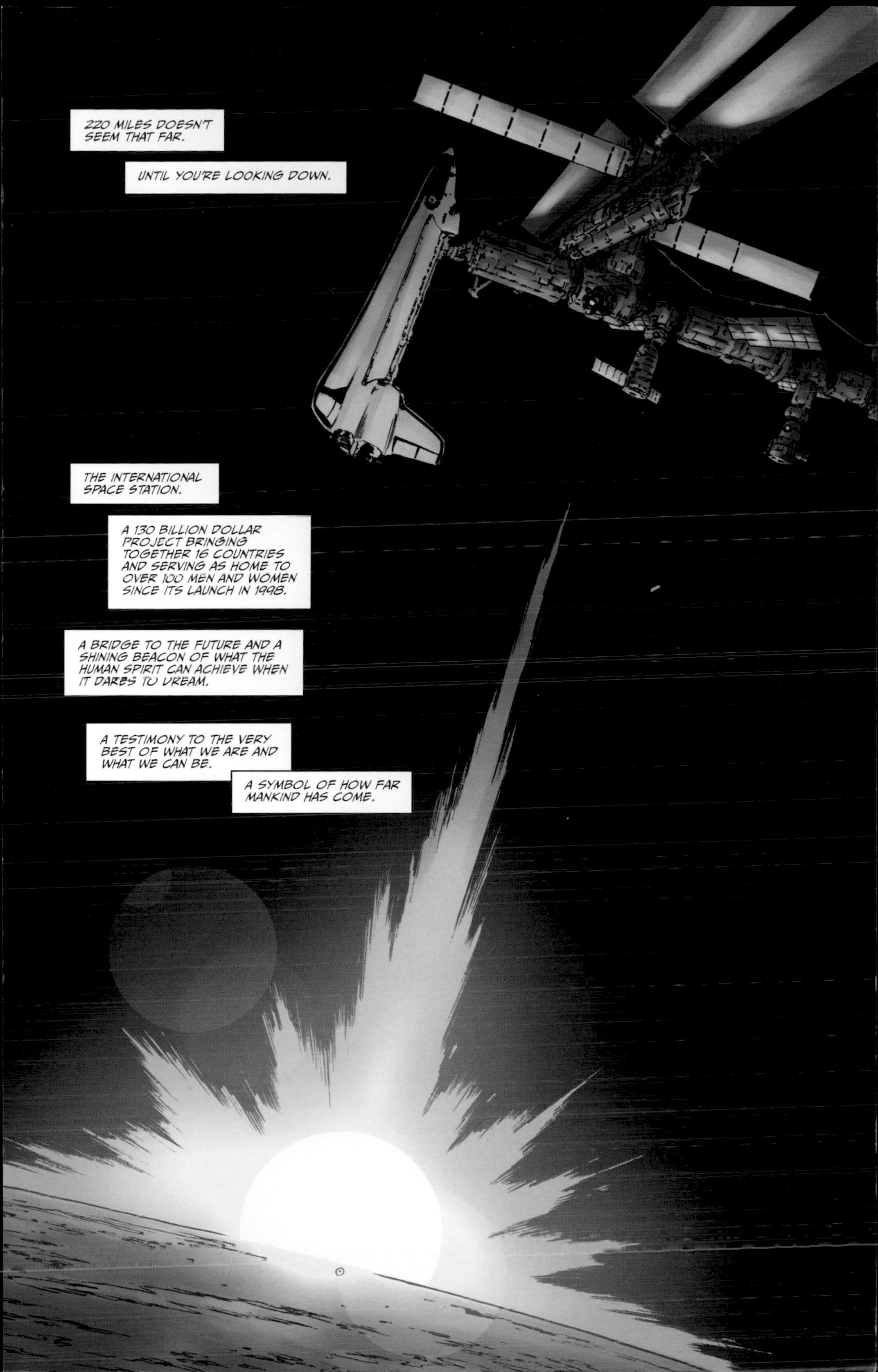
220 MILES DOESN'T SEEM THAT FAR.
UNTIL YOU'RE LOOKING DOWN.
THE INTERNATIONAL SPACE STATION.
A 130 BILLION DOLLAR PROJECT BRINGING TOGETHER 16 COUNTRIES AND SERVING AS HOME TO OVER 100 MEN AND WOMEN SINCE ITS LAUNCH IN 1998.
A BRIDGE TO THE FUTURE AND A SHINING BEACON OF WHAT THE HUMAN SPIRIT CAN ACHIEVE WHEN IT DARES TO DREAM.
A TESTIMONY TO THE VERY BEST OF WHAT WE ARE AND WHAT WE CAN BE.
A SYMBOL OF HOW FAR MANKIND HAS COME.

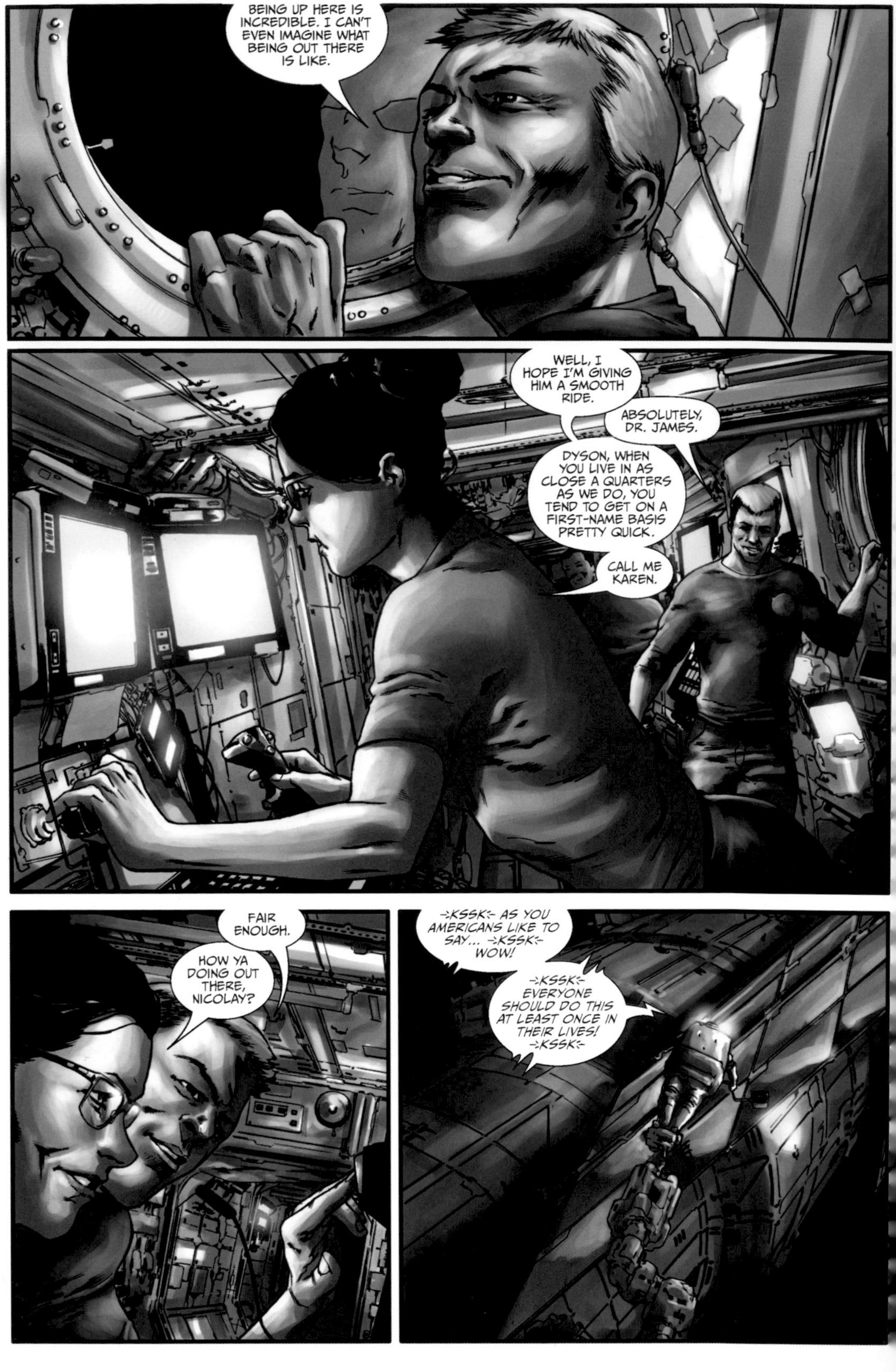
BEING UP HERE IS INCREDIBLE. I CAN'T EVEN IMAGINE WHAT BEING OUT THERE IS LIKE.
WELL, I HOPE I'M GIVING HIM A SMOOTH RIDE.
ABSOLUTELY, DR. JAMES.
DYSON, WHEN YOU LIVE IN AS CLOSE A QUARTERS AS WE DO, YOU TEND TO GET ON A FIRST-NAME BASIS PRETTY QUICK.
CALL ME KAREN.
FAIR ENOUGH.
HOW YA DOING OUT THERE, NICOLAY?
-KSSK- AS YOU AMERICANS LIKE TO SAY... -KSSK- WOW!
-KSSK- EVERYONE SHOULD DO THIS AT LEAST ONCE IN THEIR LIVES! -KSSK-

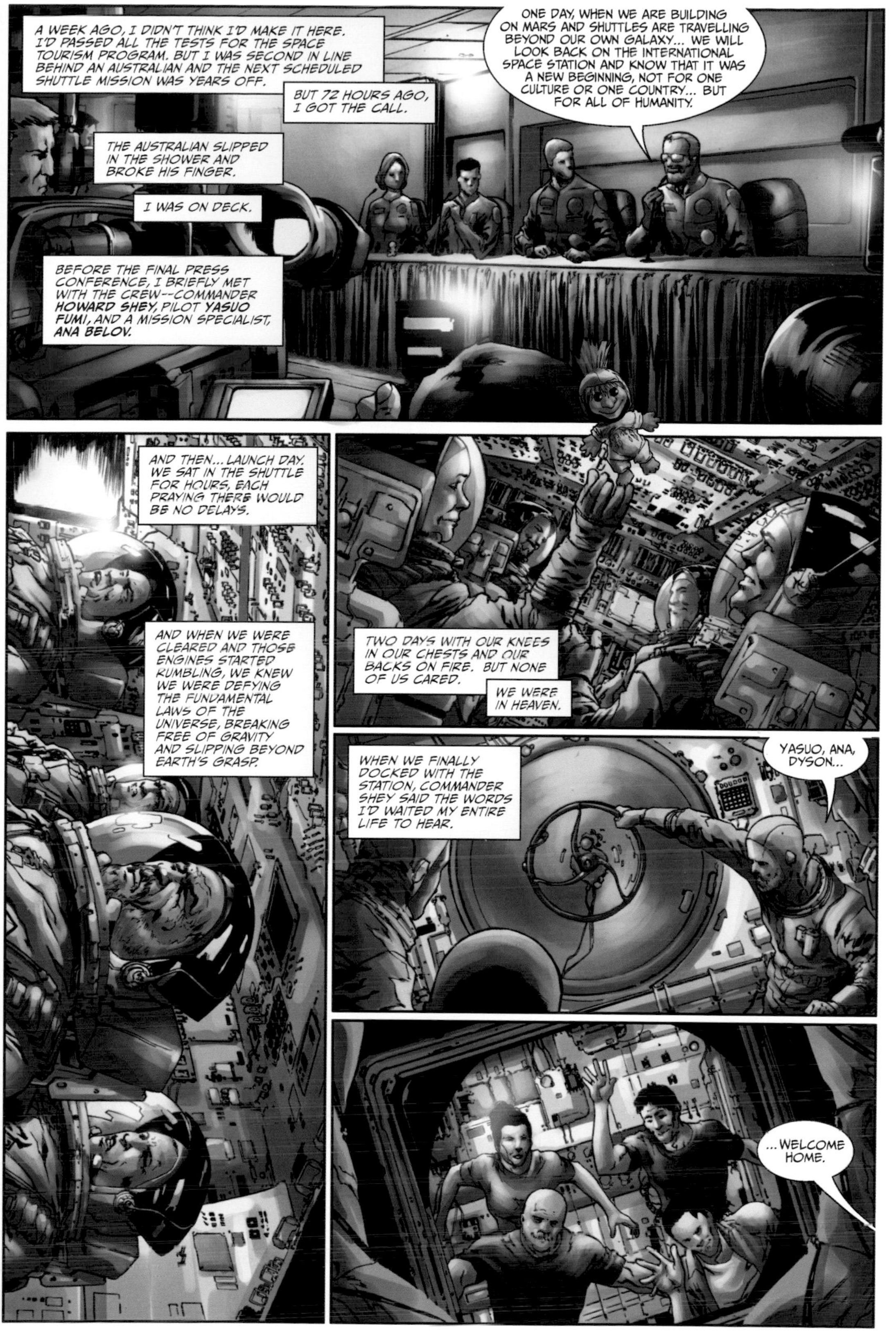
A WEEK AGO, I DIDN'T THINK I'D MAKE IT HERE. I'D PASSED ALL THE TESTS FOR THE SPACE TOURISM PROGRAM. BUT I WAS SECOND IN LINE BEHIND AN AUSTRALIAN AND THE NEXT SCHEDULED SHUTTLE MISSION WAS YEARS OFF.
BUT 72 HOURS AGO, I GOT THE CALL.
ONE DAY, WHEN WE ARE BUILDING ON MARS AND SHUTTLES ARE TRAVELLING BEYOND OUR OWN GALAXY... WE WILL LOOK BACK ON THE INTERNATIONAL SPACE STATION AND KNOW THAT IT WAS A NEW BEGINNING, NOT FOR ONE CULTURE OR ONE COUNTRY... BUT FOR ALL OF HUMANITY.
THE AUSTRALIAN SLIPPED IN THE SHOWER AND BROKE HIS FINGER.
I WAS ON DECK.
BEFORE THE FINAL PRESS CONFERENCE, I BRIEFLY MET WITH THE CREW--COMMANDER **HOWARD SHEY**, PILOT **YASUO FUMI**, AND A MISSION SPECIALIST, **ANA BELOV**.
AND THEN... LAUNCH DAY. WE SAT IN THE SHUTTLE FOR HOURS, EACH PRAYING THERE WOULD BE NO DELAYS.
AND WHEN WE WERE CLEARED AND THOSE ENGINES STARTED RUMBLING, WE KNEW WE WERE DEFYING THE FUNDAMENTAL LAWS OF THE UNIVERSE, BREAKING FREE OF GRAVITY AND SLIPPING BEYOND EARTH'S GRASP.
TWO DAYS WITH OUR KNEES IN OUR CHESTS AND OUR BACKS ON FIRE. BUT NONE OF US CARED.
WE WERE IN HEAVEN.
WHEN WE FINALLY DOCKED WITH THE STATION, COMMANDER SHEY SAID THE WORDS I'D WAITED MY ENTIRE LIFE TO HEAR.
YASUO, ANA, DYSON...
...WELCOME HOME.

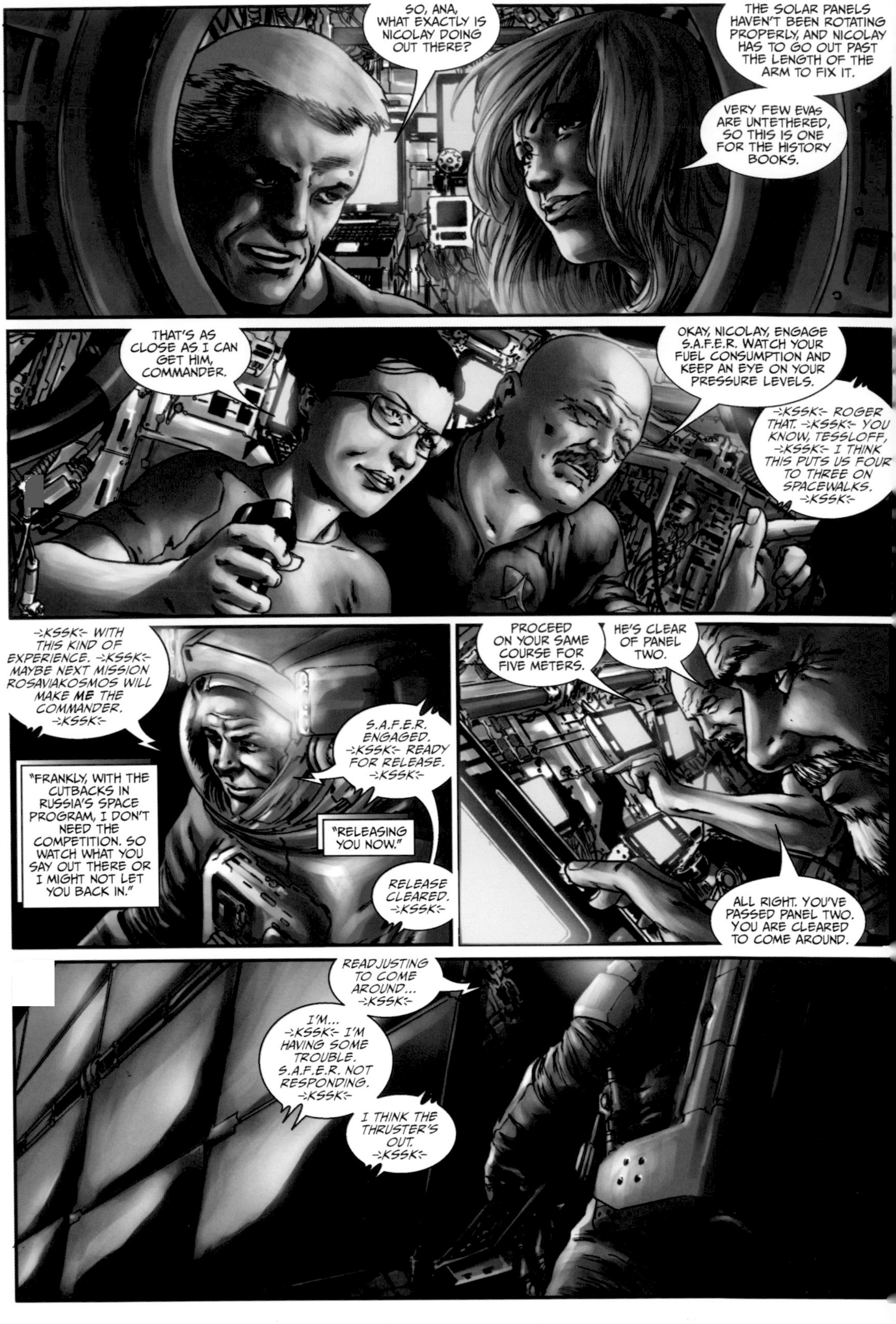
SO, ANA, WHAT EXACTLY IS NICOLAY DOING OUT THERE?
THE SOLAR PANELS HAVEN'T BEEN ROTATING PROPERLY, AND NICOLAY HAS TO GO OUT PAST THE LENGTH OF THE ARM TO FIX IT.
VERY FEW EVAS ARE UNTETHERED, SO THIS IS ONE FOR THE HISTORY BOOKS.
THAT'S AS CLOSE AS I CAN GET HIM, COMMANDER.
OKAY, NICOLAY, ENGAGE S.A.F.E.R. WATCH YOUR FUEL CONSUMPTION AND KEEP AN EYE ON YOUR PRESSURE LEVELS.
-KSSK- ROGER THAT. -KSSK- YOU KNOW, TESSLOFF, -KSSK- I THINK THIS PUTS US FOUR TO THREE ON SPACEWALKS. -KSSK-
-KSSK- WITH THIS KIND OF EXPERIENCE. -KSSK- MAYBE NEXT MISSION ROSAVIAKOSMOS WILL MAKE **ME** THE COMMANDER. -KSSK-
"FRANKLY, WITH THE CUTBACKS IN RUSSIA'S SPACE PROGRAM, I DON'T NEED THE COMPETITION. SO WATCH WHAT YOU SAY OUT THERE OR I MIGHT NOT LET YOU BACK IN."
S.A.F.E.R. ENGAGED. -KSSK- READY FOR RELEASE. -KSSK-
"RELEASING YOU NOW."
RELEASE CLEARED. -KSSK-
PROCEED ON YOUR SAME COURSE FOR FIVE METERS.
HE'S CLEAR OF PANEL TWO.
ALL RIGHT. YOU'VE PASSED PANEL TWO. YOU ARE CLEARED TO COME AROUND.
READJUSTING TO COME AROUND... -KSSK-
I'M... -KSSK- I'M HAVING SOME TROUBLE. S.A.F.E.R. NOT RESPONDING. -KSSK-
I THINK THE THRUSTER'S OUT. -KSSK-

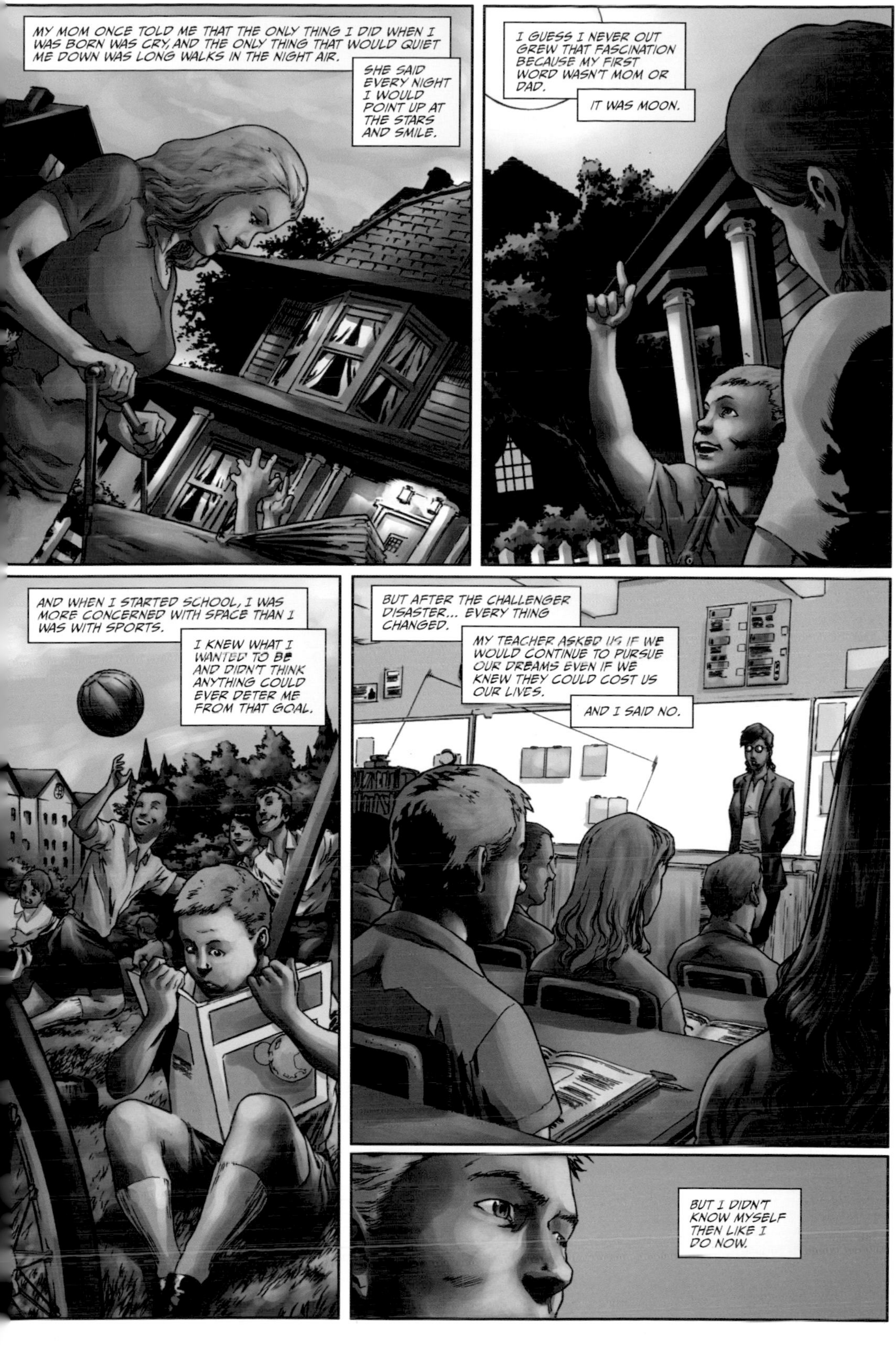
MY MOM ONCE TOLD ME THAT THE ONLY THING I DID WHEN I WAS BORN WAS CRY, AND THE ONLY THING THAT WOULD QUIET ME DOWN WAS LONG WALKS IN THE NIGHT AIR.
SHE SAID EVERY NIGHT I WOULD POINT UP AT THE STARS AND SMILE.
I GUESS I NEVER OUT GREW THAT FASCINATION BECAUSE MY FIRST WORD WASN'T MOM OR DAD.
IT WAS MOON.
AND WHEN I STARTED SCHOOL, I WAS MORE CONCERNED WITH SPACE THAN I WAS WITH SPORTS.
I KNEW WHAT I WANTED TO BE AND DIDN'T THINK ANYTHING COULD EVER DETER ME FROM THAT GOAL.
BUT AFTER THE CHALLENGER DISASTER... EVERY THING CHANGED.
MY TEACHER ASKED US IF WE WOULD CONTINUE TO PURSUE OUR DREAMS EVEN IF WE KNEW THEY COULD COST US OUR LIVES.
AND I SAID NO.
BUT I DIDN'T KNOW MYSELF THEN LIKE I DO NOW.

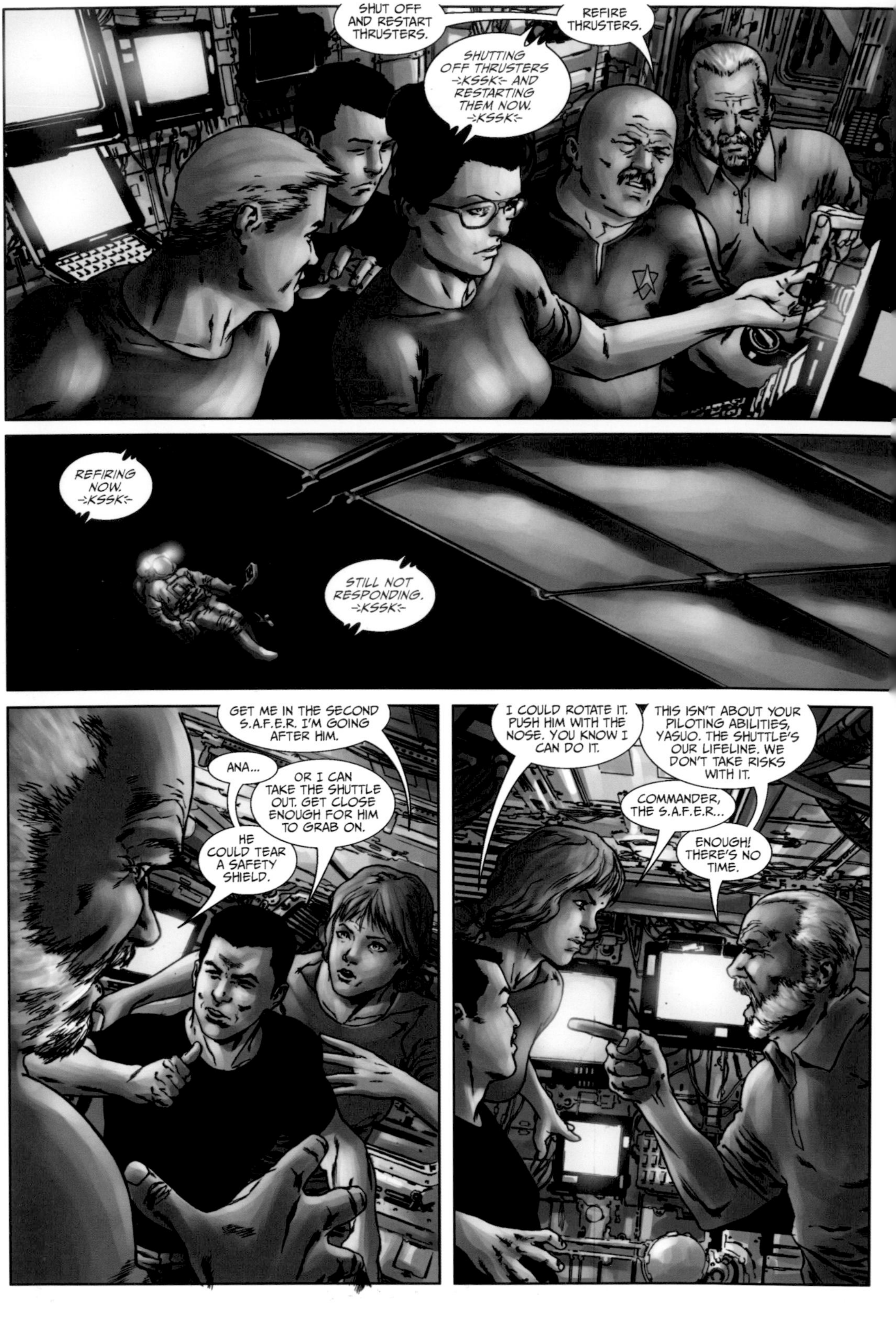
SHUT OFF AND RESTART THRUSTERS.
REFIRE THRUSTERS.
SHUTTING OFF THRUSTERS -KSSK- AND RESTARTING THEM NOW. -KSSK-
REFIRING NOW. -KSSK-
STILL NOT RESPONDING. -KSSK-
GET ME IN THE SECOND S.A.F.E.R. I'M GOING AFTER HIM.
ANA...
OR I CAN TAKE THE SHUTTLE OUT. GET CLOSE ENOUGH FOR HIM TO GRAB ON.
HE COULD TEAR A SAFETY SHIELD.
I COULD ROTATE IT. PUSH HIM WITH THE NOSE. YOU KNOW I CAN DO IT.
THIS ISN'T ABOUT YOUR PILOTING ABILITIES, YASUO. THE SHUTTLE'S OUR LIFELINE. WE DON'T TAKE RISKS WITH IT.
COMMANDER, THE S.A.F.E.R...
ENOUGH! THERE'S NO TIME.

"NICOLAY, CHECK YOUR READINGS. ANY INDICATOR LIGHTS?"

NEGATIVE. ->KSSK<-

"THE S.A.F.E.R. CONTROLS? ANY VISIBLE DISCONNECTIONS?"

NOT THA ->KSSK<- I ->KSSK<-AN SEE.

"NI->KSSK<-OLA->KSSK<-"

COMMANDER ->KSSK<- MY RESEARCH ->KSSK<- ->KSSK<- THE TELOMERE STUDY ->KSSK<-

LOOK TO THE A.L.T. PATHWAYS ->KSSK<- THE REPLICATIVE SENESCENCE FOR CELL ->KSSK<- DIVISION ->KSSK<- TRANSCRIPTIVE ENZYME ->KSSK<-

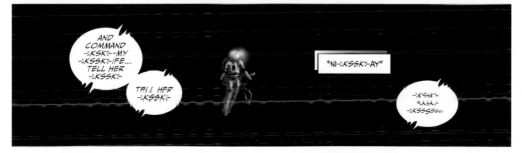

AND COMMAND ->KSK<-MY ->KSSK<-IFE... TELL HER ->KSSK<-

TELL HER ->KSSK<-

"NI->KSSK<-AY"

->KSSK<- ->KSK<- ->KSSSSSS<-

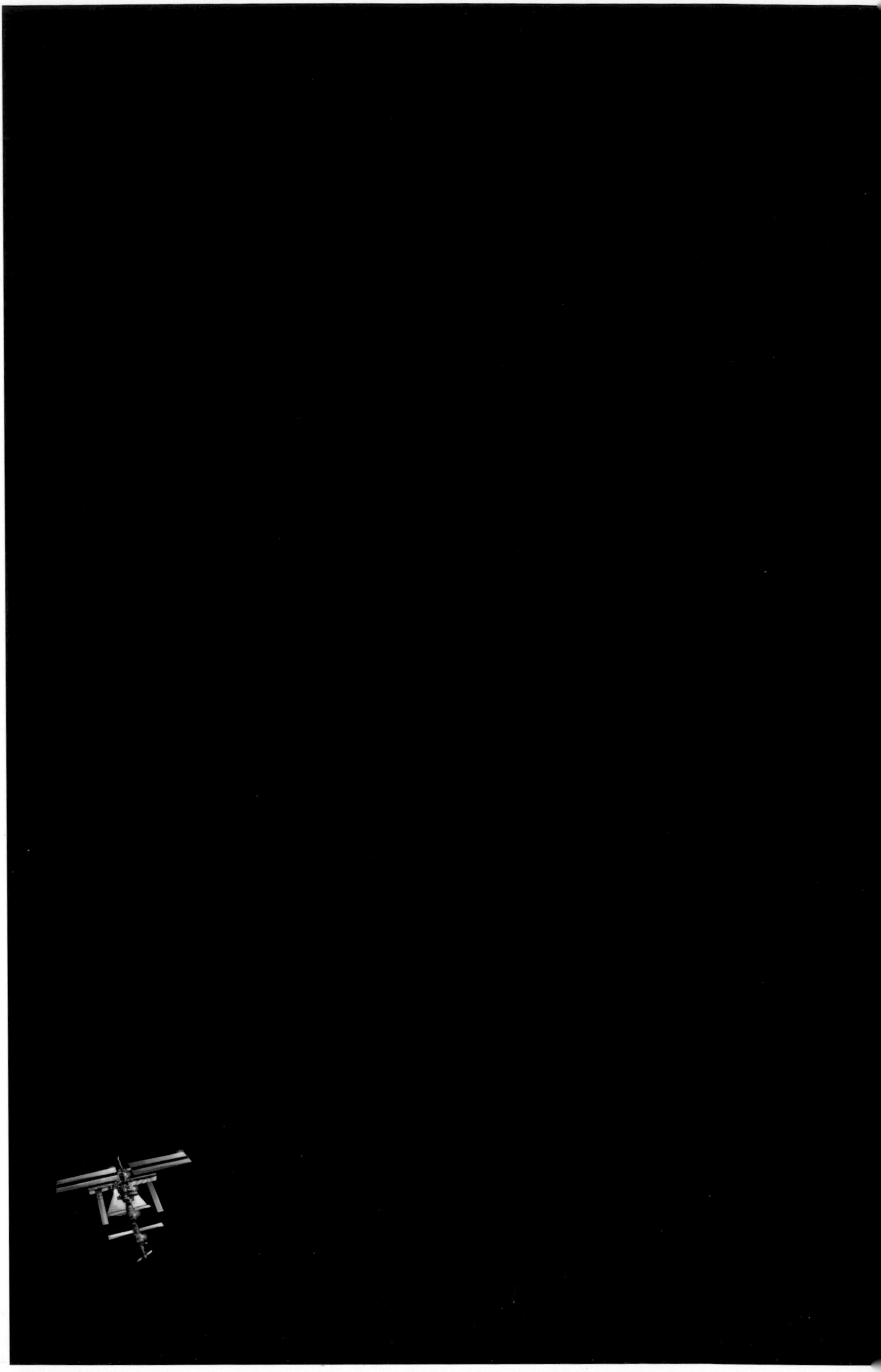

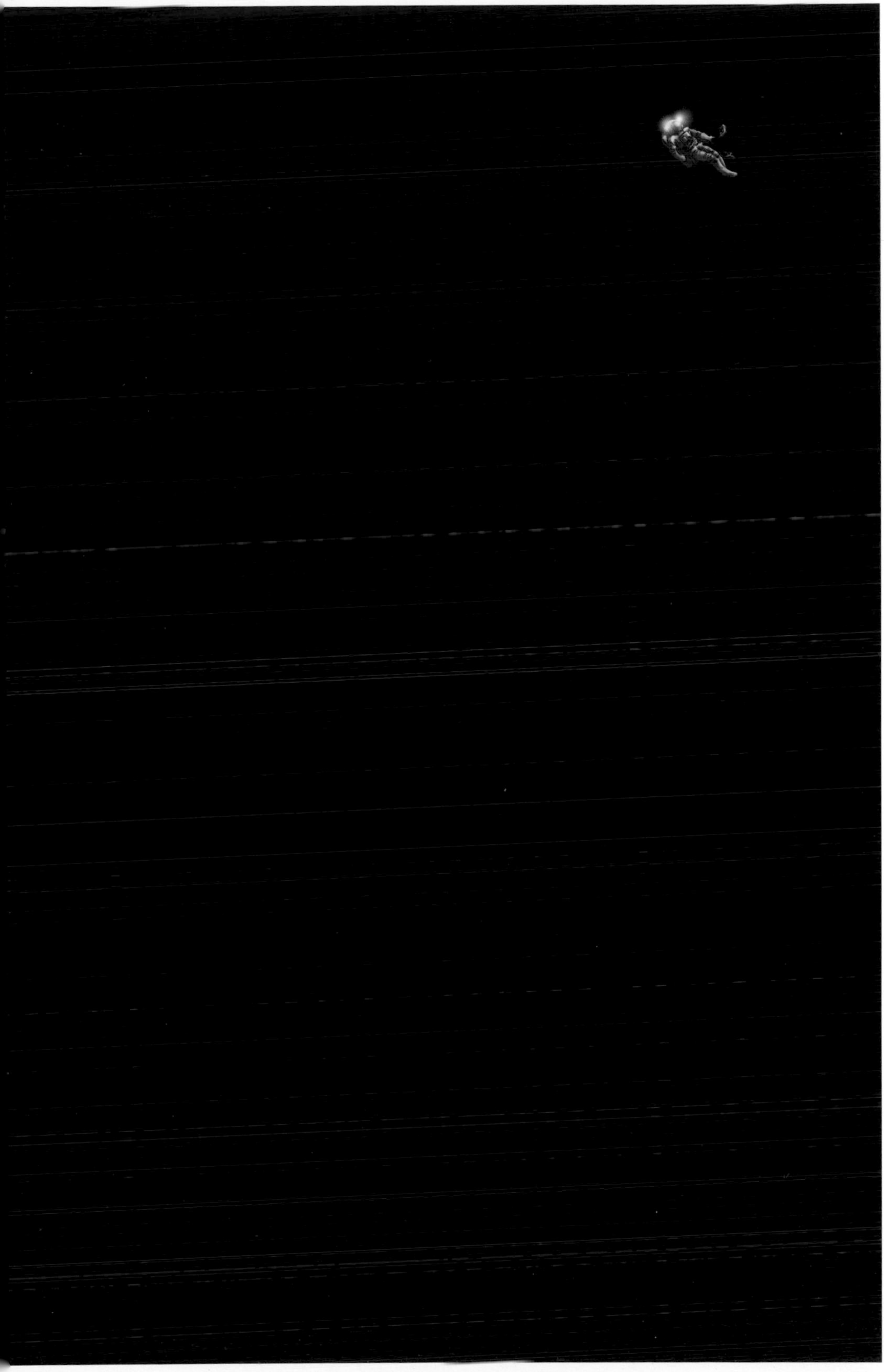

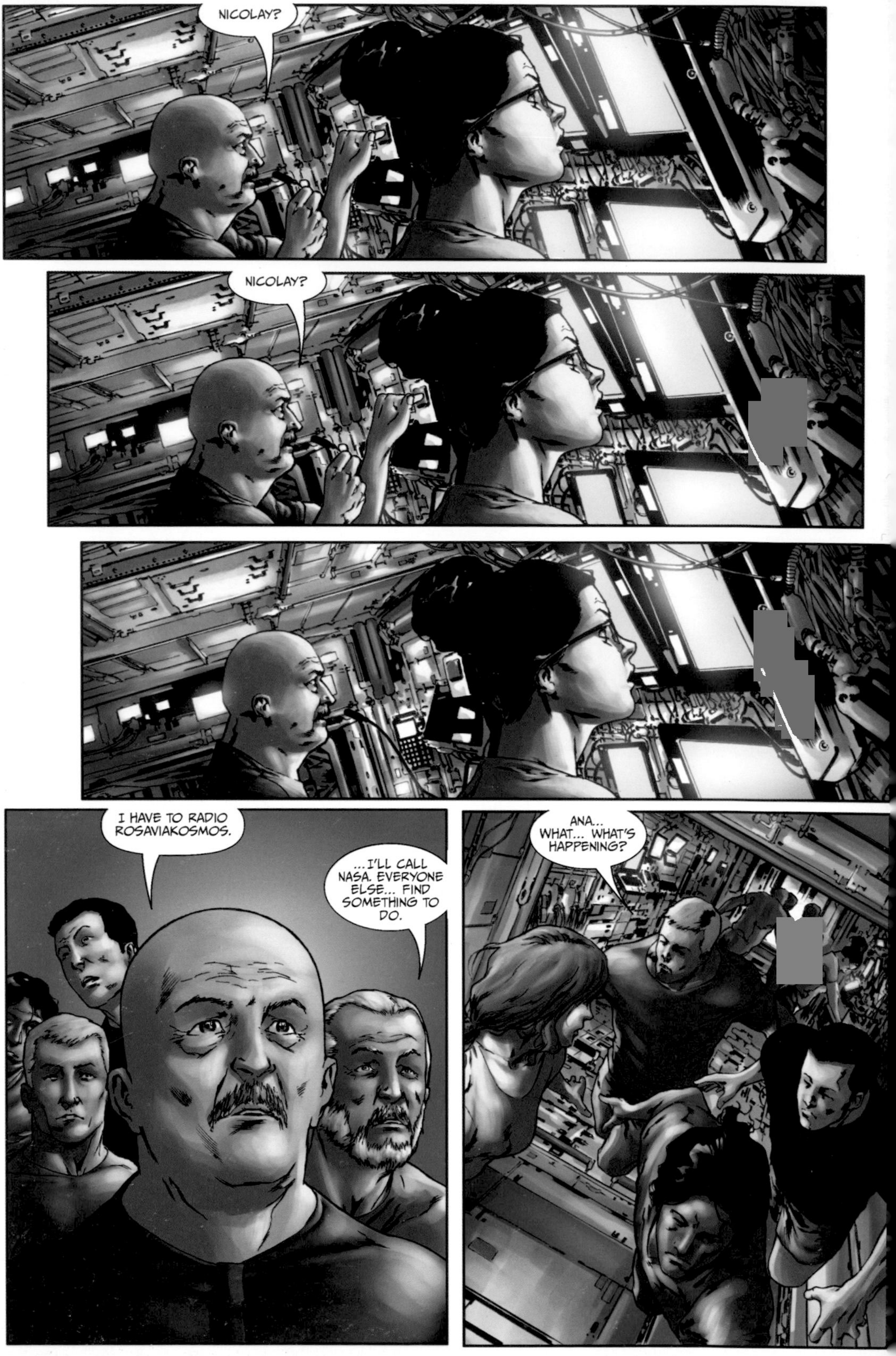
NICOLAY?
NICOLAY?
I HAVE TO RADIO ROSAVIAKOSMOS.
...I'LL CALL NASA. EVERYONE ELSE... FIND SOMETHING TO DO.
ANA... WHAT... WHAT'S HAPPENING?